THE GERMAN NEW RIGHT

JAY JULIAN ROSELLINI

The German New Right

*AfD, PEGIDA and the Re-imagining of
National Identity*

HURST & COMPANY, LONDON

First published in the United Kingdom in 2019 by
C. Hurst & Co. (Publishers) Ltd.,
41 Great Russell Street, London, WC1B 3PL

Printed in the United Kingdom by Bell & Bain Ltd.

Distributed in the United States, Canada and Latin America by
Oxford University Press, 198 Madison Avenue, New York, NY 10016,
United States of America.

A Cataloguing-in-Publication data record for this book
is available from the British Library.

ISBN: 9781787381407

www.hurstpublishers.com

For
Eleanor, Alissa, and Stefan

CONTENTS

PREFACE

In an Op-Ed piece for *The New York Times* in 2016, Austrian-German author Daniel Kehlmann asserted that Chancellor of Germany Angela Merkel's "impractical humanism [...] saved the soul of Europe."[1] He was referring to Merkel's 2015 decision to allow close to a million refugees to enter Germany in search of asylum, or at least safety. Germany has been named the most popular country in the world in several Country Ratings Polls conducted by the BBC; in 2011, the wording was as follows:

> Germany is seen as having the most positive influence in the world among all countries evaluated. This has been the case since tracking began in Germany in 2008. Globally and in the 24 countries surveyed both in 2010 and 2011, 62 per cent of people rated Germany positively, which represents a three-point increase since last year.[2]

After Donald Trump's election victory, *The New York Times* even went so far as to proclaim that Merkel "may be the liberal West's last defender,"[3] amounting to what is arguably the most incredible image shift ever recorded.[4]

During a tour of Germany in May/June 2016, I encountered many of the aspects of this new image: long-distance train trips provided views of seemingly innumerable solar panel installations and wind turbines; banners welcoming new arrivals proclaimed: "Refugees welcome. Bring your families;"[5] old cities full of cultural monuments from the past (such as Bamberg, Freiburg, or Heidelberg) were crammed full of tourists from around the world. The lives of many old friends bore the stamp of multiculturalism, be it daughters-in-law stemming from what contemporary Germans call a 'migration background' (*Migrationshintergrund*), or the tutoring of young asylum seekers in youth centers. The shops displayed fan gear in the national colors for the upcoming European Soccer Championships, not as a sign of nationalistic fervor, but rather as an expression of 'normal' national pride found across Europe; vacationing Germans were returning from the far corners of the globe (positive for global awareness, but less welcome in the form of greenhouse gas emissions); and the capital Berlin, despite problems like its new airport's delayed opening, continued to exert a powerful fascination on the young and creative from many lands.

One might well assume that the 1989 fall of the Berlin Wall and ensuing reunification of Germany have facilitated a cultural cohesion and societal consensus that is the envy of many. It is certainly true that the vast majority of Germans are satisfied with the direction that their country has taken since reunification, but there is a dissenting minority which cannot be overlooked; it is this minority that is the subject of the present study. Some Germans long for the days when their country was more culturally and ethnically homogeneous; they disparage the effects of the various New Social Movements that have swept through Germany since the 1960s; and they see evidence of cultural decline wherever they turn. This is of course not a purely German phenomenon: the effects of globalization are being felt practically everywhere, and a feeling of powerlessness in the face of rapid change can be found among disparate groups. In a world where sixty million refugees are on the move—a number hitherto unheard of—feelings of anxiety are not unusual. So-called right-wing populist parties have found success in Austria, Belgium, Denmark, France, the Netherlands and elsewhere, and now Germany has its own such grouping: the Alternative for Germany (*Alternative für Deutschland*). The citizens' group PEGIDA, Patriotic Europeans against the Islamization of the Occident (*Patriotische Europäer gegen die Islamisierung des Abendlandes*), has taken to the streets in many German cities (mainly in former

East Germany, but not exclusively), leading to confrontations with leftist counterdemonstrators, one of which I witnessed in Dresden in May 2016.

In the following, I will analyze the motivations and actions of those who are not in agreement with the construction of a Germany characterized by a generous welfare state, environmental consciousness, a striving for gender equality, a marginalization of the military, and a blending of cultures (including religious culture). I do not proceed from the premise that today's Germany is an ideal society—how could one, in light of the scandals involving Volkswagen diesel emissions or the Deutsche Bank, and all-too frequent torching of asylum seekers' homes?—and I will attempt to objectively portray the mentality of the dissenters rather than simply condemning them (as is often the case in the German media). Former President Gauck's characterization of Germany as a divided society,[6] with good Germans on the one side and bad Germans on the other (*helles Deutschland* and *Dunkeldeutschland*), disregards gray areas.

I begin with Thilo Sarrazin, an economist and Social Democratic politician who stirred up a furor with his 2010 polemic *Deutschland schafft sich ab* (a suitable translation would be: *Germany Is Digging Its Own Grave*). Sarrazin has put forth his views on immigration, intelligence, education, and economic efficiency across several books and as a frequent guest on the ubiquitous political talk shows on German television. He generally attracts many vociferous critics and few defenders. A person who strives to be a worthy successor to Sarrazin is the Turkish-German author Akif Pirinçci, whose 2014 volume *Deutschland von Sinnen* (approximately: *Germany Is Out of Its Mind*) carries the notable subtitle *Der irre Kult um Frauen, Homosexuelle und Zuwanderer* (*The crazy cult about women, homosexuals and immigrants*). His tirades stem from the pen of a child of immigrants, bringing to the fore a seldom-thematized facet of the multicultural discourse: 'new' Germans who have become completely assimilated and who fear the arrival of masses of immigrants from radically different backgrounds. To put Pirinçci's incendiary rhetoric in a broader context, I will compare it to a related example from France, Éric Zemmour's *Le suicide français* (*The French Suicide*). Another figure worthy of attention is acclaimed author Botho Strauß, whose provocative 1993 essay

'Impending Tragedy' ('*Anschwellender Bocksgesang*') was a foundational text of the post-Wall cultural pessimist intellectual scene. His recent essay 'The Last German' ('Der letzte Deutsche') is seen by many as the last gasp of the culturally conservative educated middle class (*Bildungsbürgertum*); Strauß wonders if anything will remain of the cultural artifacts treasured by previous generations of Germans. After a discussion of these three figures, I will turn to the political arena, highlighting the origins and ideology of the Alternative for Germany and its evolving relationship with PEGIDA.

For decades, even centuries, the 'German question' was on the minds of policy makers and thinkers throughout Europe. Various scenarios were played out, attempting to discern what the extent of German territorial expansion might be; fear of German dominance was part and parcel of European discourse. At time of writing, all this seems very much a thing of the past, though many southern Europeans, as objects of austerity policies, would surely disagree. The final setting of national borders after 1989 did not entail an end to the search for an 'authentic' German identity, however; some observers attribute this to the relative isolation and provincialism of the new federal states in the east, but Sarrazin, Pirinçci, and Strauß are West Germans. At present, Germany is a prosperous consumer society, but there are clouds on the horizon in the form of growing US-style income inequality and demographic distortions (too few children, too many elderly). Fear of Islamic extremist terror—despite Germany not experiencing attacks like those in France or Belgium until the summer of 2016—is also rampant. It is hardly surprising that certain people view a return to traditional values and a respect for authority (once Germany's hallmark) as an antidote to what ails contemporary society; to borrow a term applied to an earlier period, one could speak of a certain "authoritarian imagination."[7] The fact that any restoration is highly unlikely (barring the self-destruction of the capitalist system) does not mean that we can simply ignore those who dream of it.[8]

Most of the materials discussed below are unavailable in English translation, so one of the purposes of this study is to make them accessible for non-German speakers. All of the translations (from German and French) are my own.

THILO SARRAZIN
THE UNLIKELY TRIBUNE

Thilo Sarrazin (b. 1945) hardly fits the profile of a rabble rouser. An economist by training (Ph.D. Bonn, 1976), he has been a member of the German Social Democratic Party (hereafter: SPD) since the early 1970s. Most of his professional life was spent as a civil servant, and he held several posts in government as well, most notably as Finance Senator in Berlin from 2002 to 2009. He first came to the attention of a broad segment of the German populace in 2004, when he called for a phasing-out of pensions for civil servants,[1] and especially in 2008, when he appeared to ridicule people living on *Hartz IV* (basic social welfare) by demonstrating that one could easily prepare nutritious meals on a budget of about four Euros per day.[2] Despite media coverage of such incidents, it is highly unlikely that he would have been considered a significant voice in German social discourse if he had not published the 463-page book *Deutschland schafft sich ab* (*Germany Is Doing Away With Itself*, or in my own reading, *Germany Is Digging Its Own Grave*) in 2010.[3] This non-fiction volume became a runaway bestseller, though to this day there is debate about whether Sarrazin's detractors or supporters actually read it. The close reading that follows here will aim to determine if the controversial volume is a right-wing populist manifesto or something else.

The contours of the 'Sarrazin case' began to emerge in 2009 before *Deutschland schafft sich ab* (hereafter: *DSSA*) went on sale. The cultural journal *Lettre international* published an interview with Sarrazin about Berlin twenty years after the fall of the Berlin Wall.[4] The journal issue in which it is found examined many aspects of life in Berlin, including the city's role in Europe, its relationship to the former German Democratic Republic, cold-war economic subsidies for the Berlin economy, urban elites, immigration and integration, and provincialism. It is safe to say that the only piece that has remained in the German collective memory is the Sarrazin interview, or at least parts of it. Some may have found Sarrazin's comments on modern architecture amusing or old fashioned (like Prince Charles, he claimed that 80 per cent of it consisted of "functional and esthetic mistakes"), but many were enraged by one passage in which he offered his assessment of certain immigrant groups in the city:

> A large number of Arabs and Turks in this city, whose numbers have increased due to misguided policies, have no productive function beyond fruit and vegetable stands, and it is unlikely that their prospects will change. [...] The Arabs and Turks make a contribution to the city's birthrate that is two to three times higher than one would expect for their portion of the overall population. Large segments [of their groups] are neither willing to be integrated nor capable of working. [...] I must not recognize someone who does nothing. I don't have to recognize someone who lives off the state while rejecting that state, who does not see to it that his children are properly educated and who constantly produces new little head-scarf girls. [...] The Turks are conquering Germany just the way the Kosovars conquered Kosovo: by a higher birth rate. That would please me if they were Eastern European Jews with an IQ 15% higher than that of the German population.

As one might well imagine, the final statement in this section has been just as controversial as the preceding ones.[5] The interviewer Frank Berberich later lamented that there had been "an outrageous sensationalization of the interview using 'hot passages' taken out of context,"[6] but very few commentators appeared to be interested in contextualization; this mode of 'non-reception' was to be all-too-often employed vis-à-vis *DSSA* as well.

With regard to his demeanor and temperament, the politician and banker Sarrazin is usually described in the media as coarse and insensitive, but after the *Lettre* interview, he felt the need to apologize:

"The reactions to my interview in *Lettre International* have made it clear to me that not every formulation in this interview was an appropriate one." He did not, he went on to say, wish to discredit "individual ethnic groups," thus "if this was the impression, I regret this very much and apologize for that."[7] It is also telling that he added a preface to the revised versions of *DSSA* in which he spoke of the "unexpectedly violent reactions" to his book. Once again, Sarrazin assured his critics that this was all a misunderstanding: "When the media presented my theses, selective citation led in part to my views being transformed into the opposite of what I had actually said. [...] In no part of the book do I assert that certain ethnic groups are genetically 'dumber' than others" ('*Vorwort zur neuen Auflage*', 2010, p. 4). Is this merely a failure to communicate or a clumsy attempt at obfuscation? What are the views that are expressed in this controversial book? Can one speak of a scandal, or are we dealing with a straw man constructed by the media?

As the subtitle *Wie wir unser Land aufs Spiel setzen* (How we are putting our country at risk) suggests, the author Sarrazin is not one of those who would be pleased if the end of the national state were on the horizon. We learn in the introduction that a country is "that, which it is, due to its inhabitants and their vibrant intellectual and cultural tradition" (p. 8); it is not surprising that Sarrazin would say this, given that the mottos of the various chapters often stem from German high culture (Goethe, Schiller).[8] Beyond the cultural sphere, it is certain civilizational achievements that make up the essence of the German nation, namely "the specific German strengths—a high standard in science, education, and training, a productive economy, and a well-qualified bureaucracy" (p. 13). What concerns Sarrazin is an increasing indifference to such matters in the age of cosmopolitanism and multiculturalism: "It is almost considered politically incorrect to worry about Germany as the land of the Germans" (p. 18). It is of course especially noteworthy that such worries are weighing on a Social Democrat from the educated middle class (*Bildungsbürgertum*), since the SPD, in earlier times, was defamed by the conservative establishment as a motley collection of "stateless fellows" (*vaterlandslose Gesellen*).[9] Sarrazin is one of the rare representatives of the German political left for whom the concepts of homeland (*Heimat*) and love of the fatherland are not taboo. This is not to say that he is a glowing patriot or cheerleader: sometimes he sounds positively Brechtian ("Things never stay the way they are, and no social configuration is worth conserving"; p. 17).[10] He is also anything but a demagogue: "It cannot hurt to question one's cherished views over and over again, because in the world of social reality, there are only a few definitive and final answers" (p. 410). Just the same, this does not keep him from pointing out problems and offering solutions. It should be emphasized at this juncture that *DSSA* was not conceived as a missionary project; instead, Sarrazin was approached by a publisher: "The idea for this book came up in May, 2008, and it was not my own. The publisher asked if I wanted to write a book as a contribution to the political debate about the German social welfare state" (p. 409).

In fact, the German social welfare state is the focus of the entire enterprise. In contrast to conservative Republicans in the US, Sarrazin considers the social welfare state to be an example of civilizational progress, as evidenced by the first sentence of the fourth chapter: "Those who are weak and helpless, those who experience misfortune, those who cannot support themselves and their families in a manner befitting human dignity should and must be helped" (p. 103). Put another way: "Among the varied promises of the social welfare state, the core promise is freedom from material need: No one should have to be hungry, thirsty, or cold" (p. 103). Things get a bit more complicated, however, when the author attempts to define what poverty and hardship actually are; it eventually becomes clear that "intellectual" poverty concerns Sarrazin at least as much as "material" poverty (p. 113). From his perspective, help should ideally be help that leads to self-help (*Hilfe zur Selbsthilfe*), that is, "benefits for doing nothing" (p. 127) are in the end counterproductive, whereas the attempt to "make people capable of leading a self-determined life that makes them proud of their way of life" (p. 133) would serve the common good. The framework for this thinking is provided by Amartya Sen's theory of poverty and the ideas about the nature of happiness put forward by the Freudian leftist Erich Fromm. (As an aside, it should at least be mentioned that Sarrazin overestimates the success of so-called "workfare" programs in the US.)

Sarrazin's interpretation of social welfare is hardly original, and it would only be controversial in certain circles if an additional dimension were not involved: his theses about the meaning and tasks of the social welfare state are discussed in the context of immigration; in doing this, he takes a position that must be characterized as rather ambivalent. In principle, Sarrazin declares: "Diversity is desirable" (pp. 57, 60). He admires the industriousness of the expellees and refugees who contributed so much to the reconstruction of Germany after 1945 (p. 14), and asserts that the integration of *Spätaussiedler* (people of German origin who left Eastern Europe and the Soviet Union after the end of the Cold War) and non-Germans from Eastern and Western Europe has presented few problems. The same is true for "people from the Far East or India" and the "children of Vietnamese refugees in the German Democratic Republic" (p. 59). Problems with immigration and integration lie elsewhere: "The German immigration policies of the previous decades did not attract the achievement elite [*Leistungsträger*] from other countries, but rather rural residents from more archaic societies who found themselves at the bottom of the social and educational ranking scale" (p. 58). Sarrazin is referring mainly to Africans, Arabs, and Turks, whom he accuses of resisting integration, refusing to learn German, isolating their wives from society, having too many children in order to obtain more financial support from the state, and generally contributing very little to German society. Can one characterize this stance as racist or even *volkish*? If that were the case, Sarrazin would surely agree with the views of the US political scientist Samuel Huntington, who interpreted the Latino immigration to the US as a symptom of cultural decline.[11] One does not find such a position in *DSSA*; on the contrary, "The Hispanic immigrants strengthen and enrich the Western [*abendländisch*] culture and civilization of the US, instead of questioning its validity" (p. 265). This formulation highlights the fact that Sarrazin has nothing against recruiting productive individuals from foreign lands; time and time again, he argues that the Canadians have the right approach in that they steer immigration "very restrictively according to the educational level and qualifications" of the prospective citizens and with regard to "professions not well represented on the labor market" (p. 58). The term "archaic" (see above) should be interpreted to refer to societies that are based on neither a secularization of the public sphere nor a system of checks and balances. Sarrazin's societal model is modern Europe ("The geographic and cultural border of Europe is [...] clearly the Bosporus and not, as one finds in many statistics, the Turkish border with Iraq and Iran"; p. 258), and this is a model that must be defended: "Muslim immigration and the growing influence of Islamist schools of thought are confronting the Occident with authoritarian, premodern, and antidemocratic tendencies that not only challenge our self image but also represent a direct threat to our way of life" (p. 266).[12] In making this assertion, Sarrazin emphasizes that he is doing so as a representative of the European Enlightenment: "*Certain points are non-negotiable*" (original italics; p. 274). His Social Democratic colleague, (former Chancellor) Gerhard Schröder, had criticized the Swiss decision to stop the building of minarets by saying that "The concept of the Enlightenment may not be used for the purposes of exclusion."[13] Sarrazin's response was: "Oh yes it can! The attitude [of immigrants] toward the Western Enlightenment is the gist of the matter" (p. 270). Of course, Sarrazin's view of the Enlightenment is rather naive; it appears unaware of (or intentionally ignores) glaring deficiencies pointed out by Adorno/Horkheimer and others.[14] Is it still possible in our day and age to defend the Enlightenment without reservations? To be sure, but perhaps one must have some experience of premodern society so that a comparison can be made.[15] This is clearly the case with regard to the Turkish-German sociologist Necla Kelek, who defends Sarrazin against his critics; it is hardly a coincidence that her words are cited in *DSSA*: "Islam has not gone through a comparable Enlightenment yet" (p. 276).[16] Kelek fears that the "Age of Enlightenment" could be replaced by a "culture of anything goes [*Beliebigkeit*]."[17] For Sarrazin, the "value canon of human rights" is still binding (p. 30).[18]

The conflicts revolving around multiculturalism and relativism are not a purely German phenomenon, but rather a global one. The advocates of a 'canon of values' are generally relegated to the right of the political spectrum, but Sarrazin would hardly count himself among the rightists. In *DSSA*, he draws a clear line between himself and the radical right: "The radical right feared by many is not promoted when we express our legitimate preferences clearly and let our political activities be guided by them, but rather when we let things go" (p. 309). By this he means that the passivity of the established politicians or their inability to understand the cares of the 'little people' are responsible for the success of the radical right. Those who speak this way in

Germany are often considered illiberal; Sarrazin, however, considers himself a true liberal, one who views limitless tolerance as a great danger: "Liberality may not be extended to those who will not tolerate alternative convictions and ways of living" (p. 279). He is thinking here of the outrage of honor killings in general and the murder of the young Turkish-German woman Hatun Sürücü in particular.[19] A 'real' rightist would hardly call for the right of all women to lead an independent life, as Sarrazin does without exception.

Many of the observers who reacted to *DSSA* concentrated primarily on two themes: demography and education. Sarrazin cannot abide the fact that the Germans (like the Italians and Japanese) have had an extremely low birthrate for many years, and he fears that, in the course of time, the Germans will become "foreigners in their own country" (p. 309). What could be undertaken to stop this trend? In any case, Sarrazin does not recommend mandatory measures: "If people have no interest in producing offspring of their own, that is completely their business" (p. 344). Speaking as a cultural pessimist, Sarrazin laments that "as a people and society, we are too sluggish and indolent to worry about maintaining a birthrate that would maintain the population in the future, so we more or less delegate this task to migrants" (p. 360). Why is this? For Sarrazin, the culprits are decadence and comfort: "The German middle and upper classes live, either childless or with few children, comfortably in their suburban villas and tasteful Gilded Age apartments" (p. 361).[20] Although Sarrazin is an economist by trade, he is primarily concerned with the preservation of a "German language and culture" (p. 346) that has made unique contributions to world culture and should continue to do so in the future. This in no way implies that everyone should 'become German,'[21] but that which is specifically German should not disappear any more than that which is specifically Danish, Russian, or Turkish.[22] To some ears, that may sound too ethnopluralist, but in practically all countries, the inhabitants are proud of their national culture—why should Germans be any different? (It goes without saying that in the German case, national pride must involve an ongoing attempt to come to terms with the horrors of the recent past.) In order to ensure that there will still be a critical mass of Germans in the future, Sarrazin proposes "a high-quality system of childcare, whenever possible on an all-day basis" (p.

380); this was actually promised by the German government as part of the reunification project, but never came to fruition. Sarrazin also demands "a complete transformation of the school system to all-day schools following the Anglo-Saxon or French model" (p. 381). Beyond such reasonable proposals, there is little chance that his plan for a "premium" (p. 390) for educated women who have children would ever be acceptable. Making use of theories of inherited intelligence (including questionable ones such as the American "Bell Curve"; p. 417, note 61[23]), Sarrazin attempts to demonstrate that the intelligence level of the general population will continually drop due to the immigration of uneducated or poorly educated (*bildungsfern*) people, but this is less than convincing. As a great friend of the United States, he should know that many children and grandchildren of uneducated immigrants have obtained advanced academic degrees and achieved high social status.

It troubles Sarrazin greatly that the so-called secondary virtues, "punctuality, reliability, accuracy, affinity for order, toleration of frustration, sense of community and subordination" (p. 170) are gradually being devalued. As a person who experienced the reconstruction of Germany after 1945, he considers "traditional German industriousness" (p. 13) to be a key virtue. But can this virtue be passed on to the coming generations? Despite his criticism of the immigration into Germany during the past decades, he still imagines a well-functioning society with a significant immigrant population:

> It is sufficient if Muslims respect our laws, refrain from oppressing their wives, do away with forced marriages, keep their children from engaging in violent acts, and earn their own living. That is the key. Anyone who criticizes these demands as forced assimilation definitely has a problem with integration. (pp. 291-292)

It is remarkable that he can paint such a picture after having sharply criticized Islam as a faith and guide for living. All in all, *DSSA* must be characterized as a highly ambivalent work bearing the stamp of nostalgia, discontent, and even resignation. Sarrazin, who himself is not a 'pure' German (his ancestry includes French, English, Italian, and Slavic roots; p. 392), does not wish for a homogeneous society, but rather one in which there are no isolated enclaves or parallel societies encompassing several generations. Diversity is acceptable, but social cohesion is of central importance. This is clearly the norm in the 'classic' immigration countries like the US or Canada.

Public debates in Germany and other democracies focus on issues of general societal concern, but the way in which debates are carried out (*Streitkultur*) is usually not of great interest beyond the academy; regarding the "Sarrazin case," however, one must pay close attention to both the content of the various critiques and the tone of the remarks. In 2010, the German Integration Foundation (*Deutschlandstiftung Integration*) published a collection of responses to DSSA under the title *Sarrazin. Eine deutsche Debatte* (*Sarrazin. A German Debate*).[24] Its first sentence contains an important subtext: "Germany has every reason to be thankful to Sarrazin" (p. 9). In many ways, Germany is still a rather formal country (one still uses the formal "*Sie*" form when addressing someone whom one does not know), and titles are much more important than in the US. Thilo Sarrazin is an economist with a Ph.D., but here he is not referred to as "Dr. Sarrazin," or even "Herr Sarrazin." An attentive reader would notice this immediately, and the implication is that when discussing this author and very public figure, the usual rules of engagement do not apply. (The German term *Freiwild*, or fair game, comes to mind here.) Beyond this, it is no less than amazing that some of the critics included in the volume did not read the book in question at all or limited themselves to a few selected passages. In a country long considered to be the land of poets and thinkers (*Land der Dichter und Denker*), that is nothing less than scandalous.

The 'non-readers' do not hesitate to pass judgment: "Thilo Sarrazin's book is—to the extent to which I am familiar with it—an aggressive pamphlet, a tirade of hate" (Arno Widmann; p. 13); the historian and publicist Götz Aly, not known for his timidity, provides an assessment despite not getting past the title: "I haven't yet found time to read his book. The title, which reminds one of Oswald Spengler's *Decline of the West*, smacks of cultural pessimism, and I don't like it" (p. 140). Frank Schirrmacher, then one of the co-publishers of the influential *Frankfurter Allgemeine Zeitung*, rejected such intellectual sloth as "the termination of debate" (p. 198); Schirrmacher was simply astounded when Chancellor Angela Merkel appeared to share Aly's position, saying that she did not need to read the book to form an opinion (he quotes an interview where Merkel claimed that "the pre-publication excerpts are more than sufficient and quite telling with regard to the thesis, core, and intention of his argumentation"; p. 197). Launching salvos against the governing body of the SPD, which had considered expelling Sarrazin from the party, and against the president of the German National Bank (*Bundesbank*), Schirrmacher concluded: "The most dangerous books are those that no one knows, about which, however, everyone has an opinion" (p. 198). His role in the Sarrazin debate demonstrates how much his absence from the German cultural scene (he died in 2014) has left a real gap, as he was one of the few observers who attempted to come to a balanced judgment regarding *DSSA*. He could not help but reject Sarrazin's supposed "juxtaposition of genetics and culture" (p. 24), but that did not determine his overall assessment: "Sarrazin describes the results of catastrophic immigration, family, and integration policies, and one cannot dispute his findings" (p. 23).

Attacks and reproach were, despite Schirrmacher's intervention, the order of the day. Steffen Grünberg (of the leftist-alternative daily *TAZ*) was incensed that *Der Spiegel* chose to promote the "radically racist populism" of the "old rowdy" Sarrazin (pp. 16, 18) by printing excerpts before his book hit the bookstores; Robert Misik (also from *TAZ*) embellished his invective with a whole collection of derogatory terms: "so stupid that it makes you want to tear out your hair," "disgusting Thilo," "cold misanthropy," and "racism" (pp. 53f.); and the writer Feridun Zaimoglu saw Sarrazin as "a perfect racist" and "arsonist" (the latter apparently refers to the epithet launched at writer Martin Walser by Ignaz Bubis, the chair of the Central Council of Jews in Germany;[25] p. 56). Directly and indirectly, Sarrazin is connected to National Socialism, and there is hardly a stronger repudiation for any German. Arno Widmann (see above) believes that he has discovered in Sarrazin a "race and class conceit" that once became a main component of Nazi ideology (p. 89), and he maintains that the old Federal Republic (of the 1950s and 1960s) that Sarrazin allegedly wished to recreate was "the Germany that had been murdered into racial purity by the Nazi state" (p. 12). In saying this, Widmann evidences no interest in such phenomena as reconstruction, division, and the 'economic miracle.' Even a well-respected journalist such as Heribert Prantl (of Munich's *Süddeutsche Zeitung*) feels the need to mention that Sarrazin was invited to join the governing board of the neo-Nazi NPD as an honorary member[26] (p. 161); in the end, however, Prantl does not brand Sarrazin as a rightist. Rafael Seligmann, now the editor of the *Jewish Voice from Germany*, claimed that "the assembled might of public opinion," from the "*Süddeutsche to the FAZ*," accuses Sarrazin of proximity to Social Darwinism and thus by implication to Nazi thought (p. 111). That is, however, fairly exaggerated, since Sarrazin did enjoy some support in the mainstream media.

Most of the unorthodox commentators who dared to deviate from the consensus view in the German media were people who had played such a role for a long time; there appear to be few such successors in the younger generations. That is not to say that they belong to a cohesive group. The Turkish-German sociologist Necla Kelek (b. 1957) is a passionate defender of the Enlightenment; the journalist and professional provocateur Henryk M. Broder (b. 1946) participates in every cultural and political debate in Germany; the Holocaust survivor, author, and political activist Ralph Giordano (1923–2014) was long considered a moral authority in Germany until he became a sharp critic of Islam in his final years; the German-Egyptian political scientist Hamed Abdel-Samad (b. 1972) can be seen as the most prominent critic of Islam 'from within' in Germany; the dissident writer Monika Maron (b. 1941), who left East Germany in 1988, has never made her peace with West German 'political correctness.' Finally, one must mention the long-time SPD politician Klaus von Dohnanyi (b. 1928, brother of the famous conductor Christoph von Dohnányi and son of the anti-Nazi resistance fighter Hans von Dohnanyi), who represents the left wing of his party.

Kelek, who in Germany plays the role with which Ayaan Hirsi Ali is associated in the English-speaking world ("I define Islam not only as a faith, but as a political ideology and a social system"; p. 35),[27] views Sarrazin as a victim of defamation and describes him as a classic Social Democrat who supports education as a vehicle for social mobility. She pillories the educational deficits in the Arab world and asserts that "The Muslims in Germany have to decide if they wish to become part of this society with all that entails or want to go down in history as the first group of migrants that disdain the country that has taken them in. Sarrazin calls upon the Muslims to 'show what they can do'" (p. 38).

Long before the refugee crisis of 2015, she declared: "the 'all can come in' policies of the Greens have failed" (p. 217). Monika Maron defends Kelek's right to free expression and perceives "on the Muslim side" the lack of "readiness and ability to engage in self criticism" (p. 213); she is appalled by a Muslim "image of women that we fortunately have long since left behind" (p. 215); and as an author, she is—like Sarrazin— also worried about the continued viability of literature written in German (p. 217). Henryk M. Broder finds himself confronted with an "outbreak of collective hysteria in which especially the representatives of the informal and intellectual elites are losing their composure" (p. 90); he is amazed that not only the intellectuals, but also mainstream politicians attempt to silence Sarrazin and hinder a discussion of his ideas, viewing this as evidence of a "new East Germany" (p. 92). As a Jew, he is alienated by the fact that Dieter Graumann (the vice chairman of the Central Council of Jews in Germany) and the controversial media figure Michel Friedman felt justified in denouncing Sarrazin (p. 116). In Broder's opinion, Sarrazin "probably was right on most counts" (p. 117), and Islam is "an authoritarian, archaic system that utilizes the tools of modernity without accepting its spirit. It is not compatible with democratic values and structures" (p. 118). His main criticism of Sarrazin is that he implies this without stating it directly; it is obvious that the real agenda here is not defense of Sarrazin, but rather an attack on Islam (Broder's favorite hobby-horse). It is a similar situation regarding Ralph Giordano, who rages against "Germany's multiculturalists, partially blind xenophiles and professional welcomers" as well as "the enormous integration deficit of the Muslim minority in Germany" (pp. 93-94). In contrast to Broder, however, Giordano is capable of viewing minorities as individuals:

> I would have liked Sarrazin to be more emotional in public and more aggressive in the debates, with more personal empathy for the innumerable people from our Turkish-dominated Muslim minority who are very endearing but have, thanks to cultural differences, problems with the majority society—just as we have problems with them. When I see children from the Muslim milieu, then my very first thought is: Damn it all, they should all be doing well, today and especially tomorrow [...], leaving Allah and Mohammed out of it! The fact that Sarrazin did not express this does not have to mean that such thoughts are foreign to him. (p. 96)

Klaus von Dohnanyi protests against a campaign of ostracism conducted by the media and draws a parallel to the reactions to Martin Walser's 1998 Peace Prize speech (p. 128). He maintains that it is not racist to discuss "the cultural characteristics of ethnic groups" (p. 129), and he criticizes the German Greens for weeping "crocodile tears about insufficient integration" while deriding the duty of immigrants to learn German as "forced Germanization" (p. 130). Finally, Hamel Abdel-Samad, the only Arab (now: Egyptian-German) in this group has a unique perspective: for him, Sarrazin is neither a "redeemer" nor a "problem," but instead a "catalyst" (p. 109); in his view, there is no "real debate about Islam, migration, and the organization of the social welfare state" (p. 109) in Germany, so the clash about *DSSA* could perhaps initiate such a debate. In contrast to Necla Kelek, whom he characterizes as an "enraged critic of Islam" (p. 177), he strives for nothing less than a fundamental renewal of Islam: "My dream is indeed an enlightened Islam without sharia and jihad, without gender apartheid, missionary zeal and a mentality geared to entitlement" (p. 179). Sarrazin supposedly has a "fear of the Islamic world," but Abdel-Samad "fears for that world" (p. 179).

Sarrazin responded to his critics at length in his book *Der neue Tugendterror* (*The New Terror of Virtue*).[28] An analysis of that volume cannot be presented at length here, but one must at least mention that a sort of 'anti-Sarrazin industry' was hastily built up in Germany after the publication of *DSSA*. Here are some of the titles churned out by that industry: Klaus J. Bade, *Kritik und Gewalt* (*Criticism and Violence*);[29] Charlotte Halink, *Kontra Sarrazins Thesen* (*Against Sarrazin's Theses*);[30] Dorothée Lange, *Politisch inkorrekt* (*Politically Incorrect*);[31] and Andreas Kemper, *Sarrazins Correctness*.[32] One observer who made a real attempt to come to terms with Sarrazin's ideas was the political science professor Gerd Krell, whose volume *Schafft Deutschland sich ab?* (*Is Germany Doing Away With Itself?*)[33] is just as ambivalent as Sarrazin's. Krell explains this ambivalence by claming that there are "two Thilo Sarrazins," namely

> a cool observer and a contentious provocateur; the classic Social Democrat (emancipation and social mobility via education) *and* the reactionary Prussian junker [...]; the serious *and* resentful non-fiction author; the

know-it-all who supposedly never errs *and* the skillful discussant; the cosmopolitan *and* the nationalist with xenophobic subtexts. (p. 8)

Krell believes that Sarrazin is capable of differentiation with regard to the pros and cons of immigration (p. 65), and takes a critical stance himself with respect to contemporary Islam, a faith that "faces fundamental challenges" (p. 77). At the same time, he can discern "no epidemic" of Islamic fundamentalism (p. 79). Like many social scientists who study religion, he decries the dark past of Western Christianity (anti-Semitism, authoritarianism, repression) without acknowledging that major changes have taken place, especially in the past fifty years of ecumenism, and like many German scholars, he believes that the threat from the German extreme right is much more serious than that stemming from Islamic extremists (p. 99). When listing the major problems that Germany will face in the future, Krell puts climate change at the very top of the list; this is significant, since in *DSSA*, Sarrazin astoundingly views environmental concerns as secondary to the survival of the German nation. Krell ends his analysis with a call for Germany to address 'real' issues, rather than "spurious problems of German identity" (p. 107). One need not agree with all of his conclusions to profit from reading his book, but it is puzzling that he recommends Patrick Bahners's *Die Panikmacher* (*The Panicmongers*; see note 27), one of the most brutal hatchet jobs to appear in the context of the Sarrazin affair. Bahners places Sarrazin, Necla Kelek, Ralph Giordano, Bassam Tibi and others firmly in the unholy tradition of German xenophobia and hyper-nationalism; Hirsi Ali is also ridiculed as a "heroine of anti-jihadism" (p. 46), but as an antidote to this, there is praise for Angela Merkel for rejecting Sarrazin's arguments out of hand (p. 35). For some reason, the persecution of Christians in Muslim lands is trivialized (p. 56). Bahners is upset that critiques of Islam have now become "socially acceptable" (p. 73), although he would probably not be disturbed by studies linking Christianity to colonialism and imperialism. To sum up: "In the universe of Islam critiques, each point is only a short distance away from the 'lunatic fringe'" (the final two words are in English in the original; p. 86). In other words, there exists no legitimate method of criticizing Islam as a faith, nor the relationship between Islam and Islamic extremism;[34] the Germans have a chilling term for this sort of censorship: *Denkverbot*. For someone supposedly defending liberal society, Bahners is certainly attached to illiberal means. It is one thing when a journalist like Bahners engages in polemics, but it is much more troubling to find comparable language in a book by a respected scholar and public intellectual: Wolfgang Benz, a historian who has written extensively on the Holocaust and became known for his work at the Center for Research on Anti-Semitism at the Technical University of Berlin, takes on not only Sarrazin, but also Necla Kelek, Ralph Giordano, the Dutch populist Geert Wilders, and many others in his book *Die Feinde aus dem Morgenland. Wie die Angst vor Muslimen unsere Demokratie gefährdet* (*The Enemies from the Orient. How the fear of Muslims is endangering our democracy*).[35] Judgment is already passed in the preface, where one learns that the discourse about the integration of migrants and the future of Germany as an immigration society is "excessively loud and polemical, but mainly without historical consciousness or expertise" (p. 7). Benz speaks of "cultural racism, which portrays itself as a critique of Islam as a religion" (p. 14);[36] by comparing current critiques of Islam to nineteenth-century anti-Semitism in Germany, he in effect attempts to cut off all further discussion. For him, Sarrazin is an "amateur social scientist" (p. 93)[37] whose eugenics and Social Darwinism reap applause from the radical right, whereas his defender Kelek means well but fails to differentiate between "Islam" and "Islamism" (p. 117). Neither Benz nor many other observers are able to tell us just what the relationship between the two phenomena is.

If Thilo Sarrazin were mainly interested in money and notoriety, he could make a quiet exit from the public sphere and enjoy his now well-funded retirement. He has recently demonstrated, however, that he longs for a very different legacy: beyond scandals, he clearly hopes to be considered a significant political theorist. The most recent evidence of this is his 2016 volume *Wunschdenken* (*Wishful Thinking*),[38] a tome even longer than *DSSA*. The subtitle is *Europa, Währung, Bildung, Einwanderung—warum Politik so häufig scheitert* (*Europe, currency, education, immigration—why politics so often fails*): this is a handbook for active politicians and citizens, containing not only a historical overview, but also an appendix addressing morality, humanity, and action in politics. Does he succeed in taking on the roles of both a modern Cassandra and a political advisor?

Perhaps the main reason why *Wunschdenken* is so long is that Sarrazin wants to demonstrate that he is a serious thinker who has read widely beyond his field of specialization. (Some observers of the German cultural scene will sense in this a similarity to the writer Günter Grass.) Many readers will doubtless skip over the first two chapters, which are reminiscent of Jared Diamond (b. 1937)[39] and Karl Popper (1902–1994)[40] respectively. The first seeks to explain why certain societies succeed and others do not (with discussions of climate, geography, the environment, culture, traditions, religion, et al.), whereas the second offers an overview of utopian thinking and attempts to put it into practice. In the introduction, Sarrazin already puts forth a rather modest explanation of this quest: "If I think that communism is a mistake, if I reject the Islamic model, if I am against the spread of more and more stupidity, that does not imply that I know what a 'good' society should look like" (p. 11). What appears modest turns out to be something quite different: what he really means is that no interpretation of history can include a teleological component; it is thus no surprise that he mentions Marxism and Nazism in the same breath (p. 22). Instead of ideology, a society primarily needs "cognitive capital" in order to grow and prosper (p. 45). This time around, Sarrazin is careful not to open himself up to criticism for overemphasizing genetics, so he presents a whole catalog of factors that determine this capital, including "genes, health, education in the family and in school, individual capability, classmates" (pp. 45-46). The framework for the development of society must be a "strong state" that guarantees "freedom and security" (p. 51); Sarrazin is aware that this entails a balancing act, for on the one hand, he is (displaying his libertarian side) reluctant to regulate any "convictions, inclinations, and behavior," but on the other, he accepts the monitoring of citizens by the state. This vision stems from Jeremy Bentham (1748-1832), and then Immanuel Kant is added to the mix: "If one combines Bentham's definition of prosperity with Kant's categorical imperative, a whole moral philosophy takes shape" (p. 52). This juxtaposition is far from the world of the radical, populist right.

The same is true of Sarrazin's analysis of utopian thought. We are treated to a summary discussion of utopian thinkers, including Plato, Saint Augustine, Thomas More, and Karl Marx. There are no new insights here, but the purpose of the survey is to provide background for Sarrazin's rejection of all attempts to put utopias into political practice. A direct line is drawn from Plato and Marx to Auschwitz and the Gulag, and this is portrayed as a necessary development:

> Utopia begins for me there, where the social order that one draws up does not proceed from nature and human impulses—as one has comprehended them to the best of our abilities—but rather to serve the objective of changing human beings and subordinating them to a higher purpose. (p. 73)

Among the 'social engineers' condemned for such projects are the Nazis, Lenin, Stalin, Mao, and the Cambodian communists (pp. 74-75), all of whom are in the past. Yet Sarrazin does not fail to condemn the misguided utopian strivings of our own time, including "a conservative interpretation of Islam" (p. 78) as a platform for terror,[41] the "ideology of equality" (subcategorized as gender politics, inclusion, and quotas; p. 80), which he sees as a danger to personal freedom, the dream of a society without economic growth and the drive to acquire possessions, which must, he asserts, end in poverty, backwardness, and the end of the Western model of societal organization (pp. 84-85) and a "world without borders" (p. 85). This particular topic gives Sarrazin the opportunity to excoriate German Chancellor Angela Merkel for her "utopian experiment" (p. 91), that is to say, opening the German borders for over a million refugees,[42] which he maintains is tantamount to questioning each and every state's sovereignty over its territory. The final current utopia treated here is unique, in that Sarrazin admits that he "hesitated" before including it: under the rubric "A World Without CO_2," he denies that Germany can do anything to halt climate change, a phenomenon whose existence "no rational person" could possibly doubt (p. 91). He sees correctly that the fate of the global environment will be determined in China, India, and Africa, and he can only hope that what he views as inevitable economic growth in these areas will be based upon power produced with the lowest CO_2 emissions possible (p. 92).

If utopias are by definition dangerous, what is the alternative? Not surprisingly, Sarrazin turns to Karl Popper for answers. The road to the future is one of "piecemeal social engineering" (the German translation of Popper used here is "*Stückwerk-Sozialtechnik*"; p. 100), a cautious method of trial and error; the layperson in the UK would speak of "muddling through." In contrast, Sarrazin constructs a rogue's gallery of utopians, beginning with the protofascist Plato and ending with Vladimir Putin, Benito Mussolini, Hugo Chávez, Recep Tayyip Erdogan, and the attempts by extremists to create an "Islamist theocratic state" (p. 105); the inclusion of Putin demonstrates once again how far Sarrazin is from the populist right, which tends to praise Putin as a strong nationalist leader. As an addendum to Popper's vision of an "open society," Sarrazin praises Friedrich von Hayek for highlighting the dangers of totalitarianism in his book *The Road to Serfdom*.[43] Like Popper and Hayek, he views a nonviolent "decentralized market economy" (p. 114) as the prerequisite for a truly open society. This does not, however, keep him from warning against possible distortions of such a system, as illustrated by the "world financial crisis 2008/09" (p. 115). In the end, we are left with no alternative (not in the sense of Fukuyama, whom Sarrazin obliquely criticizes; p. 99)[44] to the strengthening of democratic national states — and their borders — in the context of global capitalism. It remains unclear just what such strengthening might entail, since Sarrazin rejects the social engineering of the Swedish model ("liberal paternalism"; pp. 117-118) while praising the Scandinavian countries as "model states" (p. 119). He also appears to very much admire the Danes and the society that they have constructed (pp. 133, 312, 438).

The following two chapters of *Wunschdenken* delineate the principles of good government and the nature of political errors. The "positive governance goals" listed first would hardly raise many eyebrows: in a society free of violence, the citizens should enjoy good health, freedom of speech, the right to live and express themselves as they wish (pp. 129-130); the educational system should allow "the best" to rise to the top, irrespective of social origins (p. 131); a "culture of the work ethic" should be cultivated, and a decent standard of living, a social safety net, and equality before the law are indispensable (pp. 131-132). It is noted, however, that "parasites" should not be allowed to exploit welfare, and "immigration into the welfare system" should no longer be tolerated (p. 132). Sarrazin admits that the picture he paints here, including "efficient" (p. 133) state institutions, does not, for the most part, correspond to past and present political reality. This leads to a description of "illegitimate" governmental goals; at the top of the list are megalomania, self-enrichment, and nepotism (pp. 134-135). Writing as a German, Sarrazin does not hesitate to emphasize that "subjugation and destruction" of other peoples or states must be considered barbaric (p. 135); and finally, the violent propagation of a certain religion or ideology must not be tolerated. As examples of such activity, Sarrazin mentions both the "religious war" in today's Middle East and the various attempts of the West to intervene in the "Islamic world" (p. 136). This section may well have been inspired by Kant's 1795 essay 'Eternal Peace.'

What is to be done to assure that good governance will prevail? Sarrazin provides us with "ten rules for the good regent," though it is somewhat strange that he chose the pre-democratic term "regent" rather than "leader" (p. 137).[45] Once again, the rules put forth could be found in any garden-variety civics textbook: an effective leader must possess an "inner compass" and the ability to envision the long term; must not be overambitious or tend to take risks; must have staying power, but also be flexible (pp. 138-141): all laudable but banal dictums. As Sarrazin himself states, one need not point out that he is yet again describing an "open society" (p. 145).[46] (The only assertion that goes beyond the ordinary is the recurring rejection of political Islam as an "enemy of the open society"; p. 145).[47] As an illustration of how such a society might deal with pressing problems, Sarrazin turns to the issue of climate change. He concedes that future generations will have to limit CO_2 emissions, and that this would justify putting a high tax on "products and activities that produce CO_2" (p. 147). The individual citizen would still have the right to decide how much and how far s/he might wish to travel; it does not seem to bother him that the affluent would simply pay such a tax and maintain their previous lifestyle, whereas most people would see their choices severely limited. None of this smacks of right-wing populism, and other aspects of his vision confirm this assessment: Sarrazin has a rather ambivalent attitude toward the use of referendums (pp. 150-151) in contrast to the Austrian FPÖ, for example; he warns of the danger of an inflated sense of self-worth on the part of the Germans (*"Selbstüberschätzung"*; p. 155), and sounds positively Keynesian when discussing budget deficits (p. 172). Echoing Kant's phrase "crooked timber,"[48] Sarrazin reminds us that all human endeavor is usually imperfect (p. 166).

In stark contrast to Donald Trump (this section of the present study was written during the 2016 US presidential campaign), Sarrazin characterizes his country as "successful and happy" (p. 189). As an "optimistic technocrat" (p. 192), he proceeds to tell his fellow citizens how Germany could stay that way; the theoretical framework for this undertaking is the distinction between an "ethic of ultimate ends" (*Gesinnungsethik*) and "ethic of responsibility" (*Verwantwortungsethik*) put forth by sociologist Max Weber.[49] Sarrazin lists mistakes that have been made that should be avoided in the future: since he believes— some months before the 'Brexit' vote—that a European federal state would be a "rather utopian" endeavor (p. 202), Germany must put its own house in order; instead of attempting to play the role of "global policeman" (p. 181), the German government must realize that control of the national borders is an "existential question" (p. 215). One of his illustrations of this thesis is quite intriguing for the American reader: "The downfall of the North American Indians began with the uncontrolled trickling-in of the settlers beyond one line of demarcation after the other" (p. 203).[50] He also adds—no overly Germanophile streak here—that the "uncontrolled immigration of the Germanic tribes and the Huns" was harmful for the Western Roman Empire (p. 203). The alternative is not no immigration, but rather the well-planned admission of those who can make contributions to the development of the country:[51] the examples given here are the Huguenots and the Jews. Sarrazin attributes the present crisis in Germany to the "internationalist" Merkel (p. 215), whose open-door policy is seen as a danger to both Germany as a national state and European integration. He can empathize with the people from Africa and the Middle East who want to come to Germany ("Given the conditions there, no one can blame them"; p. 218), but he is sure that the more admitted, the more will follow. He would admit only a small number and return the rest to their point of departure for Europe; he would also want to see war refugees placed in safe camps as near to their countries as possible. There thus must be an "upper limit" (*Obergrenze*), a concept that Merkel has thus far refused to consider, and which is close to what the Bavarian CSU has been demanding. Although Sarrazin takes pains to assure the reader that he does not consider all Muslim immigrants as potential terrorists, he does fear that their presence would "enlarge the Muslim parallel societies in Europe," which provide a potential basis for religious fundamentalism and even terrorism (p. 211); incidents like the attacks on women during New Year's celebrations in Cologne on the eve of 2016 contribute to this fear.

Beyond immigration, there are other concerns. Sarrazin actually admits that demography is secondary to "ability, education, and industriousness" (p. 250) when it comes to maintaining the German model, but he laments the watering-down of the educational system, specifically of the college-preparatory *Gymnasium*, by the "ideologists of equality" (p. 281), and to bolster his case, he has no compunction about citing the views of the left-liberal Austrian philosopher Konrad Paul Liessmann (p. 202). The lowering of standards at the secondary-school level leads in Sarrazin's view to a devaluing of the college degree, and is accompanied by the decline of the much-admired German model of vocational education, a devastating development for German industry (the derogatory term for this development is *"Akademisierungswahn"*, which refers to the misguided belief that as many people as possible should undertake university-level studies; p. 276). In the name of "equal opportunity" (*Chancengleichheit*; p. 314), standards are lowered, which means that both Muslim immigrants and their children and lower-class Germans have less chance to better their lot. It is obvious that Sarrazin would be opposed to affirmative action if he were active in US politics. Instead of pursuing social justice, which Sarrazin considers illusory, a society should strive to build prosperity to the greatest extent possible; this is proclaimed with a further nod to Jeremy Bentham (p. 311). On an international scale, Sarrazin asserts that each and every society has the "moral right" (p. 316) to utilize its resources and the fruits of its labor for the benefit of its own citizens. Those countries that cannot provide a decent life for their people have no one to blame but themselves:

> The peoples or societies in Nigeria, South Africa, or even Greece are at liberty to organize their societies according to German or Central European principles and to put in motion a corresponding socialization. If they are successful at that, then the typical level of prosperity found in Central Europe will be attained anywhere in the world. (p. 316)

In other words, Sarrazin is an unrepentant Eurocentrist who does not believe that the legacy of colonialism (an enterprise in which the Germans—compared to those from Britain, France, Spain, Portugal, the Netherlands, and Belgium—played a relatively minor role) has any relevance for a discussion of contemporary world affairs.[52]

It is also true that Sarrazin dismisses the so-called "gender debate" (p. 317) as irrelevant. He is convinced that there are fundamental differences between men and women with regard to "talents and inclinations," but he does accept the principle that men and women should have the opportunity to develop their given potential on an equal basis. He cannot avoid a jab at feminists who supposedly strive for freedom of choice for women while accepting the fact that in Islam, women's choices are severely limited (p. 318). With respect to environmental policies, he takes a much more differentiated view, accepting the notion that climate change has been a direct result of human activities since the industrial revolution, but he believes that ongoing rapid population growth is "the greatest threat to the environment" (p. 325). As a "non-expert," he feels that he must accept the "overwhelming view of the experts" (p. 332); this is of course also not a typical position taken by the radical right (look only to Donald Trump's assertion that climate change is a Chinese conspiracy designed to ruin the US economy). He accepts the fact that alternative energy sources must be maximized (though this includes, for him at least, nuclear energy), and that energy storage will be a key component of any plan to halt climate change. He is correct in saying that Germany cannot solve this problem on its own, given the relatively small size of its economy, but believes it can be a "model" (*Vorbild*; p. 335) for other highly developed countries. Sarrazin rejects the German "energy shift" (*Energiewende*) as a failure due to its closing of nuclear plants, but he does praise Germany's role in providing impulses for "innovation and new technologies" (p. 339); with the exception of the nuclear issue, he is close to the position of the German Green Party in this area, which amounts to quite a change from his earlier disparaging remarks about ecologists.

Deutschland schafft sich ab concluded with a clear choice for future generations, imagining what Germany might look like a hundred years from its time of writing. *Wunschdenken*'s fifth chapter fulfills a similar function, with the title 'How I view the world scene and what I wish for Germany.' Unfortunately, there is little new material in this chapter and in the appendix 'Explaining Politics;' repetition does not seem to bother Sarrazin or his editors. We do not really learn anything new about Sarrazin's likes and dislikes (he is against uncontrolled immigration, Islam, gender studies, fanatical environmentalists and dictatorial leaders like Putin; he is for hard work, an open society, pragmatic politics, and encouraging educated women to have more children).[53] Sarrazin discusses with some pride what he has accomplished as a politician and bureaucrat, but this is peripheral to his overall presentation, and many will likely disagree with his personal account. If anything, a conundrum emerges from his concluding chapters: Sarrazin has a rather dark view of human nature, one in which the capacity for evil, or at least damage, is greater than that for good.[54] (This is not far from the young Martin Luther, who makes a brief appearance in *Wunschdenken* as the first "media star"; p. 495). Here is one characteristic formulation: "Man is so contradictory and the realities of his environment are so unmanageable that politics without inner contradictions would not even be possible if it had to serve only one person in the whole world" (p. 485). Given this, he prefers opportunists to zealots, because they generally will be responsible for less suffering (p. 456). Strangely enough, Sarrazin views the "technological/scientific revolution," not democracy,[55] as the main contribution of the West to human civilization (pp. 347, 482); he exhibits no interest in examining any negative effects of that revolution, a surprising absence given that it is a product of flawed human beings. His exhortation that "our fate lies mainly in our own hands" (p. 405) is thus hardly comforting, even though it is clearly meant to be.

Sarrazin's brief observations about right-wing populism, direct democracy, and PEGIDA will be taken up below. At this juncture, it is helpful to examine the reaction to *Wunschdenken* in the German media. In this case, it was not *Der Spiegel*, but rather the infamous tabloid *Bild* that featured pre-publication excerpts from *Wunschdenken* on April 19 2016. In typical fashion, it was proclaimed: "This book will start arguments!"[56] That was certainly the case after the appearance of *DSSA*, but this time the situation was more complicated: six years after *DSSA*, Sarrazin was a known quantity rather than an obscure politician. By pure coincidence, *Wunschdenken* made its debut on the bestseller lists along with the new scholarly edition of Hitler's *Mein Kampf*; as one can well imagine, this was duly noted by those observers who hoped to dismiss Sarrazin as a latter-day fascist. On the whole, however, the media buzz was not as intense as it had been in 2010; as Alexander Kissler put it in the magazine *Cicero*, "There was more alarm before."[57] He went on to maintain that the Berlin Republic had decided to make the "taboo breaker" one of their own, though of course not everyone could accept this cooptation model.

On the extreme right, the controversial journalist and author Udo Ulfkotte could hardly find enough superlatives to express his admiration; for him, *Wunschdenken* was a "treasure trove of intellectual delights" with "unassailable figures and facts," even "mathematically precise."[58] The journal *Junge Freiheit* (Young Freedom), often involved in disputes about whether it is an organ of the extreme right or not, began its announcement of the publication with the headline "*Wir schaffen das nicht!*" (We can't manage this), negating Angela Merkel's famous 2015 assertion that the Germans could manage the refugee situation.[59] The blogger "conservo," who characterizes himself as a "Catholic, joyful *Rheinländer*," reposted a review by Ellen Kositza, whose words originally appeared on the site *PEGIDA Bayern*. Kositza believes that "hardly anyone" is capable of analyzing contemporary problems like Sarrazin, who combines "scientific methodology, political experience, and the courage to speak the truth."[60] This is surely the stuff of which prophets are made, but Sarrazin would feel uncomfortable donning that particular mantle.

Deutsche Welle, the German international broadcasting company, opined that the new book would "fail to attract as much attention" as *DSSA*, because Sarrazin was clearly "beyond his peak;"[61] this view itself turned out to be wishful thinking, as most important media outlets joined the discussion. In the *Süddeutsche Zeitung*, Detlef Esslinger predicted that *Wunschdenken* would be torn to shreds by the reviewers, but his own piece was far from that.[62] He pointed out that Sarrazin was writing neither for *Wutbürger* (in other words, enraged activist citizens who believe that the government is ignoring their input in important matters) nor the supporters of the AfD. What Sarrazin writes is "funny, frightful, and good;" in other words, the book is a rather ambivalent affair, not a mere rant. Esslinger often disagrees with Sarrazin, but he takes him and his positions seriously and believes that engaging with them helps form one's own positions — that is, he does not dismiss Sarrazin out of hand. Writing in the rival *Frankfurter Rundschau*, Arno Widmann (see above) chose to forgo such niceties: "In his new book, Thilo Sarrazin has perfected the art of selling the crudest stupidities as differentiated analysis."[63] Widmann stated flatly that the new book was the same as the old one (*DSSA*). Sarrazin is a "man possessed," so his best readers would be those who are plagued by the "same demons." In closing, Widmann informed his readers: "The Germany in which we live today is no longer the racially pure one in which Thilo Sarrazin and I grew up. Nostalgia is out of place." Reading this, one would never guess that Sarrazin has called for the planned immigration of productive people from all over the globe; beyond that, Widmann has basically internalized Hitlerian ideology: Germany has never been racially pure. A competing polemic appeared in *Der Spiegel*, where Nils Minkmar attempted to psychoanalyze Sarrazin, maintaining that all of his books were basically about himself and his "aggression" vis-à-vis the world.[64] The magazine framed the piece with the phrase "more nonsense from Sarrazin" and dubbed the book "a collection of cognitive errors;" in case this wasn't explicit enough, a photo of Sarrazin sitting next to AfD leader Frauke Petry is placed at the beginning of the article. Minkmar emphasized that Sarrazin's books are only worth reading because there are others who share his "dark" world view, and the AfD attempts to profit from that. Minkmar even had the cheek to enlist Frank Schirrmacher as an ally here, without bothering to mention that Schirrmacher's assessment of *DSSA* was not uniformly negative (see above). As for immigration, Minkmar pointed to the US and Canada as success stories, without realizing that the two models are distinctly different. He also seemed to know more about the tragedy in Syria than anyone else, because he felt justified in berating Sarrazin for not considering that "these refugees will return to Syria if peace were to rule in their homeland,"[65] an eventuality that no one can possibly predict with certainty. The weekly *Die Zeit*, long seen as the *Bildungsbürger*'s organ of choice, was equally merciless: its author, Mark Schieritz, offered his comments under the headline "To all: Put on a sweater!"[66] This was meant to make Sarrazin look ridiculous for having advised impoverished Berliners to put on a sweater if their heating costs were too high, a recommendation previously given by US President Jimmy Carter during energy shortages in 1977. Schieritz portrayed Sarrazin as a typical colonialist who represses the consequences of his actions, such as wars of intervention; the problem is that Sarrazin has spoken out against such wars himself. Schieritz criticized Sarrazin for not wanting to spend German tax dollars for foreign aid, even though he admitted that such aid has not brought about the desired results. In general, he found Sarrazin to be naive in thinking that the individual national state could still act independently in an increasingly interdependent world. Sarrazin's "fundamental" critique of the 'German way' puts him, according to Schieritz, in the same camp as the many citizens who have turned away from the mainstream political parties. What is not said here is that not all of those citizens have turned to the right for solace. However, Minkmar and Schieritz seem tame compared to Jakob Augstein; to him, Sarrazin is simply a racist, and not only that:

> Thilo Sarrazin currently occupies the top spot on the SPIEGEL list of bestselling non-fiction books. In second place is Adolf Hitler. The great right-wing publicist just ahead of the great seducer. There are clearly continuities in German reading habits. With tongue in cheek, one could say: The right people are next to each other.[67]

Sarrazin's way of thinking (and that of Necla Kelek, Augstein adds) is an expression of "contempt for humanity," and Sarrazin "systematically teaches racism" to his readers. To counter Sarrazin's critique of Islam, Augstein relates the success story of Sadiq Khan, the child of Muslim immigrants who was elected mayor of London in 2016; such success must be a "puzzle" to people like Sarrazin, Augstein opines. However, Sarrazin had already written in DSSA: "Liberal Muslims resist those who attribute certain characteristics to Islam per se, and they are right to do so" (p. 268). In this passage, the potential for a modernization of Islam is not denied: "*Most* streams of the Islamic faith have *yet* to go through the societal developmental process that most streams of Christianity have completed in the past 500 years" (my italics; p. 269). In other words, there is room in this picture for Sadiq Khan and others like him. Augstein also recycles Wolfgang Benz's comparison of anti-Semitism and Islamophobia and raises the bar, claiming that

Islamophobia has "long since supplanted anti-Semitism as the most dangerous racism in Germany". Where Angela Merkel once deemed *DSSA* "not helpful," Augstein's diatribe is pernicious, pure and simple.

Not all of the reactions to *Wunschdenken* ignored grey areas. *Die Welt* is a conservative newspaper, but its contribution to the debate did not paint everything black and white. Even though Sarrazin's overinflated sense of self-importance and his misuse of genetics in the discussion of inherited intelligence were criticized there, it was conceded that his intentions were serious (no "Facebook flaneur," but rather a "*Bildungsbürger*"—no ironic undertone here), and that the issues that he addressed were substantial.[68] A similar stance was taken in the conservative Catholic newspaper *Rheinische Post*, where it was pointed out that *Wunschdenken* contains "much that is stimulating and much that must be taken seriously" along with "analytical nonsense."[69] It is noted that Sarrazin's views on the environment and climate change have become more sophisticated. One intriguing statement made here is that Sarrazin "does not fulfill the expectation that [his new book] could serve as a broad scientific basis for contemporary right-wing populism." The question is: whose expectation? That of the media, or that of the populists themselves? Finally, even the left-leaning magazine *Freitag* did not feel the need to take *Wunschdenken* very seriously: Michael Angele wrote there that the only readers who would be able to get through the entire book were probably "a few extremely conscientious retired civil servants (his core following)."[70] The book itself "seems like the monstrous blog entry of a highly conscientious retired civil servant with modest authorial talent," whom the reviewer rather patronizingly wishes "a few nice long trips with many interesting and enlightening encounters." Or, as Stefan Wagstyl put it in the *Financial Times*: Sarrazin is "at heart a grumpy old man," and: "He raises important questions. But his reactionary and sometimes brutal answers are of little relevance to modern Germany."[71]

Is the Sarrazin case a mere tempest in a teapot? If it had occurred in any other developed industrial democracy, the answer would probably be yes; long books crammed full of statistics written by retired civil servants do not usually drive social change—of course, they do not normally become bestsellers, either. One source of the hostility toward Sarrazin has to do with the fact that he cannot be simply dismissed as a crank: he is a Social Democrat and an educated member of the middle class who values the culture of his country and strives to preserve it for the coming generations. (It is another question whether or not said generations will appreciate his efforts or at least allow him to take their attention away from their electronic devices for a brief period.) He is an advocate for high culture, which is often considered elitist in today's Germany. Another country-specific factor also comes into play: even though Germany has been a united country for more than twenty-five years, and even though the Third Reich disappeared over seventy years ago, the German public sphere remains unique. As philosopher Jürgen Habermas put it when reacting to *DSSA*: "social and political developments in Germany, given its ghastly history, do not necessarily have the same significance as in other countries."[72] Or, as Michael Slackman wrote in *The New York Times*: "[*DSSA*] for the first time since World War II made it socially acceptable in Germany to single out a particular minority for criticism."[73] In the title of his article, Slackman made sure that his readers understood exactly what he meant: "Opening a door long shut." With that, Sarrazin becomes a link, even a continuation of the dark past; very few contemporary Germans would appreciate being characterized in that way, and those who would welcome the comparison are not Sarrazin's colleagues or comrades (and they certainly do not share his ambivalence about many issues). What can be said without qualification is that Sarrazin represents a group of people who cling to their national identity in the face of ever-accelerating globalization[74] and a record number of refugees on a global scale. In the United States, such a stance would hardly be controversial, but in Germany, it is still a red flag, at least in certain quarters. One knows that Sarrazin was quite upset about Chancellor Merkel's now famous dictum "We can manage this" (*Wir schaffen das*). Is he now heartened by her later statement ("Germany will remain Germany, with everything that is dear and precious to us"[75]) as a reaction to criticism of her refugee policy?

Thilo Sarrazin is not a prophet or even a veteran political consultant. He is, however, a citizen who feels the need to speak out about the course that the political elites are charting for his country. Does such activity not belong to the essential attributes of a democratic society? Sarrazin has written books that should be taken seriously, analyzed, and criticized.[76] It is disturbing that in Germany, a country that has been the home of so many important thinkers, so few people have been willing to engage in a serious dialogue with him. Is this a symptom of cultural decline? At any rate, Sarrazin is not a representative of the extreme right, and the pundits who claim that he is do a disservice to those who want to understand and struggle against that particular camp, both in Germany and elsewhere.

2

AKIF PIRINÇCI
THE MIGRANT PROVOCATEUR

The national and international discourse about immigration often revolves around two concepts, namely assimilation and integration. Should an immigrant be allowed or even encouraged to retain certain aspects of his or her original culture and socialization, or should a border crossing entail a sort of rebirth? This question usually leads to another: is it possible to construct a multicultural society? Canada, the country whose immigration policies are admired by Thilo Sarrazin, has put into law the directive to "recognize and promote the understanding that multiculturalism reflects the cultural and racial diversity of Canadian society and acknowledges the freedom of all members of Canadian society to preserve, enhance and share their cultural heritage."[1] This wording makes it eminently clear that Canada does not strive for the assimilation of its new residents/citizens. But what of those who do wish to assimilate? The Turkish-German writer Akif Pirinçci (b. 1959), who was born in Istanbul and came to Germany with his parents at nine years old, can be considered an extremely successful example of complete assimilation. He is a prolific author whose books have sold millions of copies, both in Germany and abroad, and some of these have been made into films; his works have made him prosperous; and his command of the German language is more sophisticated than that of many native Germans. He has truly lived the German version of the

American dream, and was described by one critic in 2006 as "a fully integrated and respected member of society in the Federal Republic."[2] However, in 2014 something happened that turned his life upside down and transformed him into a social outcast. How did he become "perhaps the best-known provocateur in Germany after Thilo Sarrazin?"[3]

Pirinçci had to self-publish his first book, the autobiographical novel *Tränen sind immer das Ende* (*Tears Are Always the End*) in 1980.[4] Some observers were surprised that the author seemed uninterested in examining the lives of Turks in Germany, something that was *de rigueur* for writers of a migrant background at the time.[5] It was the series of detective novels about the cat detective Francis and his feline milieu (*Katzenkrimis*) that brought Pirinçci to the attention of a wider reading public. A brief look at *Felidae*, the first volume in the series,[6] can be instructive with regard to later developments. Right from the outset, we learn that Francis inhabits a decidedly dystopian world: "The world is hell! What does it matter what happens in it? It is set up so that one woe follows another" (p. 9). The clever and heroic Francis spends his life pursuing murderers and love and uncovering a sinister feline plot for world domination. The two overriding themes are sex and violence, both of which are described in great detail.[7] Here is one example:

> I will kill him! [...] I will make ground meat out of him and cook his entrails in the microwave! I will bite through his throat and drink his blood! I will rip out his balls and have him eat them. (p. 150)

Anyone familiar with Thilo Sarrazin's works will know that one would never find such language used, and the level of emotionality in *Felidae* and elsewhere is completely foreign to Sarrazin's world. The German philosopher Ernst Bloch once used the terms *Kältestrom* (cold current) and *Wärmestrom* (warm current) to describe two opposing methods of analyzing the economy and society;[8] it is clear that Sarrazin represents the former and Pirinçci the latter. There is one other facet that sets the two polemicists apart: Sarrazin resides exclusively in the ethereal realm of high culture, whereas Pirinçci constantly mixes high culture (in *Felidae*, he references Nietzsche, Mahler, and Richard Strauss) with the popular (Woodstock, Deep Purple, *The Aristocats*).

In 2014, the German cultural scene was shocked by the publication of a tirade when Akif Pirinçci's seething polemic *Deutschland von*

Sinnen. Der irre Kult um Frauen, Homosexuelle und Zuwanderer (*Germany Is Out of Its Mind. The crazy cult about women, homosexuals and immigrants*, hereafter *DvS*)[9] was brought to market by a rather obscure conservative publishing house. (One recalls that Sarrazin's *DSSA* was distributed by Random House, one of the largest publishers in the world.) Without Sarrazin as a trailblazer, the new volume might not have come into existence; Pirinçci makes this quite clear in his own book:

> Sarrazin's name has in the meantime become separated from his million-selling book *Deutschland schafft sich ab*, and it stands in public discourse not only as a synonym for "misanthrope," for the worst form of right-wing radicalism, but it is also one of the most effective Nazi clubs[10] with which one can thrash unpleasant critics of the multi-culti church. As soon as someone comes under suspicion of being a Sarrazin supporter, he is for all practical purposes already dead. *Despite this, I fervently hope that I will, with the present volume, outstrip Sarrazin.* (My italics; p. 214)

Why does Pirinçci feel that such outstripping is necessary, given the overwhelming resonance of *DSSA*?[11] He offers an explanation right after the above passage:

> Thilo Sarrazin has actually written a rather dry book with many soporific numbers, statistics, and diagrams. [...] Not even he, the supposedly right-wing radical demon, has dared to say what every normally thinking person—including the majority of the immigrants in this country—believes: One should give tickets to a few million of the people with migration background here and send them home again without delay before they eat us out of house and home. (p. 215)

Even the self-styled hyperradical making this proposal is not unaware of how such pronouncements might be received in Germany, so he hastens to add: "Just so I am not misunderstood: We need everyone here—no matter what skin color they might have—who is useful for us, but not a single one who is useless" (p. 215).[12]

Just as Sarrazin's *DSSA* was preceded by controversy involving an interview, Pirinçci's *DvS* appeared after a media brouhaha. On March 25 2013, Pirinçci published the text 'The Slaughter has Begun' (*Das Schlachten hat begonnen*) on the liberal/libertarian site "The Axis of Good" (*Die Achse des Guten*).[13] This was a reaction to the attack on the young German Daniel Siefert by the Turkish immigrant Cihan A. and others in the town of Kirchweye in Lower Saxony; Siefert died as a result. The aim of Pirinçci's blog post was not to express grief or even outrage, but rather to declare that migrants are at war with ethnic Germans. There is, he asserted, a campaign of "creeping genocide" underway directed against young German men. Beyond that, there is supposedly a media conspiracy designed to play down the role of migrants in this campaign—all in the name of political correctness. This is seen as a result of the socialization of young Germans, "trained from kindergarten on to hate their own ethnic origin" (*Volkszugehörigkeit*); such a statement is of course connected to the agonizing postwar discourse about what it means to be German. The blog contains other themes that will reappear in *DvS*: the denigration of German men by gender studies, the "left-green" dominance of the public sphere, the German overdependence on the state, the "insanity" of the "anti-fascist gangs," and the use of brutal language, as illustrated by one particular passage:

> [...] even in the course of evolution, it seldom occurs that they [a group under attack] simply let themselves get fucked and then kiss the dick of the rapist. And in no case would they lick the dick of the one who has murdered their own son.

Despite such fighting words, Pirinçci's closing statement is not a call to arms, but rather a resigned prophecy that the Germans will have to get used to the takeover of their country. He advises them not to have sons anymore, since they will be killed anyway; future daughters will "at least survive," to be (ab-)used by the conquerors. Such formulations are not uncommon on sites run by conspiracy theorists and/or white supremacists, but no one in Germany could have predicted that an assimilated Turkish-German author would harbor such sentiments. No one could have imagined that the book-length amplification of this brief blog would become a bestseller in Germany, either.[14]

Whatever else one might say about the two books by Thilo Sarrazin discussed above, they do have a clear structure, meant to be a reflection of the 'rational' analysis provided by the author. In contrast, Akif Pirinçci's *DvS* is an eruption. If one were to speak in terms of literary history, Sarrazin feels an affinity with the Enlightenment, whereas Pirinçci writes like a latter-day representative of the *Sturm und Drang*. One can read his book from beginning to end or from the middle, since the level of emotional turbulence remains constant. The final chapter is entitled 'The Slaughter has Begun,' and it contains the full text of the blog post of the same name. In his prefatory remarks, Pirinçci mentions that he had to pay a fine of 4,000 Euros; later one learns what led to the penalty: it was not the views expressed in 'The Slaughter has Begun' (though Pirinçci claims that legal action was considered), but the result of another text about Professor Monika Sieverding of the University of Heidelberg. What Pirinçci is railing against here is the theory and practice of gender mainstreaming,[15] but something else becomes immediately apparent: whereas Sarrazin felt the need to lecture his fellow citizens, Pirinçci is more of an aggressive loner who feels persecuted and is always ready for battle. His various interventions are difficult to assess, however, because it is not always obvious whether or not he is being completely serious.

Perhaps the best way to access Pirinçci's world is to compare it with Sarrazin's, and the aforementioned topic of gender mainstreaming is a good place to start. The European Institute for Gender Equality defines the term as follows:

> The systematic consideration of the differences between the conditions, situations and needs of women and men in all Community policies and actions. Gender mainstreaming is the (re)organisation, improvement, development and evaluation of policy processes, so that a gender equality perspective is incorporated in all policies at all levels and all stages, by the actors normally involved in policy-making.
>
> Mainstreaming a gender perspective is the process of assessing the implications for women and men of any planned action, including legislation, policies or programs, in all areas and at all levels. It is a way to make women's as well as men's concerns and experiences an integral dimension of the design, implementation, monitoring and evaluation of policies and programs in all political, economic and societal spheres so that women and men benefit equally and inequality is not perpetuated. The ultimate goal is to achieve gender equality.[16]

Sarrazin praises Hirsi Ali and Necla Kelek as "pioneering champions for women's rights" (*DSSA*, p. 274) and at the same time criticizes

Islam for "limiting women's freedom" and making them subordinate to men (*DSSA*, p. 313). Calling for the universal availability of all-day childcare, he observes that the "classic division of labor—the man as the provider, the woman takes care of the household" is now passé (*DSSA*, p. 380). Although he is unhappy about the fact that educated (German) women have few children, he does not really believe that this could change. He endorses equal opportunity for men and women, although he cannot help adding an aside that "even the most pigheaded gender debate" cannot deny that women have different "talents and inclinations" than men (*Wunschdenken*, p. 317). In the end, he categorizes what he calls "genderism" as a "special variant of equality mania," one of the "hobbies of conviction fetishists" or naive idealists (*Wunschdenken*, pp. 402-403). In other words, he considers such 'post-materialist' pursuits to be rather insignificant compared to economic growth and stability and the preservation of cultural heritage. No such subtleties (if that is the correct term here) are to be found in Pirinçci's *DvS*. The fourth chapter is entirely about women ('*Über die Frauen*'), but the fundamental proclamations are found in the final chapter:

> Whether the female reader of this text likes it or not, being a woman is primarily creating life, giving birth to life; everything else must be subordinated to this goal and purpose. No woman is more beautiful than when she has a baby bump [...]. (p. 246)
>
> Gender Mainstreaming is a rubbish theory that was farted into the world by lesbians who are aggressive, even though they do not want to work. It says that the sex[17] of a person is a learned "social construct" that one can change according to desire or whim like tampons. [...] In short, the identity as a combative lesbian (*das Kampflesbenartige*) is supposedly the only true sex, and everything else is pure shit. (p. 245)

Given such eruptions, one wonders what else could be said in an entire chapter. In this final chapter, one immediately encounters a very personal account about the author's own life. This is not the place for amateur psychoanalysis, but what Pirinçci relates here is clearly connected to the motivation behind his book. He describes a beautiful blond woman sleeping peacefully after a night of "vigorous" sex;[18] we then learn that he is speaking of a summer day nineteen years previously. In the meantime, "the usual" has happened: namely, she has left him, even though Pirinçci swears that he was a "responsible father" and "a good lover" (p. 129). How could this have happened? In the course of his search for answers, Pirinçci mulls over the changes in gender roles over the past century. He assures the reader that he does not wish to criticize women's emancipation per se; the real problem is "contemporary prosperity:" "Back then, people, especially women, had very different problems than worrying about gender roles, since their lives were too short. Above all, it was about getting enough to eat, a roof over one's head, and getting through life relatively healthily" (p. 136). Why do today's women question traditional roles? One factor is their supposed gullibility (women are more "manipulable" and have more "illusions"; p. 133), and another is connected to what Pirinçci calls the "gabbing sciences" (Geschwätzwissenschaften: the humanities and social sciences). He claims that young women today are mainly attracted to young men who study such fields, which contribute nothing to "surplus value" or "prosperity" (p. 137), and in contrast to earlier times, these men, who are rather "feminized," assert their dominance via verbal "manipulation" (p. 138). He claims such men are also not interested in having children; in one fictional example, a smooth-talking man is able to convince his girlfriend to have an abortion (pp. 142-144). Although Pirinçci does not say so directly, the implication is that 'real' men—the "nerds" ("naturally 'white,' Asian, above all ones of Jewish descent") would be better partners (pp. 138-139). In one of his many asides, he points out that on a global scale, women hold only 4 per cent of all patents. It is not necessary to speak of Pirinçci's theories about sexual practice, but his comments about the men whose wives/partners have left them are certainly noteworthy: such men are not only "disillusioned," but also suffer from "traumas" (p. 150); they restlessly search for new relationships, but they are so damaged that they are attractive to no one. Among the types described are "the pervert," "the desperate phoney," "the slimy one," "the sender of penis photos," and "the braggart" (pp. 147-150). In other words, the transformation of gender roles has made both women and men into rather pathetic figures, or "emotional zombies" (p. 152).[19] Pirinçci's yearning for the 'good old days' is expressed in his lament that the proverbial saying "Let's grow old together" could soon become a "humorous anachronism" (p. 152). Beyond nostalgia, there is one conundrum regarding women which refers us back to Sarrazin; as will be discussed below, Pirinçci is highly critical of the subordination of women in Islam.

DvS begins with a paean to "Germany, my mother" that would in all likelihood embarrass many 'native' Germans, especially those of the left-liberal persuasion: "Germany, oh you golden Elysium! You powerful steer! You are the power that carries all of Europe! You are the most beautiful of all the beautiful countries!" (p. 11). The novelty lies in the fact that the author behind this apotheosis is not a 'blond beast' (neither ethnically nor in Nietzschean terms[20]), but rather an immigrant from Turkey who has embraced his new homeland without reservation. Or has he? In responding to a journalist from Bremen who had criticized his text 'The Slaughter has Begun' as basically proto-fascist, Pirinçci declared: "You have chosen the wrong opponent. [...] If you fuck me, then I will fuck you. [...] And don't forget, at the bottom of my heart I am still a Turk, so watch out!" (p. 243).[21] The writer with this hybrid identity proceeds to explain the shocking pallor of "Germany, dearest mother"[22] with reference to demographics: instead of praising procreation as the sine qua non of national life, the German media are, he claims, fixated upon the deviant (*das Abseitige*) forms of sexuality and their "myriad deformations" (p. 12). The only form of heterosexuality supposedly worthy of mention is that of the country's Muslims, who defend their wives' head scarves "tooth and nail". Heterosexuality as the *locus* of procreation is for Pirinçci not only "normal," but even "sacred" (pp. 12, 19); using this model as a yardstick, judgment is passed on institutions, intellectual activity, and political parties. Perhaps the most crass example of this practice is the characterization of the German Greens (*Bündnis 90/Die Grünen*) as the "sex-with-children party" (p. 13); aside from the fact that Pirinçci misses no opportunity to denigrate environmentalists,[23] this particular instance illuminates his methodology. There was a discourse about the nature of pederasty/pedophilia in Germany from the 1970s onwards (including the aspect of decriminalization), and there were factions in the Greens who advocated for the general liberation of sexuality. This topic gradually faded into the background, and the party itself commissioned a study by independent experts, the results of which can be examined in book form and in a useful summary.[24] There can be no doubt that the Greens (and other individuals/groups in Germany) were on the wrong side of this issue, but that does not justify an overall condemnation of their efforts in the environmental arena. Such niceties do not interest Pirinçci; the same is true for the policy of Gender Mainstreaming, which is dismissed here as a "mental illness" (p. 16). The German Protestant Church, which has been open to a discussion of the varieties of sexuality, looks like a "nothing" to Pirinçci, whereas the Catholics exercise their right to defend their doctrine (p. 14). The author comes out against gay marriage, the right of homosexual couples to adopt children, transsexuals, the "psychic hell of *anything goes*" (p. 22) and even AIDS research, which takes away resources from research and treatment for the straight majority.[25] Not for the first time, however, he also issues a disclaimer to ensure that his readers understand him 'correctly;' he emphasizes that he does not wish to "defame" homosexuals (p. 22), given that homosexuality has "always existed," and that society would be less "innovative" and more boring without "the other" (p. 23); he also does not want to "play down" the persecution of minorities in the past (p. 15). What could explain this contradiction? Perhaps it is Pirinçci's solemn vow that he will protect "our gays, lesbians, and others" against "the very dangerous and more and more aggressively spreading Islam" (p. 23). This leads us directly to the second and perhaps most important chapter of the book, which is entitled 'Islam belongs to Germany like the Reeperbahn belongs to Mecca' (the *Reeperbahn* is the legendary red light district in the port city of Hamburg).

When Thilo Sarrazin warned of "authoritarian, premodern, and antidemocratic tendencies" in certain strains of Islam (*DSSA*, p. 266), he did so from a distance, like an anthropologist describing an exotic civilization. In contrast, Akif Pirinçci approaches the subject as a 'member of the tribe' who has intimate knowledge of its rituals; it is thus not surprising that he includes his own family history in the account, and this inclusion appears with a characterization that it is normative with respect to Islamic immigrants to Germany:

> In 1969, my parents, with a cardboard suitcase in hand, came with their children to this country. Turkey offered us nothing [...] We were so poor that in the end, we could not even afford coal for heating in the winter.

39

We felt that it was an incomprehensible gift that Germany took us in. [...]
We were simply told: Work, go to school, make something of yourselves,
you owe us nothing except possibly that you can become a productive,
creative, and enriching part of this country and can even put down roots
here if you like. My parents were not unemployed for a single day of
their working life in Germany; they did not hear that the state pays social
welfare to people who do nothing until long after they had returned to
Turkey, where they enjoyed their retirement. Our family had neither the
leisure time for nor interest in religious matters. [...] Yes, in some ways
we were of the Islamic faith that we had been born into. [...] Although
we had still been cultural Muslims in the homeland, in Germany the last
traces of religiosity disappeared from our family life, especially in the case
of the younger people. That is how it probably went with almost all of the
Turkish immigrants of my generation. (pp. 31-32)

It is no accident that the name Richard Dawkins appears in this chapter,
for Pirinçci has clearly become an atheist in the meantime. He not
only rejects Islam, but any religion that strives to play a role in public
life—asserting that no one pays any attention to Buddhists or Taoists
because they don't "cause any irritation" (p. 34). European Christianity
is for him nothing more than a historical relic, albeit an imposing
one: "wonderful cultural manifestations like cathedrals, breathtaking
paintings, and of course classical music. [...] The rest is history,
ironically cultivated tradition [...], folklore" (p. 28). Given this stance,
he sees no reason to speak respectfully of the various religious faiths
or their followers; with respect to Islam, this manifests itself in such
terms as "Allah app" (p. 35), "M people" (p. 36), "Mohammed fans" (p.
39), or "Mohammed's checklist" (p. 54). As youths, Pirinçci and his
peers were supposedly no more interested in "the prophet" than they
were in "Grandpa's smelly boots" (p. 32).[26] All this was before the rise
of Islamist terror; the main terror that young Pirinçci was confronted
with stemmed from the "tyrannical regime" of his father's "Muslim-
oriental-authoritarian-Turkish mentality" (p. 32); the new gods were
Genesis and Pink Floyd, representatives of Western culture, "the freest
in human memory" (p. 33). Pirinçci makes it abundantly clear that he
cannot imagine why anyone would turn away from this culture and
embrace Islam, which produces a culture without inventiveness or
creativity (p. 39), despises women (p. 54), and propagates a "highly

sexualized, politically aggressive, and religiously grounded community ideology" (p. 50). Addressing a typical Muslim immigrant to Germany, Pirinçci berates him/her: "You belong to a religion in whose name each and every day people around the world are blown up, beheaded, executed, subjected to genital mutilation, tortured, senselessly murdered on a mass scale, and finally robbed of their beautiful and noble humanity" (p. 66). This searing indictment reads like a clarion call for a sort of 'anti-jihad' against the Muslims in Germany, but that is actually not the case; Pirinçci is speaking of a specific subgroup, namely those

> who actually practice Islam, demonstratively carry it into the public sphere and have the gall to call for special treatment allowing for the disdain of human beings and especially women. There are more than a few of these, but they are by no means the majority of the M people who live in this country. (p. 36)

The vast majority of Muslims in Germany, we are told, are "peace-loving, decent, and live for the moment,"[27] as opposed to those "who act as Stone-Age religious agents of divisiveness [Spaltpilze] in our modern age" (p. 42); many of the latter are simply "not civilizable" (p. 41).

As in Sarrazin's writings, the tone at one point turns pessimistic. Pirinçci thinks it is already "too late" (p. 41) to do anything about this situation, short of a declaration of war, which will not happen. The reason why it will not happen is almost a greater source of rage than the radical Muslims themselves: Pirinçci's beloved Germany is being undermined from within, subverted by a cabal of leftists, Greens, apostles of religious tolerance, and advocates of integration and inclusion. Thanks to "feminist-pacifist brainwashing," German men have become completely emasculated (p. 41). The "systematic destruction" of German society began in the mid-1980s, when the Greens and the "left-leaning media," purveying a kind of "hippie and communist way of thinking," pushed for technophobia and German self-hatred (p. 50); hand in hand with this went the "exaltation of the others" (p. 50). In Pirinçci's mind, one of the biggest lies was the talk about the environment: a long list of 'non-existent' problems is provided, including air and water pollution, the dangers of nuclear power, acid rain, chemicals in food, and GMOs (p. 51). The pre-apocalyptic mood set the stage for the gradual takeover of the country by Muslim immigrants,[28] facilitated by feckless German politicians, a justice system that "looked the other way," and the miserable journalists with a "tolerance fart in their heads" (p. 52). If the country does not heed the warnings issued by Pirinçci, Germany and Europe ("Eurabia"; p. 68) will be unrecognizable by 2030. A detailed description of life under the new regime is intended as a wake-up call: most of the German place names have been forgotten; women are intimidated by TV shows portraying rape as punishment for straying from the right path; the infrastructure is falling apart; garbage is everywhere; and corruption is the order of the day (pp. 69-71). The final image is that of a gay man who has been tortured, executed, and finally put on display in a public square to warn others against sexual deviation. What Pirinçci does not tell us is what the Germans' reaction to this wake-up call should be.

However, in the next chapter, 'Fear is a Decision,' Pirinçci does disclose what kind of Germany he would prefer. Even though he assures us that he would never emigrate ("I could never live in any other country in the world"; p. 125), that does not mean that he accepts the status quo. It is perhaps no accident that the United States is mentioned more than once. If Sarrazin put forth a vision of an open society, Pirinçci's version is much more libertarian; in the wake of Donald Trump's election victory, it is almost eerie to read that "tax evasion is not a trifling offence [*Kavaliersdelikt*], but rather a heroic deed" (p. 125). Pirinçci's "mortal enemy" is the EU, which hates Germany (p. 81); taxes, "the cause of all evil in the country" (p. 85), are taken in by the "predatory state" (p. 89). In the best of all worlds, this state

> should, as far as possible, stick to its own shit, to securing the borders, a military, (real) police and justice, the handicapped and truly needy, well-maintained streets, and sexy uniforms for policewomen. That is enough! It should not guarantee that there is a kindergarten spot for my child. (p. 91)

Given his affinity for the American way of life,[29] one could think that Pirinçci's vision is close to the Tea Party world view (minus the uniforms, of course), but that would ignore the issue of religion. Since Germany is for him a "completely secularized society," state and religion must be "strictly separated" from each other (p. 115). The radically reduced state apparatus would need much less revenue—so little, in fact, that there would only be a flat tax rate of 5% for both individuals and corporations (p. 109); this is a proposal that would make even Steve Forbes blush.[30] The dismantling of the social welfare system would allow for the flowering of old-fashioned solidarity in families and communities; this is because "almost all people" have a "big heart," which has been suppressed by the nanny state (p. 111). Many fewer politicians would be needed, and the remaining ones would be men, since women in politics, with the "maternal gene," would be too inclined to give away the citizens' hard-earned money (p. 98). Women would be too busy taking care of their children anyway, since they would no longer need to work; the 'woman whisperer' Pirinçci is convinced that working women are an aberration. The "normal" women "would prefer to raise their children, decorate their (middle-class) houses, take care of the garden, plan vacations, spend a few hours with a blah-blah activity in order to get some contact with other people, and perhaps write a novel" (p. 101). All of the subsidies for the arts, including public television and movie production, would be eliminated, leading to "good art and entertainment" that would succeed on its own merits (p. 115); Pirinçci's use of the derogatory term "state artists" in this context is reminiscent of the rhetoric of the late Austrian populist Jörg Haider. Finally, environmental protection and ecological thinking would disappear, since climate change is a "lie," and renewable energy is "nonsense" (p. 86); all environmental legislation passed since 1975 is to be declared invalid (p. 112), and the nuclear power plants are to be restarted (p. 113). It is not enough that Pirinçci is determined to turn back the clock—it is also the way in which he expresses this wish that is extremely troubling. One of the best examples of this is a passage in which he dismisses the notion of 'buying local' produce: "The slogan 'local produce' is just as spurious as me in the brothel demanding to fuck only local whores instead of Ukrainian ones because they are not compatible with me down there" (p. 112). Some might say that such thuggery should be censured, but it is actually important to be aware that this sort of brutal misogyny stems from someone who wants to consign Western liberal society to the dustbin of history. We have been warned. It is nothing less than a travesty that Pirinçci ends the chapter containing such language with the phrase "Bury my heart at the bend of the Rhine" (p. 125), since this recycles most of the German title of

43

Dee Brown's *Bury My Heart at Wounded Knee*, implying that Germans face the same sort of cultural genocide that was imposed on Native Americans in the nineteenth century.

Pirinçci's all-out attack on the German media (under the heading "You can see better through your asshole"; pp. 155-193) contains multiple usage of the word "lie," but the Nazi term *"Lügenpresse,"* now favored by the US alt-right, does not appear—though this is hardly significant, because it would be difficult to imagine a more negative portrayal anyway. The Germans, Pirinçci maintains, are suffering under a "media dictatorship like in Hitler's time" (p. 164) This situation is expressed in the kind of sexualized imagery that one comes to expect in the volume: German public media are "fucked over and over like a whore who has been in the business for thirty years" (p. 173), and the perpetrator is none other than the German political establishment. There follows a long litany of the truths being withheld from the German media consumers: the media are run by "a bunch of super ugly ass kissers and untalented people, usually crypto-communist geezers with dementia" (p. 158); Fukushima was not a disaster, since no one was killed by radiation (p. 158); nuclear power is the "the cheapest, cleanest, and most harmless way of producing energy" (pp. 159-160); the Germans have invented "almost everything that has radically changed human life for the better" since the nineteenth century (p. 161); and the Third Reich ended in catastrophe because the Jews were exterminated: "Believe me, with them, they could have with absolute certainty won the war" (p. 163). He adds that it is a shame that the entire Jewish entertainment elite left for Hollywood, because without them, no highly developed entertainment industry can function; the *Rundfunkrat*, the supervisory body of German public media, now contains "Muslims, Sinti, and Roma," as well as too many environmentalists (pp. 180-181); the opposite model is found in the US, the "homeland of independent productions" (p. 190). Even though German intellectuals are fond of disparaging Hollywood, Pirinçci tells us that, in reality, Germans are "addicted" to US "films and TV" (p. 185) (It is more than a little strange that this passage contains a positive reference to filmmaker Michael Moore, since his films strive to dismantle the very system that Pirinçci praises so much.) The solution, according to Pirinçci, is for the commercial TV channels and print media to mount a relentless campaign against the public media (p. 192). To show that he is not pursuing a specific political agenda here, he calls upon the resistance to be undertaken by "leftist, libertarian, and conservative" media (p. 193). Of course, the agenda is actually quite political, namely an attempt to limit the power of the state in favor of private interests, and in the end, Pirinçci admits that it is highly unlikely that anything will change.

In contrast to Thilo Sarrazin, Pirinçci does not emphasize the importance of high culture in German society. He does, however, briefly discuss cultural issues in a chapter about German intellectuals; this is somewhat confusing, because no distinction is made between culture and civilization. The chapter begins with this statement: "German culture is an export hit" (p. 197). Reference is made to such phenomena as *Oktoberfest*, Christmas markets, *Currywurst*, copies of the Munich *Hofbräuhaus* or King Ludwig's *Neuschwanstein,* fairytale parks inspired by the Brothers Grimm, Bavarian beer, or *Lederhosen*, none of which would be found in Sarrazin's ranking. Pirinçci is aware of this, so he then provides a panorama of elite culture, which encompasses giants of classical music (Bach, Beethoven, Wagner, Brahms), literature (Goethe, E.T.A. Hoffmann), cinema (Murnau's *Nosferatu*, Fritz Lang), and finally Kurt Weill's influence on popular music. Although he claims that he could easily provide "pages and pages" of more examples (p. 198), one has the impression that his heart is not really in it. He even remarks that his readers will have noticed that he is speaking of "'old' German culture;" no dedicated advocate of elite culture would speak in this manner. The true agenda then becomes clear: very little of consequence has supposedly been produced in Germany after 1945, though a few exceptions are mentioned, such as the early Günter Grass, the band *Kraftwerk*, the filmmaker Rainer Werner Fassbinder, and the author Christian Kracht. The cause behind this sorry state of affairs (which would of course be rejected out of hand by serious cultural observers) is the mutation of the German intellectuals from unconventional thinkers and providers of impetus for public discourse to hostages with no will of their own. And who are the hostage takers?

> The seducers and hostage takers are those people who have studied some useless field and pay tribute to the leftist-green way of thinking,

political correctness, German self-hatred, and especially schizoid ideas and concepts [...] Not artists, not great thinkers and visionaries set the tone in today's cultural life and media, but rather some lesbians with university chairs in Gender Mainstreaming, bureaucrats involved in equality and anti-discrimination issues, organizations like *Pro Asyl*, refugee mentors, solar and wind [power] barons, Greenpeace & Co., sociology professors and appointed experts for the migrant and welfare industry (poverty report, criminality of foreigners, etc.), environmental groups, hardline communists on the left, a justice system that is an enemy of the state, crypto-fascist mobs like the *Antifa* [anti-fascists], and finally a *Gutmenschentum* [knee-jerk liberalism], installed mainly by the Greens in the course of the past thirty years, whose foundation consists of nothing but lies. (pp. 199-200)

In case the reader has not grasped the gravity of this situation, Pirinçci later provides one designation that applies to all those listed above: "traitors to the fatherland" (p. 200). In the past, such traitors have been routinely convicted of treason and executed, but this is not being done in contemporary Germany. What is the hindrance in this case? For Pirinçci, it is clearly German guilt, or, to be exact, "the indelible [*untilgbare*] German guilt" (p. 204). This is used as a club by those who wish to 'keep Germany down,' to prevent the country from reaching a status commensurate with its many achievements. Is there a way out of this dilemma? According to Pirinçci, it is a very simple: "Well, dear Germans, don't let yourselves be told by some moral apostles from elsewhere that you have to bear any guilt because of the Third Reich" (p. 206).[31] By saying this, Pirinçci is either betraying his own ignorance or suppressing the truth: German politicians routinely proclaim that those citizens who were too young to have participated in Nazi war crimes (former Chancellor Helmut Kohl famously spoke of the "grace of the late birth" in his 1984 speech before the Knesset and elsewhere) or were born after 1945 do not bear guilt, but they do indeed have a special responsibility to stand up for peace and justice in their time. This stance has gained much respect in the postwar world, and Germany has become a model for dealing with a difficult past (as opposed to Japan, for example). This status, acquired despite much initial skepticism from abroad, obviously means nothing to Pirinçci, who is more concerned with transporting both Germany in particular and the West in general back to the conditions that prevailed before the cultural and societal changes brought about by the social movements associated with 1968. Does he really believe that this could be done? At the end of the chapter, he remarks that German intellectuals cannot be brought to their senses by a box on the ears, but perhaps a "powerful blow to the head with an iron bar" might be sufficient (p. 228). That would be more reminiscent of 1928 (when SA thugs roamed German streets) than 1968.

What is to be done? In a final section of *DvS*, Pirinçci speaks directly to his fellow citizens, returning to the images that he used at the very beginning:

> Germans, this is *your* country. [...] It is the most beautiful country in the world! Yes, there are many other beautiful countries, but this one surpasses all of them in beauty, because it is your homeland, because you were born naked and bloody in it and grew up in it, and the spirit of your forebears lives here. [...] This German land belongs to neither the enemies from the EU, who want to enslave it, exploit it, and sooner or later lay claim to it, nor to some so-called immigrants, who are penetrating it each and every day with political lunatics and notorious traitors to the fatherland. [...] You are Germans, not cowardly rats. Long live sacred Germany! (p. 269)

After reading this stirring appeal, one almost expects Emperor Frederick Barbarossa to rise from the dead and lead the Germans to victory over their foes. That is not Pirinçci's universe, however; he is a man of the present, and he calls upon his compatriots to fulfill the roles for which they are destined. German men must once again embody the strength of the country, shaking off the shackles of gender discourse; they "alone" are responsible for the wealth of the country, so they should "arise" (pp. 269-270). The verb used here, "[*sich*] *erheben*," is used in connection with such key events in German history as the Wars of Liberation against Napoleon and the revolution of 1848/49, but in the mind of many, it is associated with its most recent usage, the Nazi term "national uprising" (*nationale Erhebung*). German women are "the most beautiful under the sun," whose "primary task" is to found a family with their loving husbands, and to bear children. That is the "female way of the world," according to

47

Pirinçci: women should accept traditional roles, because "provider" is a "noble word" (pp. 270-271).

After addressing German men and women, the author turns to "Germans with foreign roots" (pp. 271-272). This is difficult terrain, since for such people, Germany is neither the land of their birth nor the home of their ancestors (see above). In this case, Pirinçci's advice is clear and simple: "Forget your country of origin" and "Kindly assimilate! At the latest, your children should do that" (pp. 271-272). This refers only to those who have come to contribute something and better themselves; the ones in this category are even allowed to practice their religion, as long as they do not "overdo it" (p. 272).[32] Those who come in order to "live off us" (p. 272) should get out. Turning to German gay men, Pirinçci is surprisingly tolerant, largely because he views them primarily as German men. They should be "tough" (*hart im Nehmen*)—as all German men supposedly are by nature—and not complain about non-existent discrimination; they may live as they wish, as long as they do so "in the shadows" and do not bother Pirinçci (pp. 272-273). Conversely, he has very little succor for *German lesbians*, who "hate men," know nothing about marriage and family, and look strange; he believes they should "disappear" into their lesbian realm and stay there (p. 274). As bad as this sounds, it is trivial compared to the epithets directed toward "Green Germans" (p. 274). Pirinçci's kindest words are that they will not be "punished" once the fatherland has regained its former glory; however, they will be required to leave, because their "dirty lies" have destroyed Germany's "moral, spiritual, and technical/infrastructure foundations;" they should simply "go to hell" (pp. 274-275). Just after that admonishment, the term "Judgment Day" is used (p. 276). Pirinçci never explains exactly what he means by this, leaving the reader to imagine what sort of country German would be if people of his ilk held sway. Despite all the homage to the blood-and-soil rhetoric of the past, Pirinçci doubtless believes that his status as an "adopted" German (p. 66) will not prevent him from contributing to the shaping of the country's future. Perhaps *DvS* should be interpreted as Pirinçci's attempt—as a person with a so-called migration background—to present his credentials to those who will determine the course of a new nationalist, neotraditionalist Germany.

Just as Sarrazin's *DSSA* was followed by a volume containing critical responses, Pirinçci's *DvS* was maintained in the public eye by the publication of *Attacke auf den Main-Stream.* *"Deutschland von Sinnen" und die Medien (Attack on the Mainstream.* "Germany Is Out of Its mind" and the media).[33] The two accompanying volumes could not be more different, however: whereas *Sarrazin. A German Debate* contains the full text of responses from a broad spectrum of standpoints, *Attack on the Mainstream* provides some complete texts, but far more commented excerpts. Pirinçci's co-editor Lombard (the chief editor of the publisher *Manuscriptum)* contributes not only a preface, but also three other longer pieces. Since Pirinçci himself also adds a preface of his own and an exchange of letters with his publisher Thomas Hoof, one cannot avoid the impression that the purpose of the enterprise was not dialog, but rather a defense of *DvS* against its critics. A brief look at the two prefaces illustrates this: Lombard relates how he and his colleagues got the idea to ask Pirinçci to write the "pamphlet" (Lombard's term) after the appearance of the text 'The Slaughter has Begun.' We learn that the published work reached rank #4 on the German Amazon bestseller list, and that it was meant to be an attack on German politicians and journalists as "organizers of a feeble-minded feminist, homo, and migrant cult" in the country (pp. 7-8). Lombard adds disingenuously that in *DvS*, "not a single evil word was directed toward women or homosexuals themselves" (did he read the section on lesbians?), and that Pirinçci's "rude remarks" were reserved for "hack writers and spokespersons" (p. 8).[34] It does not bother Lombard that *DvS* is an expression of "contempt for journalists" (p. 9). He accuses Pirinçci's critics of wanting to send this "author without an Aryan certificate [*Ariernachweis*] who has gone crazy" right back to Turkey (p. 9); this particular statement is especially worthy of note, because it puts Nazi terminology into the mouths of anti-fascists. In the end, Lombard's main regret is that *DvS* did not change Germany, but he predicts that many similar efforts will follow (p. 10). Pirinçci's own preface is a melange of obfuscation and aggression. He begins by expressing amazement that anyone could imagine that he has misogynistic leanings, because, as he describes it, "In the course of my life, it was always women [*die Weiber*] who helped me along" (p. 11). (This includes the one who "sweetened" his weekends after a week of writing.) Pirinçci chooses not to bore his readers with justification for what he has written, because he sees no need to defend his clear statements. The actual writing of the book was "fun," since he was writing not a sober non-fiction work, but "a very personal speech" (pp. 12-13). He is especially proud of the fact that the epithet "Nazi" has (supposedly) lost its sting after the appearance of his book (in other words, one can no longer do away with uncomfortable right-wing foe by calling them that); the real fascists are the anti-fascists, he maintains (p. 15). Left-leaning journalists are in his view "perverse, pedophile, addicted to drugs, and impoverished" (p. 16), a rather curious statement, since the "mainstream" mentioned in the title implies that the establishment media, by definition agents of the left, do not pay well! Finally, Pirinçci points out that the whole edifice inhabited by the knee-jerk liberals (*Gutmenschen*) has proved to be rickety. He hopes that the publication of "thousands, even tens of thousands" of successor volumes to *DvS* will bring it tumbling down (p. 17). His last bit of advice? "Always attack head-on!" (p. 17).

One instructive way to access *Attack on the Mainstream* is to examine how Pirinçci is characterized. Interestingly, there is no consensus, either among his supporters or among his critics. With regard to the question of assimilation vs. integration, a list of terms is fascinating:

- "foreigner" (Pirinçci speaking about himself; p. 12);
- "a Turk" (p. 26);
- "a Turk, more German than the Germans" (p. 29);
- "a child of guest workers" (p. 42);
- "a Turkish migrant" p. (79);
- "a native Turk, not equipped with the German 'murderers' gene'" (p. 97);
- "no roots of his own in this country" (p. 112);
- "a former Turk" (p. 139);
- "a German with Turkish roots" (p. 141);
- "a model immigrant" (p. 203).

The most accurate one is "a German with Turkish roots," which was used by Arnulf Baring (1932–2019), a well-known conservative intellectual and social commentator, rather than a prominent left-leaning proponent of multiculturalism. Beyond identity questions, the terms used to describe Pirinçci's political stance are colorful, to say the least. His supporters see in him many postures, including:

- a writer in the tradition of Bukowski, Céline, Burroughs, or Ayn Rand (pp. 23, 86, 197);
- "a passionate and romantic realist" (p. 43);
- an "empiricist" (though he provides no data à la Sarrazin; p. 122);
- "a person who loves freedom" (p. 173);
- "an arch-liberal, self-ironic romantic" (p. 184);
- "a lonely voice in a cultural and spiritual wasteland" (p. 212).

His opponents, by contrast, speak of:

- "the writer as thug" (p. 41);
- "an autodidact gone crazy" (p. 63);
- "a drunken and whoring Turk" (p. 67);
- "a Turkish rapper who hates Germany" (p. 112);
- "a clown" (p. 193);
- "an intellectual arsonist" (p. 128);
- "a pre-fascist conformist pseudo rebel" (p. 159).

This compilation should make it clear that the reactions to Pirinçci have been much more visceral that those to Thilo Sarrazin, which should come as no surprise, since the former makes his case with much more vehemence and in language more suited to the pub than the auditorium. After publisher Thomas Hoof has painted a picture of a dystopian future in which people will be "determined by nothing, no origins, no place, no gender, just a cosmopolitan-hermaphroditic potential" (p. 23), and co-editor Lombard has opined that Pirinçci's views should be compared with those of "the assimilated German-nationalist Jews in the decades before the Holocaust who did not want to be lumped together with the Eastern Jews (*Ostjuden*) who came after them" (p. 29),[35] the first formal review of *DvS* is provided. It stems from the *Süddeutsche Zeitung*, one of the most liberal daily newspapers in Germany. Is this not counterintuitive, given the title of the volume? The choice is actually a quite clever one, because the author, Marc Felix Serrao, is not a 'knee-jerk liberal' at all, but more of a liberal without any firm convictions. Serrao takes the trouble to interview Pirinçci at his home in Bonn, giving the reader much more than a book review. The journalist encounters a man who seems more interested in attractive women than in politics, including that of the AfD (the extreme-right Alternative for Germany). After calling *DvS* a "brawl" and proposing a more appropriate title ("Akif is out of his mind"), Serrao immediately plays down his criticism by injecting rather inappropriate humor: compared to Pirinçci, Sarrazin is about as controversial as the Count (*Graf Zahl*) from Sesame Street (p. 34); Serrao also seems to find it humorous that Pirinçci's hobbies are "insulting leftists and panting after young women" (p. 36). Given this tone, the more serious parts of the review appear as afterthoughts: the author is "too clever and eloquent" to use the jargon of the right-wing website "Politically Incorrect" (p. 40); he is an "extremist" in terms of language, but not a "right-wing extremist" (p. 36). It is difficult to believe that a summary statement such as the following appeared in the *Süddeutsche*: "One leafs through, one grins, one is sometimes carried away by the ruthlessness of the analysis and the many wild ideas" (p. 39). A similar example of the tameness of the mainstream media can be found in a report about Pirinçci's appearance on the noontime show (*Mittagsmagazin*) of the ZDF (Second German Public TV Station) on April 2 2014.[36] In a brief video summarizing *DvS*, shown before the actual interview, it is stated that "No one has written so unsparingly about the Turks in Germany." There is absolutely no critical discourse to be found in the conversation between Pirinçci and the moderator, Susanne Conrad, who laughs on several occasions, including at Pirinçci's statement that he immediately fell in love with Germany: first with the nature, later with the women; and later, when he calls the "rubbish" writings of sociologists about immigrant ambivalence "nonsense." Conrad does say—with tongue firmly in cheek—that *DvS* is "politically very incorrect," but she is not insulted when Pirinçci characterizes the mainstream media—including of course the ZDF—with the chapter title 'one sees better through the asshole;' in the end, she tells her interviewee that it was "interesting" to hear his theses. The treatment of Pirinçci by the *Süddeutsche* and the ZDF would be enough to refute the assumption underlying *Attack on the Mainstream*, but the volume is still a telling compendium.

If one wishes to find the best example of a critique written by the kind of person that Pirinçci despises (*Gutmensch*), one need look no further than Ijoma Mangold's "Full Load of Hate," which was originally published in the leading liberal weekly *Die Zeit*.[37] Mangold finds *DvS* so extreme that he is convinced of Pirinçci's absolute honesty (p. 59), seeing it as a campaign of revenge against "all of the progressive-emancipatory social policy" in contemporary German society (p. 60). What surprises Mangold is that Pirinçci does not appear to be a traditional conservative, given the "incomparably obscene sound" of his book (p. 61); like Sarrazin, he believes that he is speaking for the "silent majority" (p. 62) usually ignored by the media. (If this reminds the reader of Donald Trump's presidential campaign, it should.) Mangold points out correctly that Pirinçci's xenophobia does not include anti-Semitism (p. 63), and his dissection is generally on the mark, although his conclusion that *DvS* will have little impact remains to be seen. Unfortunately, he also makes himself an easy target for scorn from the Pirinçci camp, because he makes the fatal error of comparing *DvS* to Hitler's *Mein Kampf* (remarking that he has never made this comparison before; p. 63). It is one thing to say that both Hitler and Pirinçci are mainly self-taught (Pirinçci struggled through the lowest rung of the German school system) but quite another to compare an ideologically driven politician with a thirst for absolute power over people's lives with a self-styled radical libertarian bent on reducing the power of the state to a minimum. Hitler of course did not praise the high achievements of Jews or defend homosexuals against persecution by religious fanatics; by using the so-called 'fascism club,' Mangold has enabled Pirinçci and his supporters to completely ignore his generally insightful analysis.

Perhaps the most characteristic defense of Pirinçci stems from Felix Honekamp under the title '*Deutschland von Sinnen*—better late than never. An Assessment,' which originally appeared on the website *The Free World. The Internet & Blog Paper for Civil Society*.[38] Honekamp reports that *DvS* is a 'hot item' in conservative circles as well as among libertarians and Christians (p. 168); he attributes this in part to Pirinçci's readable style and clarity, in contrast to Sarrazin. Astonishingly, Honekamp maintains that "neither women, nor homosexuals, nor immigrants" are subject to criticism, instead:

> It is the state itself, or rather its organs. [...] They, namely, do everything in order to limit freedoms, to turn the populace into new human beings who reject rationality as reactionary, and act as if it were one of the greatest achievements of mankind to have replaced normal light bulbs with highly toxic, but supposedly climate-friendly dim lights. And it is the people who, due to a fear of having to take their economic and social existence into their own hands, go along with this game like lemmings and let themselves be led—as if by a nose ring—through the arena of a welfare and nanny state that is out of control. (p. 169)

What makes Honekamp's advocacy effective is the fact that he has reservations about certain aspects of Pirinçci's world view. He seems uncomfortable with Pirinçci's rejection of religion as a mere relic of the past, fearing that a world without transcendence would be a hedonistic one (p. 170); although he generally finds the analysis in *DvS* to be "correct" (p. 173), he does not agree with everything, rejecting also the use of provocative sexualized language. In the end, however, he recommends the book, and even adds that "everything is not yet lost in Germany" as long as such works are published and read (p. 174). Honekamp, others like him, and Pirinçci himself clearly believe that Germany, the economic motor of Europe and a much-admired modern democracy, stands on the brink of self-destruction.

Extreme reactions from advocates and opponents alike can be found throughout *Attack on the Mainstream*. Ellen Kositza wonders why Pirinçcis are not ubiquitous, given the "hair-raising conditions" in Germany (p. 45); according to Werner Reichel, *DvS* "has gotten something going by breaking up the politically correct crust that covers and crushes *everything*" (my italics; p. 91); Thorsten Hinz is pleased that Pirinçci has "thrashed" (*vermöbelt*) his critic Jochen Grabler (see above; p. 124); Arnulf Baring believes that *DvS* is actually a "relatively mild" piece of work that was only controversial because the Germans have lost the ability to "openly discuss controversial topics" (p. 142); Erwin Leibfried defends Pirinçci by asserting that "The wife at the stove is now being discriminated against, although that is the old European model of living" (p. 149); Marina Tenger thinks that *DvS* is a "super-funny" read (p. 176); Pirinçci is, says Alexander Marguier, "a master of enraged speech [...] he takes no prisoners" (p. 185). On the other side, Robert Misik of the leftist *Tageszeitung* sees Pirinçci as a "preacher of hate and smear writer" (p. 78), and he calls for a form of censorship called "gatekeeping" (p. 79), which will be discussed below; Jakob Hein, also from *Tageszeitung*, is incredulous but unsure whether or not to take Pirinçci seriously: "Mr. Pirinçci, tear down this joke!" (p. 84); Alan Posener accuses Pirinçci of being a self-styled "martyr" (p. 82); in the Berlin *Tagesspiegel*, Pirinçci was even compared to the Norwegian terrorist and mass murderer Anders Breivik (p. 98); and Lisa Inhoffen (*Bonner Generalanzeiger*) fears that *DvS* could be interpreted by "crazies" as a "call to use violence" (p. 178). Not surprisingly, the site *queer.de* speaks of "macho homophobia" and warns that Pirinçci's "misanthropy" bordering on "incitement" (*Volksverhetzung*) is too often played down as a mere "opinion" by the mainstream media (p. 57).

Perhaps the most significant fact with regard to *Attack on the Mainstream* is that major opinion leaders and well-known public figures are missing, standing in stark contrast to the reactions to Thilo Sarrazin. The only contributor who would be recognized outside of Germany is not a contributor at all, but rather a controversial Russian-American: in an afterword, André F. Lichtschlag, the editor of the series *Lichtschlag in der Edition Sonderwege* in which both *DvS* and *Attack on the Mainstream* appeared, claims that Akif Pirinçci is "Germany's Ayn Rand" (p. 197). According to Lichtschlag, both Rand and Pirinçci are "immigrants who love and cherish their new homeland more than anything else" (p. 201); Rand, however, exhibited "not a trace of humor," a deficiency made up by Pirinçci, who is capable of formulating his "libertarian manifesto" in such a way that it can reach non-academic readers (p. 201). Why would the Germans need a stiff dose of Randian hyper-individualism? It is supposedly because they have somehow lost a "striving for happiness with all its risks and dangers" (p. 199); in other words, there are too few 'heroic capitalists' in Germany, a country where "productive people" (p. 200) are not given the admiration they deserve. To be fair to Lichtschlag, one must point out that Volkswagen CEO Martin Winterkorn's role in the highly risky and dangerous diesel-deception ploy had not yet come to light when he wrote his afterword.

Just as Thilo Sarrazin was not content to publish only one bestselling and controversial book, Pirinçci has tried to keep himself in the public eye. One year after *DvS*, he wrote a polemic entitled *Die große Verschwulung: wenn aus Männern Frauen werden und aus Frauen keine Männer* (*The Great Gay-ification: When men turn into women and women don't become men*).[39] Pirinçci's views about gender roles, sexuality, and the nanny state have already been presented, so it is not necessary in the context of this study to discuss this particular book. What is remarkable, however, is how an attempt was made to silence the author now infamous for *DvS*; one recalls that Misik of the *taz* had called for some kind of "gatekeeping" after the publication of *DvS*. For a time, *amazon.de* would not list the new book, and it also disappeared from bookstores; Random House/Bertelsmann even cancelled the contract for publishing Pirinçci's cat detective novels. These amazing steps—amazing, if not absolutely scandalous in a liberal democracy—had less to do with the new book than with a speech that Pirinçci gave in Dresden on October 19 2015, on the occasion of the first anniversary of the PEGIDA movement. Pirinçci was only one of many speakers on that evening, but his remarks were so controversial that PEGIDA founder Lutz Bachmann asked him to stop speaking before he had come to the end of his manuscript.[40] The media immediately focused upon Pirinçci's use of the term "KZ," namely *Konzentrationslager* (concentration camps). It was initially reported that he was calling for them to be used again,[41] and the Dresden public prosecutor began an investigation regarding possible prosecution for incitement. It later came out—something that should have been immediately obvious to anyone who watched the speech at the rally or on video—that what Pirinçci actually said was that some German politicians would like to put critics of their policies (about the refugee crisis, for example) in concentration camps, but those, "unfortunately, are not in service." The misquotation in news reports only served to strengthen Pirinçci's conviction that the media are biased.[42] In the end, a court in Dresden came to the conclusion that the content of the speech constituted an act of disturbing the peace, and sentenced Pirinçci to a fine of 11,700 Euros.[43]

Although Pirinçci told his audience in Dresden that he would be offering them "an original speech," he began by reading a long passage from the manuscript of his new book about the future of Germany and Germans. This volume, *Umvolkung* (see translation below)[44] was published by Verlag Antaios, because Pirinçci's previous publisher, Manuscriptum, had decided to cut its ties with him. Whereas Sarrazin wrote *Wunschdenken* to secure his role as a kind of *éminence grise* among conservative pundits and political consultants, Pirinçci stayed the course and produced an angry elegy, if one can imagine such a thing. There is little that is new in this book, but the level of intensity (or fanaticism, depending on one's perspective) is even higher than before. The subtitle explains the title: *Wie die Deutschen still und leise ausgetauscht werden* (*How the Germans are quietly being replaced*, that is to say, exchanged for another populace). The title term *Umvolkung* was coined by the conservative historian Albert Brackmann (1871–1952), who was active in the Nazi period until his retirement in 1936. Pirinçci provides a definition of *Umvolkung* late in the work itself:

> The term "Umvolkung" stems from the National Socialists and means the exchange of populations and re-Germanization in the areas that had at that time been conquered by the *Wehrmacht,* where *Volksdeutsche* [i.e., people of German ethnicity who had been living outside the borders of the German *Reich*] replaced unwanted groups of people who were sent to other areas assigned to them. (p. 89)

The formulation is similar to the one found in *wikipedia.de*. Radical conservatives in Germany are often accused of wanting to re-implement Nazi policies; in this case, Pirinçci not only condemns such policies, but goes on to claim that it is present-day German politicians who want to revive the past—only in reverse, expelling their own people in favor of newcomers.

It is at first glance surprising that a book revolving around such a claim would begin with a discussion of a Hollywood film (even given Pirinçci's preference for US popular culture), but that is exactly what *Umvolkung* does. Pirinçci utilizes the film in question, Michael Cimino's *The Deer Hunter*, as a platform for discussing another term that is at the core of his own beliefs, namely *Heimat* (homeland). The American soldiers portrayed in the film are of Russian descent, and due to the immigration of their families to the US, they have lost their roots and traditions (despite certain remnants like a Russian Orthodox wedding ceremony). After horrifying experiences in Vietnam, the only thing that keeps them going is the sense of belonging in their new homeland, the US. *Heimat* is for Pirinçci "this conglomerate made up of feelings, experiences, perceptions, familiar landscapes, climate conditions, and especially people and friends, with whom one has grown up" (p. 10); *The Deer Hunter* is "a fairy tale about assimilation and the healing power of a sense of belonging" (p. 10). In contrast to this positive picture, *Umvolkung* depicts "the contemporary forced de-homelandization (*Entheimatung*)—which will end in complete dissolution—by the foreign element" (p. 11). The book must be considered an elegy because Pirinçci is convinced that the process he describes is irreversible. An addendum to his definition of *Heimat* makes it absolutely clear that the process of mourning involves not only the Germans as a people, but also—and perhaps primarily—Pirinçci himself as an immigrant who has forged a new identity in Germany: "Wherever one once came from, which skin color, religion or customs one still has from the old *Heimat*, plays no role [in the process of assimilation]" (p. 10). Put another way, the country (the old *Bundesrepublik*) that made it possible for newcomers like Pirinçci to put down new modern roots, after leaving behind the ancient ones, is about to disappear. Whether this is true or not, the mere belief that it is happening is a source of trauma.

Reading *Umvolkung* in the year of the US presidential campaign and election, one cannot ignore one extremely troubling—but in our time rather characteristic—phenomenon. Whatever the topic, the self-taught author always knows more than anyone else. Pirinçci, who enjoyed very little formal schooling, is now, at least in his own eyes, a Renaissance man. Here are some pertinent examples:

- as an expert on intelligence measurement, he declares that "everyone knows that the dumbest people on earth (on average) come from Africa, Arabia, and the Islamic countries of Asia" (p. 35);
- as an expert on prejudice, he can say that "the worst racists and anti-Semites are Muslims, closely followed by Afros" (p. 47);
- as an expert on psychology, he reacts to criticisms that he is exaggerating the impact of mass immigration by saying: "If they

only knew a bit about psychology, especially mass psychology
[…]" (p. 68);

- as an expert on psychiatry, he assures us that "the Green
  movement and its followers were and are in the best case stupid,
  but primarily mentally deformed" (p. 80);
- as an expert on energy production and physics, he is sure
  that renewable energy is "a physically impossible method of
  producing energy" (p. 83);
- even though his pronouncements about the humanities are
  invariably disparaging, he is convinced that Muslims and other
  non-Westerners "in no way" provide any "cultural impulses
  for the modern world, either in the humanities area or in
  entertainment" (p. 115);
- even though he generally disdains intellectuals, he knows one
  when he sees one and calls those whose views he rejects "pretend
  intellectuals" (Intellektuellendarsteller; p. 121);
- as an expert on biology, he mocks German politicians who "were
  absent when evolution was discussed in biology class" (p. 123);
- finally, as an expert on criminology, he rejects statistics
  demonstrating that "foreigners are just as involved in crime as
  Germans" (p. 124).

Employing a tactic not unknown in contemporary politics, Pirinçci
does admit at one juncture that his calculations might not all be
completely accurate, and then adds: "Maybe I even lied. What of it?
Today's lie is already tomorrow's truth!" (p. 60).[45] This statement is
appropriate in a year when the Oxford Dictionaries chose "post-truth"
(postfaktisch) as the "word of the year."[46]

The venom directed toward the refugees who arrived in Germany
in 2015-16 knows no bounds in Umvolkung. Pirinçci even disputes
the fact that they are refugees, dubbing them "pretend refugees"
(Flüchtlingsdarsteller; p. 30). As he has done in the past, he rejects the
idea that they could contribute anything to the Germany economy (p.
12); after that, he seems bent on testing the limits of hate speech.
Beginning with the relatively mild term "incompatibles" (p. 26), he
proceeds to speak of "prick bearers" (Schwanzträger; p. 41), warning
that hordes of young, potent men will roam the German streets

looking for victims; the Biblical designation "locusts" (p. 88) is brought into play; and finally, incredibly, the male refugees (he has little to say about the females) are reduced to subhuman status, in that they are characterized as "ape-like" creatures (*Primatartige*; p. 130). Any German, or for that matter anyone familiar with the Third Reich who reads that will inevitably think of the term *Untermensch* (subhuman). The irony here is that Pirinçci asserts that the current German government is "totalitarian" (p. 16) and yearns to use concentration camps against its critics (pp. 90, 103). In other words, he may use fascist terminology, but the real fascists are the political elites and their media supporters, who are supposedly intentionally implementing the extermination of the German people. Depending on one's view of the world, this assessment is either prophetic or an expression of extreme paranoia.

The only solution that Pirinçci can envision is to "close the borders and defend them by force of arms" (p. 74). But why would he even mention this scenario if he were certain that it would never come to pass? The fourth and final chapter of *Umvolkung* is entitled 'The future belongs to the others' (p. 125 et passim). This future is clear: the Germans will be driven from their country, enslaved by foreigners, and their everyday life will be "orientalized" (p. 139). (How this could happen if they were no longer present is a conundrum.) Thanks to the pernicious influence of a "humanism divorced from reality" (p. 146), the "clever and industrious" Germans (p. 140) will be duped into believing themselves responsible for the problems of the "dumb and lazy ones" (p. 143). This will be the beginning of the end, for the Germans somehow agree "voluntarily" (p. 157) to be the slaves of the foreigners, leaving them with no "future" (p. 156) and no "fatherland" (p. 158); all that will remain is the "remembrance of a simply beautiful country" (p. 160). Since Pirinçci is such a fan of Hollywood films, he could have chosen the chapter title 'Apocalypse Now.' Importantly, however, what this is not is a manifesto for a right-wing populist resistance movement in Germany. If there were such a movement, Pirinçci could never be its public face, since his wooden style as a public speaker would produce boredom rather than fervor among his listeners, as was clearly the case in Dresden. He points out in *Umvolkung* that most Germans do not vote for the AfD, and he clearly believes that this will never happen (p. 15). Beyond seeking publicity, one wonders why Pirinçci even bothered to speak at a PEGIDA rally; it is also puzzling that Götz Kubitschek, one of the intellectual gurus of the German radical right, would choose to print *Umvolkung* in his publishing house Antaios. The first chapter of *Umvolkung* ends with the following statement about Germany: "it will already become hell [on earth] this year!" (p. 47). Even though there were several terrorist attacks perpetrated by jihadis in 2016, culminating in the horrific deaths at the Berlin Christmas Market in December, the apocalypse predicted by Pirinçci did not come to pass, and the brutal attacks on women during the 2015 New Year's celebrations in Cologne were not repeated (due in part to a massive police presence at the event). If anything, the author's own life has come to resemble a sort of hell on earth. Late in 2015, the weekly *Der Spiegel* published a profile of Pirinçci with the title "The Leper."[47] In this portrait, Pirinçci is a social outcast who hardly ever leaves his house, lamenting his fate as follows: "Akif is done for. I don't exist anymore" (p. 41). The irony lies in the fact that Pirinçci tells the interviewer Jan Fleischhauer that he has "nothing" to do with PEDIGA, and finds the people associated with the Alternative for Germany "too narrow minded and humorless." Fleischhauer adds his own assessment: "Pirinçci is not really a person who thinks politically. He has never voted, and his views about many topics are rather ordinary" (p. 42). What is typical for him is a desire to provoke, never shying away from extreme formulations. This has gained him many fans on Facebook, but few friends in the real world—friends who could tell him that he has gone much too far. His situation has become so untenable that he is considering moving to another country.[48] This is the same person who once wrote that he could only live in Germany (*DvS*, p. 125). In *Umvolkung*, he asked: "What was so bad about the old Germany?" (p. 14). It would have been better for him, and Germany, if he had asked a different question instead: What was so bad about the old Akif?

INTERMEZZO
A FRENCH PIRINÇCI?

Does Akif Pirinçci have a *doppelgänger* in Western Europe? In 2014, when his *Deutschland von Sinnen* appeared, a Paris publishing house brought out a thick volume entitled *Le suicide français (French Suicide).*[1] The book's belly band offered an 'unofficial' subtitle, namely *Les 40 années qui ont défait la France (The 40 years that have defeated France).* The author, Éric Zemmour (b. 1958), was by no means an unknown quantity: he had already published eleven works of non-fiction and three novels, and he had been a well-known figure in the French media since the 1980s, including stints at *Quotidien de Paris*, *Info-Matin*, *Le Figaro*, *Figaro Magazine*, *i-Télé*, *Canal+* and *RTL*. He was born in Montreuil, just outside of Paris, and his parents were Algerian Jews who came to France during the Algerian War. (He has stated that his parents were French, but of Berber origin.)[2] Unlike Pirinçci, who had to adapt to new surroundings and learn a new language as a boy, Zemmour grew up a Francophone and took full advantage of the educational system, finishing his studies with a degree from Sciences Po. Despite these differences, both Pirinçci and Zemmour are representatives of the assimilated 'other,' who lament the decline of the country that they love and value. We have already examined the roots of Pirinçci's rage and sadness. To what extent is Zemmour his Gallic soul mate?

Given that the contours of French and German history are so different, it is perhaps surprising that both authors are fixated on the question of guilt and its relationship to national identity. Whereas Pirinçci decries the use of the "Nazi club" (*DvS*, p. 204) to keep Germany down, Zemmour rejects the depiction of France as a country weighed down with guilt stemming from both colonialism (including the treatment of immigrants from former colonies) and the actions of the Vichy government of the 1940s. The younger generation is supposedly no longer taught about the glories of the *Grande Nation*, but rather that France is a guilty country and will remain so "in all eternity" (p. 385). One specific manifestation of this is the way in which the present-day French elites distance themselves from Napoleon, one of Zemmour's heroes. Along with the emperor, the country wants nothing more to do with "war, man, and fatherland," the demonized "trinity" of our time (p. 506). Like Pirinçci, Zemmour also is a strong advocate for assimilation and a vigorous critic of integration; he is incensed that some immigrants and their children hate France and want nothing to do with French civilization, culture, and society. One example he provides of successful assimilation is the way in which Jews living in France became French after Napoleon granted them full citizenship rights (pp. 370-371). As one would expect, he also does not believe that Islam and the concept of assimilation can be reconciled, since Islam "sculpts the landscape, mentally and morally, but also with regard to clothing, sexuality, and commerce" (p. 502). Just as Pirinçci emphasizes that Islam does not belong to Germany, Zemmour concludes: "France has not received the heritage of Mecca and Saladin, but rather that of Descartes and Pascal" (p. 482). There is an "unavoidable conflict" between the Koran and the *Code civil* (p. 481).

Pirinçci and Zemmour also generally find common ground when discussing the nature of the family and the role of women. It is surely not insignificant that the latter dedicated his book to his father. Zemmour characterizes the family as "a molding institution that permitted the founding of a people, a society, a nation" (p. 30); this institution was clearly a patriarchal one, but in the past few decades it has been replaced, he asserts, because "the father has been ejected from Western society," leading to the "death" of the family (p. 34). "Femininity" has replaced "virility" (p. 13), and the proliferation of divorce has shaken the foundations of society (pp. 102-103), while the legalization of abortion has weakened the French nation (pp. 136-140). At the same time, the immigrants from the Maghreb have maintained "the most traditional, the most archaic, the most patriarchal" form of the family (p. 142), something Zemmour views as a blueprint for "*remplacement*," or what Pirinçci has called "*Umvolkung*" (see previous chapter). A related issue is the increased visibility of people who have a non-traditional gender orientation. Although Zemmour does not engage in the sort of brutal gay-bashing favored by Pirinçci, he does lament the 'new fluidity' that is in the process of replacing the old dichotomy, envisioning a dystopian world where the margins become the norm and heterosexuality is considered abnormal (p. 270); there is another major reason for his distaste for homosexuality, but that will be considered below. In general, neither Pirinçci nor Zemmour would admit to being misogynistic, but they also show little interest in considering the experiences and views of women. For them, tradition and stability are paramount.

Other areas of agreement include Zemmour's attack on political correctness and the "faction of the good" that propagates it (p. 252), his criticism of abuse of the welfare state by immigrants (p. 310), his rejection of naive pacifism (p. 402), his mocking of anti-fascist activists ("the anti-fascist comedy"; p. 466), and his skeptical attitude toward Gender Studies (p. 406). However, such areas of congruence tend to mask the fundamental differences between the two polemicists. As a Parisian intellectual, Zemmour sees himself as part of a long and distinguished tradition of cultural and political discourse, which is reflected in the figures that he cites in his book; as if to illustrate his grasp of the material, he refers to Richelieu, Molière, Pascal, Racine, Montesquieu, Rousseau, Mirabeau, Constant, Chateaubriand, Hugo, de Tocqueville, de Musset, Flaubert, Zola, Verlaine, Jaurès, Lacan, Aron, Sartre, Beauvoir, Lévi-Strauss, Bourdieu, Derrida, and many others. To demonstrate the breadth of his knowledge, he also looks beyond the borders of France to Hegel, Schopenhauer, Marx, Nietzsche, Thomas Mann, Dickens, O. Wilde, Chesterton, Golding, Gramsci, Solzhenitsyn, Mark Twain, Samuel Huntington, Tom Wolfe, and Angela Davis. As opposed to Pirinçci (an isolated individual writing from provincial Bonn), he truly wishes to be taken seriously by the intellectual establishment, even as he criticizes it (as in the remarks on Bernard-Henri Lévy; pp. 191-196). His distance from the vulgarity and brutality of Pirinçci's writing can be seen in his homage to the singer Charles Aznavour, who is "subtle, precise, elegant. Literary. So French." (my emphasis; p. 69).[3] Zemmour's familiarity with elite culture does not prevent him, like Pirinçci, from referring often to popular culture—mainly films and songs—to undergird his arguments, but his examples usually are taken from French culture. This leads us to a fundamental difference between *Deutschland von Sinnen* and *Le suicide français*: the assessment of the culture, economic system, and politics of the United States. One recalls that the libertarian Pirinçci views the US as a sort of promised land; for Zemmour, just the opposite is true. If one were to choose one phrase that provides his critique in a nutshell, it would be this one: "consumerist bulimia" (p. 45).[4] In a world of "casino capitalism," the "insatiable cupidity" of Wall Street investors is shaping a world in crisis (p. 51). In place of the *citoyen* (citizen) willing to put patriotic concerns first, zombie-like consumers are obsessed with material goods that they hope to obtain at the lowest possible price. This is the brave new world of globalization,[5] where profit margins have absolute primacy. This is not to say that Zemmour is anti-capitalist, although he was once attracted to leftist ideas, and he twice voted for François Mitterrand.[6]

With reference to French conditions, he describes what has been lost in the wake of the economic transformation and dislocation of the past several decades: "[A]fter 1968, the new internationalist and libertarian bourgeoisie [...] dislodged the old Catholic, conservative, and patriotic bourgeoisie" (p. 56). Zemmour's interpretation of the 1968 upheavals is much different from Pirinçci's: whereas the latter sees the sociocultural shift as the beginning of the end of civilization, the former views the activists and participants as 'useful idiots' who did not realize they were simply paving the way for the next stage of capitalist development.[7] One illustration of this shift relates to gay liberation: according to Zemmour, gays are "the best and most active consumers" (p. 72).[8] In contrast to the world of the "new *condottieri* capitalists, Bill Gates, Steve Jobs, etc" (p. 49), the French model of "traditional state capitalism" (p. 282) was rooted in the nation-state and shaped by the historical development of France, something that

Zemmour refers to as "the good old French archaism" (p. 86).[9] For many years, the symbol of such "archaism" was Charles de Gaulle, who relentlessly pursued French interests; in many ways, Zemmour's entire book is an act of mourning for the de Gaulle era. The general, an "emulator of Machiavelli and Richelieu," concentrated on the relationship between individual nation-states and knew that the "international community" was nothing but "nonsense, a myth invented by idealists and the naive and utilized by cynics" (p. 472). The creation of the EU is viewed by Zemmour as a sort of subset of pernicious global trends:[10] the 1992 Maastricht Treaty signals, for him, the "death" of democracy (p. 355), and de Gaulle is cited as the absolute authority: "For me, democracy is closely tied to national sovereignty" (pp. 357-358). It should be emphasized here that when Zemmour thinks of the nation, he looks beyond the elites, and is quite concerned about the plight of the French working class, which has been buffeted by both an influx of cheap labor from abroad and a loss of political influence.[11] Even though he has supposedly put his leftist sympathies behind him, he paints a sympathetic portrait of Georges Marchais, the long-time head of the French Communist Party. Marchais is almost portrayed as a proletarian de Gaulle: "Like General de Gaulle, the communists had understood that the European construct was nothing but the G-string of the Pax Americana and of the end of national sovereignty" (p. 201). Marchais, who had spoken out against immigration, was accused of racism in the media, but Zemmour sees him as a tragic figure who was unable to reconcile his "revolutionary internationalism" with his "patriotic passion" (p. 207).

Any French intellectual who chooses to write about national identity and prospects must consider the past and future of Germany, a country that has long been an object of French ambitions and nightmares. In doing so, Zemmour of course has a very different perspective than Pirinçci, whose love of his adopted country is boundless. Zemmour's rambling ruminations about Franco-German relations are framed by one overriding concern, namely domination and/or hegemony. For over two centuries—from the end of the Thirty Years' War in 1648 until the Franco-Prussian war of 1870–71—France was the dominant power on the continent. It is clear that, for Zemmour, this was the natural state of affairs in Europe, and the decline in French influence in the wake of the defeat at Waterloo is portrayed as an absolute disaster. One reason for this, beyond the perceived superiority of French culture and its accompanying way of life, is the concept of the state, which is anchored to "sovereign reason" in France and to the "cult of the law" in Germany (p. 41). Zemmour clings to the notion that the French state has been the embodiment of rationality since the eighteenth century; even as late as the 1960s, he says, the French believed that Europe would be a larger version of France; only thereafter did it become clear that what was emerging was a larger version of Germany (p. 519). The two world wars were already fought over the domination of Europe (here Zemmour is citing de Gaulle; p. 305), and after 1945, hegemony became a "German obsession" (p. 442). It is with a certain ambivalence that Zemmour regards Germany, since there are aspects that he clearly envies, including the maintenance of a strong industrial base (their technology is "the ultimate revenge"; p. 445), the willingness to limit social welfare benefits (during the Schröder chancellorship), and the enduring work ethic: the French are "cicadas," while the Germans are "busy bees" (p. 485). He would feel quite comfortable with the "Carolingian vision" of his idol de Gaulle, who had hoped to create a new Europe including Franco-German friendship, but directed by France (p. 59); the outcome was, he must admit, quite different: an "American-German Holy [Roman] Empire" (p. 339). Political developments since the election of Donald Trump have of course put such a model, if it ever existed, into question.

At present, most observers who pay attention to Zemmour are less interested in his specific ideas than in their applicability in the political sphere. First and foremost, they want to know about his relationship to the extreme-right *Front National* (renamed the *Rassemblement National* in 2018) and its leader Marine Le Pen. To cast light on that phenomenon, one must first examine how Zemmour treats the former party leader Jean-Marie Le Pen in his book. Right from the outset, it must be emphasized that the older Le Pen is a minor figure in Zemmour's portrayal of contemporary France, even compared to Marchais; he appears mainly as a person accused of unacceptable behavior, such as in the case of the desecration of Jewish graves in Carpentras in 1990 (p. 186),[12] or being labeled a "fascist" by the left (244). Zemmour's interpretation of Le Pen's main claim to notoriety, namely his remark that the Holocaust was a "mere detail" of the history of World War II, is rather tortured. He provides part of the transcript from the interview in which Le Pen made that statement and mentions that he was convicted of "trivializing crimes against humanity" (pp. 303-304). We then learn that the burden of anti-Semitism that Le Pen has carried since then was avoidable: there was a move afoot to change the FN's image with regard to the Jews, and a trip to Israel was even in the works; this was all derailed by Le Pen's one remark. Zemmour faults him for carrying on the traditional anti-Semitism of "old France" (p. 304), but he also maintains that the Holocaust was not a major factor in the Allies' wartime strategic planning, and that the Germans would have lost the war even if there had not been a Holocaust (and: "[T]he allies did not raise a little finger to save them"; p. 305). Viewed from that perspective, Le Pen was not wrong—just politically inept. Why would this concern Zemmour? The answer lies in the FN's attitude toward the EU: during the discussion of the Maastricht treaty, Le Pen was unable to escape from the political "ghetto" to which he had been consigned (p. 360); Zemmour clearly would have wanted to see a successful campaign against the EU led by the FN, but that was doomed to failure. One must conclude that he is either a supporter of the FN, or that he views them as 'useful idiots' to be employed in the battle for national sovereignty against the Eurocrats. The second interpretation is corroborated in a statement that Zemmour made in a 2010 interview: "I organize nothing, no strategy, I say what I think. [...] As de Gaulle said: The right is not France, the left is not France. I identify with a kind of gaullo-bonapartism."[13]

Despite having similar backgrounds, Pirinçci and Zemmour are not usually mentioned in the same breath, although references to both of them can sometimes be found on right-wing websites,[14] and one French publication characterized Pirinçci as a kind of "local [provincial] Zemmour."[15] The two would, however, probably have little to say to one another, especially since Pirinçci would like to slash taxes and reduce the state apparatus to an absolute minimum, whereas a strong state with broad powers is one of Zemmour's essentials. It is rather far-fetched to compare Zemmour to Rush Limbaugh,[16] but his name has been linked to Thilo Sarrazin and his book *Deutschland schafft sich ab*: *Le suicide français* has been described as a "French counterpart" to Sarrazin's work.[17] When a respected German publication tells its readers that "Zemmour is a best-selling author in France—akin to the populist Islamophobe Thilo Sarrazin in Germany,"[18] one wonders if the author of that statement has read either book. It is not difficult to imagine that the person most upset by such comparisons is not Sarrazin or Zemmour, but rather Pirinçci, left out in the cold. To a great extent, Zemmour has accomplished what Pirinçci failed to achieve: he is a highly educated—albeit also highly controversial—social commentator with the full attention of the French establishment. Some have even spoken of a so-called "zemmourisation" of French society.[19] It would not occur to anyone in Germany to make a similar statement about Pirinçci.

3

BOTHO STRAUß
FROM COSMOPOLITAN FLANEUR TO RURAL PROPHET

Thilo Sarrazin can be compared to politically active US economists like Milton Friedman, and the case of Akif Pirinçci is at least somewhat similar to that of the immigrant gadfly Dinesh D'Souza, but it is difficult to imagine an analogous figure to Botho Strauß (b. 1944) in the US context.[1] Ever since the publication of his essay '*Anschwellender Bocksgesang*' ('Impending Tragedy') in 1993, he has been linked with the German intellectual representatives of the so-called Conservative Revolution of the 1920s.[2] That particular publication came as a great surprise to most critics and readers, because up until then, Strauß had been a celebrated post-modern dramatist and prose stylist specializing in the everyday interactions of the educated urban elite. His apparent turn to the right, rather unusual for someone who experienced the student movement of the 1960s and was quite familiar with (neo-) Marxist cultural theories, continues to puzzle many in Berlin and beyond. Part of the unexpected shift included a change in residence from eclectic Berlin to the idyllic countryside of the *Uckermark* region northeast of the city.

'Impending Tragedy' appeared first in the weekly newsmagazine *Der Spiegel*[3] and was later reprinted in revised form in the anthology *Die selbstbewusste Nation* (*The Self-Confident / Self-Aware Nation*),[4] a project of the post-reunification intellectual New Right. In actuality, the Strauß of 'Impending Tragedy' has more to do with a certain strain of German culture than with contemporary rightist political agendas. He is part of a tradition that began during the Romantic era, one in which the poet is depicted as a kind of visionary who can see beyond surface phenomena, diagnose societal ills and show the way to a better future for the people (*Volk*). This tradition of course arose at a time when the French, in the wake of their revolution, were redrawing the map of Europe; the German revolution was relegated to the sphere of ideas and images. Whereas many German Romantics dreamed of a return to a pre-Enlightenment social order based on tradition, Strauß, as an intentionally detached observer, expresses admiration for the intricate workings of our capitalist democracies, but senses that crisis is nigh (hence his title, which refers to Greek tragedy). In his view, this system

> has been up until now without competition: neither totalitarianism nor theocracy could better promote the welfare of the greatest number than this system of calculated freedoms.
> Naturally, that [statement] is only valid as long as we are convinced that it is only economic success that forms, ties, and instructs the masses. (p. 202)

Strauß predicts that even a minimal reduction of our affluence will lead to "impatience and aggression," and that modern man will realize that he is not exclusively a creature of the present, but rather a juxtaposition of the contemporary and pre-modern impulses and thought patterns. These two sides, and their constant change and resistance, will at some point go to "war" with each other (p. 203).

The immediate catalyst for such a conflict will be, Strauß asserts, the arrival of "legions of refugees and those who have lost their homelands" (p. 203). A Christian Europe might have been capable of comprehending the tragic fate of such persons, but not our "modern egotistical paganism" (p. 203) . Thus a "re-Christianization" of Europe would be in order, he says, to counter "the hypocrisy of public morality, that always tolerated (if not promoted) the ridicule of Eros, the ridicule of the soldier, the ridicule of the church, tradition, and authority" (p. 203).[5] In other words, we have replaced ancient forms of faith with a belief in the civilizing effect of prosperity; this is, ironically, reminiscent of German sentiments in World War One about Britain as a place where the economy dominates all aspects of life (in contrast to the Germans, who had supposedly retained an affinity for the heroic).[6]

In discussing German xenophilia, or openness toward other cultures and their representatives, Strauß believes that one major source of German tolerance is a negative one, namely the self-hatred of those who cannot forget the crimes perpetrated by their countrymen in the twentieth century. In this model, the "foreigner" is welcomed as an agent of destruction who will destroy "that which is ours" (p. 203). As a precursor of Pirinçci, Strauß identifies those self-haters as the leftist intellectuals, and he also laments the loss of German "dignity" (p. 203). Unlike Pirinçci, however, he appears to be convinced that if the Germans were again forced to come to terms with "sudden pain or care," their dignity might be resurrected (p. 203).[7] If this were to occur, it would go hand in hand with a conservative resurgence, an act of revolt (*Auflehnung*) against "the total dominance of the present, which wants to eliminate from each individual the *presence* of an unenlightened past, historical development, and mythical time" (p. 204). Instead of pursuing utopian dreams like the left, the right would seek a "reconnection with the long past," and this process would be a "religious and protopolitical initiation" (p. 204). Strauß does not envision a mass movement, but rather the creation of an exclusive group of 'memory keepers' who will battle political oppression by preserving

> a spiritual enclave that will fight against the political relativization of [human] existence in the name of the wisdom of the peoples (*Völker*), in the name of Shakespeare, in the name of the devaluation of the secular, in the name of the improvement of the human ability to suffer. (p. 205)

At a time when "the intelligence of the masses has reached its peak" (p. 207), the group of radical individualists will meet in a garden that is "only accessible to a few," hermetically sealed off from the majority (p. 206). Once the hated system of modernity has collapsed through a "culture shock" (p. 204), the elect will perhaps be capable of rebuilding traditional society. This may remind some readers of Ray Bradbury's *Fahrenheit 451*, albeit with a very different slant.

Even though Strauß emphasized in 'Impending Tragedy' that the conservative imagination—in contrast to that of the left—is not utopian and revolves around what has been lost in the course of history, and despite his assurance that it is a poetic, not political imagination (p. 204), he was sharply criticized by those who saw him as a reactionary prophet, if not agitator. Strauß clearly anticipated this reading when he asserted that a true conservative "is as far removed from the neo-Nazi as a soccer fan is from a hooligan" (p. 204); the Social Democrat politician and intellectual Peter Glotz ignored that dictum and dismissed him as a "dangerous muddle-headed fellow,"[8] and others went much further, drawing a direct line from 'Impending Tragedy' back to the "crypto-fascist popular literature between 1920 and 1932."[9] Although there were myriad responses to Strauß's essay (including supportive ones), they did not in the end have a significant effect on the author's standing in the German cultural scene, perhaps attributable to the fact that Strauß was and remains a representative of high culture in Germany, as illustrated by the awarding of the prestigious Büchner Prize in 1989. He has also published over a dozen books since 1994, and his plays have been staged in Germany, Austria, and Switzerland. This is strikingly different from the fate of Akif Pirinçci and comparable to the postwar treatment of Ernst Jünger (1895–1998), the most prominent imaginative writer of the Conservative Revolution, who received the coveted Goethe Prize in 1982.[10]

In 2015, the German journalist Cordt Schnibben published a late response to 'Impending Tragedy' in Der Spiegel.[11] His purpose was to demonstrate that after Angela Merkel's decision to allow great numbers of Syrian refugees into Germany, the Germans had responded admirably and humanely, effectively refuting the dark prophecies of Strauß and others who had sounded the "tragic alarm bells of the fearful" (p. 105). Schnibben was upset that Strauß had found numerous "imitators" (Nachbeter) who engage in a "ridiculous battle against knee-jerk liberalism (Gutmenschentum)" (p. 105). Two aspects of this essay are worthy of note: Schnibben utilized President Gauck's formulations when he praised the triumph of 'bright Germany" over "dark Germany" (even while acknowledging that the "grey Germany of the fearful" was growing; p. 106), and he implied that humanitarian efforts vis-à-vis the refugees were even more important than environmental protection, a position that the Greens would find difficult to accept. Just two weeks after Schnibben's words appeared in print, Der Spiegel offered a platform to none other than the just-maligned Botho Strauß; twenty-three years after 'Impending Tragedy,' the sometime prophet issued a commentary (*Glosse*) that the magazine editors linked via a facsimile to the "famous essay" (the editors' words) of 1993. The rather ominous title was 'The Last German. We are being deprived of the sovereignty [that would allow us] to resist.'[12] In case *Der Spiegel* readers had forgotten the debates of the past, context was provided:

> Hardly any other text in the media of reunited Germany unleashed more outrage and discussions. Strauß's opponents declared that he was the prophet (*Vordenker*) of a new rightist Germany. [...] Now Strauß, who lives in isolation in the Uckermark, is coming to grips with his topic for a second time in light of the refugee crisis. (p. 122)

As in 1993, Strauß and *Der Spiegel* clearly collaborated with an eye to the greatest impact on the German public sphere; this is an intriguing example of a left-right or liberal-conservative tandem arranged for mutual benefit.

Many German readers who saw the formulation 'The Last German' in Strauß's title surely thought of Friedrich Nietzsche, who spoke of "the last man" in *Thus Spake Zarathustra*. By choosing his title, Strauß was playing a mind game with his audience, since he was actually turning Nietzsche's vision upside down. Whereas the philosopher used the figure of the prophet Zarathustra to express his distaste for the comfort-loving, risk-avoiding, democratically-inclined modern Germans and other Europeans responsible for the destruction of everything that he held dear, the commentator was envisioning an intellectual elite encompassing the last representatives of the traditional European civilization that he revered. Strauß's subtitle, however, was very much in line with the mindset of his predecessor: only an autonomous individual, one who has severed all ties with the 'system,' is capable of unerring analysis and true opposition.

Thilo Sarrazin utilized statistics, tables, and innumerable footnotes to underline his competence as a sober analyst; Akif Pirinçci made light of documentation and felt more comfortable using unbridled subjectivity and vulgar language to gain attention; Botho Strauß chooses to present his thoughts in a way that is difficult for most readers to understand, opting for a rather opaque mode of expression. The one term that critics have used the most often with respect to his essays is the verb *raunen*, which can be translated as 'whispering or murmuring.' Leftist observers of the cultural scene tend to use this term not to denote a quiet, modest manner of speaking, but rather a pre-modern jargon associated with myth and even the occult; it operates in the shadows, not in the light of reason exalted by the Enlightenment. 'The Last German' begins in a rather self-referential manner, as Strauß lifts a passage from an earlier work, namely *The Awkward Ones* (*Die Unbeholfenen*), a so-called "novella of consciousness" (*Bewußtseinsnovelle*) that appeared in 2007.[13] Here is the beginning of that passage:

> Sometimes I have the feeling that I am only among Germans when I am among the ancestors. Yes, it appears to me as if I were the last German. [...] A scoundrel, a vagabond rummaging around in the sacred remnants of the city, the country, and the mind. A homeless man. (p. 122)

In the novella, it is not completely explicit that these sentiments are those of the author, but in the new context, that is unequivocally the case. However, Strauß immediately adds the proviso that his status as "the last German" is a "fiction" in which he imagines himself as an "extender (*Fortsetzer*) of ways of feeling and thinking that brought forth, beginning with Romanticism, a specifically German literature" (p. 122). He adds that his life consisted of the attempt to "bring some of that back to life;" as an aside, it is rather strange that he uses the past tense here, as if his life (at least his creative life) were over, though his most recent book appeared in 2018.[14] One reason why this revival project is necessary is given in *The Awkward Ones*, namely "*Infodemenz*" (p. 65), which means that Strauß's contemporaries are so inundated with information that they are incapable of contemplation and true understanding.

As was already the case in 'Impending Tragedy,' there is no clear structure in 'The Last German.' Strauß vacillates between personal observations about his intellectual/literary life and assessments of the cultural and political status quo in Germany. One particularly jarring example of this is found in the first section, where he proclaims his affection for some of his favorite authors, only to launch into a lament about the state of German society: "I would rather live in a people that is dying out than in a vigorous one that is being rejuvenated, primarily out of economic-demographic speculation, by livening it up with foreign peoples" (p. 123). This is a typically Straußian dichotomy: cultural tradition on the one side, economic activity on the other; it is not that he is so naive as to think that a society could survive without economic activity, but rather that all areas of human endeavor are, in our time, gradually becoming subordinate to it. Remembering his own experience with the student movement of the 1960s, he decries the fact that "critical leftist intellectuals," who once fought against the "hegemony" of the economic, have in the meantime become advocates of such a hegemony (albeit in a supposedly more socially responsible form); he does not hesitate to name names: "Piketty, Stiglitz, Krugman" (p. 123). Immediately thereafter, Strauß provides a very different list, the names of those German authors who comprise his own "heroic intellectual history" (p. 123). Many of these will hardly be familiar to non-Germans, so a certain amount of elaboration is required: Jakob Böhme (1575–1624) was a post-medieval mystic of peasant stock who wrote in German, supported sects that deviated from Lutheran orthodoxy, and was frequently persecuted, and prevented from publishing his works; Böhme's philosophy of language influenced Johann Georg Hamann (1730–1788), a philosopher whose advocacy of irrationality and unconventional language was one of the pillars of the late-eighteenth-century *Sturm und Drang* (Storm and Stress) movement in Germany; Friedrich Gottlieb Klopstock (1724–1803), perhaps best known for his verse epic *Messias* (The Messiah), preferred emotional expression and wrote about the concept of poetic genius as the source of all creativity; Friedrich Nietzsche (1844–1900) was the ultimate outsider who dissociated himself from what he saw as dying culture around him. It is not surprising that Nietzsche's works have been illustrated with Caspar David Friedrich's famous Romantic painting "Wanderer above the Sea of Fog." The above-mentioned Ernst Jünger (1895-1998) was an elitist whose long life was marked by heroic service in World War One, rejection of Weimar democracy, and disdain for the uncultured, lower-class Nazis, which led to a sort of 'inner emigration' in the *Wehrmacht* (German armed forces). The final author on the list is Paul Celan (1920-1970), a Jewish poet and translator from Czernowitz who spent much of his adult life in France; he initially reacted to current events in his works but later doubted that language could truly express human feeling and suffering. This is quite a diverse group, but all of its members were fascinated by poetic language, conversant with tradition, and situated outside the mainstream of their times (with the exception of Klopstock). It is no accident that no living author is considered worthy of mention, since Strauß himself feels most at home in a past that he idealizes.

At first glance, one would be justified in asking why such ruminations would interest anyone who is not a literary scholar intrigued by underground connections between various generations of writers. There is another dimension to all this, however, which is of more than marginal import. First of all, Strauß tells us that most of today's Germans are no longer capable of feeling the "cultural pain" associated with the realization that knowledge of the great German literary tradition is slipping away (p. 123). He calls such compatriots "social Germans" (p. 123), meaning that the only aspect of their existence connected to German identity is their residence in a place called Germany; they are, he asserts, no less uprooted than the millions of refugees who are entering the country. Secondly, and much more significantly, he goes on to proclaim that the treasures that have been passed down to us (*Überlieferung*) exist outside of history and society:

> It (*Überlieferung*) exists, by the way, beyond the reach of principalities, the nation, the foundation of the *Reich*, world war(s) and extermination camps. None of that inspires or pre-determines it. It contains neither salvation nor disaster and does not put them into practice either. Just about anything can be misused. (p. 123)

The implications of this viewpoint are more than troubling: in effect, any cultured person (in the sense of high culture and sophisticated educational preparation) should live his life outside the political and social sphere, since these are mere ephemera. Thus any effort to maintain a democratic order, as flawed as it might be, would be a waste of valuable time. One cannot help but recall the situation in the Weimar Republic, when members of the educated middle class (*Bildungsbürgertum*) lost interest in the democratic process; this was reflected in the sharp right turn of the German Democratic Party (DDP), that went from a liberal defense of democracy and individual rights to an alliance with conservative nationalists. No democratic country can survive if highly educated citizens are alienated from the political process, or simply uninterested in it. This does not appear to concern Botho Strauß.

Strauß ridicules representatives of the political right who believe that it is their mission to do battle for the preservation of the German nation in light of the mass influx of refugees. For him, "Germans" and "things German" no longer exist (p. 123); the only way such phenomena might reappear would be in a situation where those people who used to be German were to become a minority in their own country. German identity might be valued again if a form of "intolerant foreign domination" were to make life unbearable (p. 123). At the present time, however, Strauß maintains that the Germans seem completely uninterested in defending themselves and even willing to view the ebbing away of their identity as a positive development, supposedly bringing them enriching "diversity" when it is actually a case of cultural decline (p. 123). This assessment is not far from Pirinçci's condemnation of multiculturalism; in stark contrast to Pirinçci, though, Strauß intimates that the strong current of "obedience" in Islam might somehow remind the Germans that tradition is important (p. 124);[15] he even compares the rule of scholars (imams) in "Islamic theocratic countries" to a Germany where "the masses and the media," who are "uneducated in all areas" hold sway (p. 124). The rule of the political parties acts as a barrier against "non-democratic (*außerdemokratisch*) ideas from the depths of time" (p. 124). What is maddening about such pronouncements is that Strauß refrains from presenting these ideas in detail. In a section where he accuses pacifists of anti-German sentiment, he does remind the reader that our values include not only freedom, but also the "fight for freedom" (p. 124); he is clearly skeptical about the ability or even willingness of his compatriots to engage in self-defense; he is absolutely shocked by both the brutality of everyday life in Afghanistan and the attacks on the quarters of asylum seekers in Germany by right-wing radicals; but he doubts that the masses of media consumers are capable of feeling pain as he does. Too many people have become "mediatized," that is, their primary access to reality is not direct experience, but rather a filtered version presented on various kinds of screens. Given that, he can imagine that a Syrian refugee who comes to Germany with a knowledge of his own traditional culture could in the end be a more educated person than a native German.

In a final passage, Strauß analyzes the hate of refugees by (German) "radicals" (p. 124). Even though the casual observer would see xenophobia as its source, Strauß offers a very different explanation for such behavior: what they are really reacting to is supposedly a "feeling of vacuum" that has been created by a political class engaged mainly in "mollification" rather than leadership (p. 124). Once again, the reader must fill in the blanks: what has the vacuum replaced? The answer cannot be found in 'The Last German,' but it is the subject of another of Strauß's books: in 2014, he published an extremely personal account of his childhood and youth entitled *Herkunft* (*Origins*).[16] This brief memoir provides a glimpse of a relatively uneventful 1950s German childhood, with one exception: Strauß's father Eduard (1890-1971) was imprisoned in East Germany after the war, and the family moved to West Germany after his release. It is this father figure and his relationship to his son Botho (an only child) that is the focus of the memoir; in fact, the book begins with the word "father" (p. 7), and Strauß's mother, while sympathetically portrayed, remains on the periphery. Eduard Strauß is an exceedingly complicated figure; in his youth, and later in life, he is "faithful to the Kaiser and a German nationalist" (p. 19), a soldier who loses an eye in World War I; he shares in the enthusiasm about the war, only to later become a pacifist (p. 27), which is contrasted with the 'automatic' pacifism of his son, who never experiences war;[17] in leaving East Germany, he loses his upper-middle class status and has to struggle to maintain a decent standard of living for his family. Through all this, he places great emphasis on presentation: even though he works from home, he dresses rather formally every single day and keeps a strict schedule of daily activities. His hands are a symbol of his character: firm and evoking trust (p. 38); they are also instruments of education: "[His] hand punished me and caressed me, it showed me my first flowers and the first line in a book" (p. 36). Although modern readers might expect some resentment of this dual function, there is no sign of this in *Herkunft*. Even though Strauß clearly had many disagreements with his father, he came to accept his authority, perhaps because he has come to be a person much like his father, someone who finds "little pleasure in present-day life" (p. 9).

Eduard Strauß is a throwback to an earlier time when there were true individuals, or as his son puts it, "an individual of the old Ibsen format" (p. 17). He represents a rapidly-disappearing "bourgeois way of life" (*Bürgerlichkeit*) grounded in "ethical values" (p. 53); it is no accident that his favorite author is Thomas Mann, famous for his chronicles of the decline of that mode of living. Eduard Strauß exhibits a "chaste and Prussian" moral code (p. 67), but is not without a sense of humor. (He bears no resemblance to "good-for-nothing" Uncle Wilhelm, who was an "enthusiastic Nazi"; p. 63). He is not only "upright," but also an "anachronism" (p. 83).[18] Finally, Eduard shows no interest in climbing the social ladder, and he looks upon those who do so with distaste (p. 77). In a key passage, Botho Strauß explains his relationship with this rather patriarchal figure:

> Perhaps since I was never a happy orphan of the rebellion [i.e. the 1960s student movement] who wanted to break with his father and who always broke out in a sweat when he was confronted with power as embodied by a powerful person, I tend to think that [centralized] power secures a better life for those who do not have it than power that is shared by many. But that is being said by someone who has always profited from authority, for whom, in education and work, models, mastery, and leadership were a given and whom they have always fostered and never oppressed. (My additions in brackets; p. 90)

In an era when one common mantra is 'speaking truth to power,' Botho Strauß is without a doubt an anachronism.

What is fascinating about all this is that Botho Strauß had to go through a long process of development and self-actualization before he realized how influential the model of his father had been. Even though he was studious enough to be given the honor of delivering the final address at the celebration of his high school graduation (*Abiturfeier*; p. 61), he grew up reading comics and watching television and was exposed to myriad influences: "[...] Grimms' Fairy Tales and Elvis Presley, Karl May and General Eisenhower, Wagner and James Dean" (p. 66); "Zorro" is mentioned in one sentence with Kant's *Critique of Judgment*. He is somewhat of a young snob—'sharing' a girlfriend with Sartre (p. 58)—but he also flirts with the family maid Dora. He is even caught shoplifting on one occasion—an activity far removed from

Prussian behavioral codes! His only experience with today's much-discussed multiculturalism comes in the form of childhood games with the children of the Italian family who run an ice cream parlor in the summer. When he returns to his hometown of Bad Ems to dispose of his family's possessions and see the apartment in which he grew up for the last time, he surveys the scene and exclaims: "How beautiful! My dear country!" (p. 45); he is honest enough to admit that when he was young, he had "no sense whatsoever" for this beauty (p. 46). One senses that he would have preferred to have been a member of his father's generation (or even a previous one), especially when he reminds us who the famous visitors to the Bad Ems spa were in earlier times: Dostoevsky, Kaiser Wilhelm I, Effi Briest (the protagonist of a famous novel by Theodor Fontane), [Richard] Wagner, Franz Liszt, Ferdinand Lassalle, Nikolai Gogol, Jenny Lind, and Alfred Krupp (pp. 24, 87). One other detail from the history of Bad Ems is perhaps significant: the house in which Strauß spent his childhood was once a hotel owned by a Mr. Levi, who provided accommodations for Jewish guests including Heinrich Heine's uncle Salomon. Strauß transforms the nineteenth century into a refuge of sorts, whose representatives were spared the horrors of the 20th. Despite all the nostalgia, Strauß acknowledges that there can be no return to the past (pp. 59-60), and as a budding young writer who moved to the cultural metropolis of Berlin, he did not at all follow his own vision as elucidated in *Herkunft*:

> Is there anything better than staying there where one was born, grew up, went to school and first fell in love? Where one's parents and grandparents lived? Why should one leave one's hereditary place? And if it has to be because one wants to learn and accomplish this or that out there somewhere, why not return home afterwards? (p. 54)

Life in Bad Ems in the 1950s was already a pale reflection of what had been; old certainties had been destroyed by the crimes of the Third Reich, but the disruptions of the 1960s were still unimaginable. For someone like Botho Strauß, overcome with sadness and a strong sense of loss and caught in sociocultural limbo, there is nowhere to turn except to the world that he has constructed for himself in the life of the mind.

German pundits did not hesitate to react to the publication of 'The Last German.' One way to explain how a "great writer" could compose such a piece is to claim that he is losing his mind, as Hans Hütt does: Strauß is 'diagnosed' with the "initial stages of dementia," or he is simply a "crazy person" who is committing a kind of "symbolic suicide."[19] Another strategy is to turn the "panic junkie" Strauß into a neo-fascist whose latest essay is almost a reprise (*nahezu deckungsgleich*) of Hitler's 1945 political testament; the blogger making these claims, Joachim Petrick, links Strauß to "volkish" ideas and "blood and soil;" he even 'jokes' about Strauß getting down his "paratrooper boots" (*Springerstiefel*, the preferred footwear of neo-Nazis) from the attic in order to practice for the coming "revolt." Petrick also intimates that Strauß is a closet Holocaust denier, since he mentions Paul Celan without quoting from his famous poem "Death Fugue" (*"Todesfuge"*).[20] In the mainstream *Frankfurter Allgemeine Zeitung*, Dietmar Dath expresses the hope that Strauß is in fact the last German, since he equates that with everything negative that has happened in the past century. Since the Germans prefer "ideals" to "reality," they have no real modern identity—unlike France, Italy, or Britain—because they were basically forced to enter the age of democracy by outside forces. Thanks to his stylistic preference for "dark murmuring," Strauß does not, we are assured, pose a threat in the end: "No one should fear that a Nazi would understand him and then yell in the streets;"[21] unfortunately, Dath himself has also not understood very much. A very similar stance is taken by Richard Kämmerlings in *Die Welt*, who confesses to being "nauseated" by much of the Strauß essay. It is "obscene," he says, that Strauß attempts to use cultural tradition to wipe away the "dark stains" of German history; the real tradition that "defines" German identity is World War Two and the Holocaust, and that will continue to be the case "as long as this country exists." What Kämmerlings accepts, and what he claims Strauß and others will never accept, is that what is German is a product of pure negativity.[22]

Many other commentators attacked Strauß, even going so far as to suggest that he and others like him be "deported,"[23] but there were also supporters. The most prominent one was conservative Catholic author Martin Mosebach (b. 1951), like Strauß a recipient of the Büchner Prize. When one reads the transcript of his interview with German Radio (*Deutschlandfunk*), one encounters an assessment of Strauß from a completely different perspective.[24] Mosebach begins by speaking of the "pain" that Strauß feels in light of the gradual but inexorable disappearance of his world, namely a literary sphere with unique roots in German Romanticism. Mosebach himself has no illusions about this sphere, commenting that only a few were ever familiar with it, and that it may be "brilliant," but also "hermetic" and not very accessible; still, he points out that in 'The Last German,' Strauß's criticism is not directed toward the numerous refugees entering the country, but rather toward the Germans themselves, who have been losing touch with their own identity—as manifested in high literary culture—for quite some time. How could the refugees be assimilated into a country that no longer has an identity that has evolved over time? Mosebach and Strauß seem to be equally skeptical about such a project. Beyond defending Strauß, Mosebach questions the ability of the media to even form an opinion about texts like 'The Last German,' given the overall devaluation of critical reading in the society. There are certain taboos in place: "In the cultural supplements (*Feuilletons*) of the German newspapers, there reigns the order to totally affirm the status quo, and anyone who has even the most modest reservations is an outlier who is by definition suspicious, dangerous, obscene." The subtext is an assertion often made by representatives of the political establishment that the current Federal Republic of Germany is the best country that Germans have ever lived in. Although it is indeed possible to marshal arguments to support that assertion, one cannot conclude that every aspect of the past is somehow tainted or at least irrelevant; put another way, a globalized consumer culture is not a stable platform upon which a society can be built, especially if one believes that crises are inevitable. Mosebach's defense of Strauß is all the more surprising when one reads that he has a very different view of Germany: whereas Strauß laments the loss of a certain cultural unity, Mosebach is torn: "I experience quite strongly the division of the country. The religious division has brought about a cultural one, and I feel this inner turmoil (*Zerrissenheit*) very, very deeply. [...] I have difficulty identifying with the whole [country]."

One other Strauß supporter—or at least sympathizer—should be mentioned here. Rolf Schneider (b. 1932), a writer who spent most of his adult life in the German Democratic Republic, reminds us that the aspiring dramatist Strauß was once a convinced neo-

Marxist. Perusing the list of intellectual forerunners provided in 'The Last German,' Schneider notes (not without disapproval) that most of them were anti-Enlightenment figures, and what they have in common is their use of the German language. Schneider's conclusion: "The national identity that Botho Strauß is concerned about can be reduced—although he does not say this and perhaps cannot even see it—to our mother tongue."[25] This is indeed a key point: although each and every language contains innumerable variants determined by class, educational level, group, location, etc., the most sophisticated means of expression are cultivated by the representatives of high culture. If one believes that nuances, profundity, and subtleties are no longer needed in our increasingly technologically driven world, then Strauß can be consigned to the dustbin of history. However, if one believes that language use shapes the mind, then those who advocate for rigor and sophistication should not be dismissed so quickly. In his article, Schneider relates an anecdote that is sure to send shivers down the spine of any culturally-inclined German: a pupil nearing completion of a college-preparatory secondary school (apparently in the Berlin area) recently asked his teacher: "Who was this Friedrich Schiller anyway?" That would be like a young French person admitting that s/he has never heard of Voltaire. In his typically reticent manner, Schneider comments: "Perhaps we should push back against that a bit."

Where are we to place Botho Strauß in the spectrum of conservative cultural criticism? Perhaps the answer lies in an article about ecology and environmental politics that he wrote in 2005.[26] Already in 'Impending Tragedy,' he had praised the German Greens:

> The ecologists were the first to impressively proclaim that things cannot continue this way, and they managed to imprint this upon our consciousness with some success. The dictum about limits could be translated into the language of politics, morality, and certainly also socioeconomics. The limits of freedom and permission seem to be clearly making their appearance in what we have brought about. (p. 205)

In 2005, twelve years later, the tone is still positive, but Strauß's words of praise are mixed with criticism: to demonstrate that he is beyond partisanship based on any one political party, he begins by chastising the Greens for their naive view of multiculturalism (as evidenced by their tolerance for the head scarves worn by some Muslim women in Germany). Despite this, he makes it clear that, at least for him, the Greens are the only "metapolitical" party in Germany. What might that mean? The Greens are characterized as "the only party in our parliament that was interested and active in a sphere beyond social questions. A Gaia party, feminine and pagan, that felt more responsibility for the elements light, wind, earth, and water than for general economic welfare." Strauß sees the origins of the Greens' ecological orientation not in the influence of various leftist groups looking for a new home after the end of the student movement, but rather in the publications of the Club of Rome (seen here as a conservative organization) that emphasized the limits of growth. Among the impressive accomplishments of the Greens are "the cleaning up of waterways, waste management, and protection of the biosphere;" all this is portrayed as a conservative project that combines "innovative technology and the ethic of responsibility." (One recalls that the latter term from sociologist Max Weber was also utilized by Thilo Sarrazin.) Strauß reminds us that one of the founders of the Greens, Herbert Gruhl, was a long-time member of the conservative CDU.

The CDU is then criticized much more harshly than the Greens, because it is a conservative party in name only, concerned with protecting the interests of those who profit from the present system. Strauß still hopes for a transformation that could put not only climate change, but also a defense of the beleaguered humanities, at the top of the CDU's agenda. The subtitle of the article in question can be read as a call for a completely different kind of politics: 'If the Greens were to become blacker [more conservative] and the Blacks [the Christian Democrats] were to become greener.' If the two groups were able to work together, it might be possible to infuse politics with "more truth and more imagination;" in German political discourse, the possibility of a Black-Green coalition government has been examined for years. (There is already a Green-Black coalition in the prosperous federal state of Baden-Württemberg, led by Green politician Winfried Kretschmann, a devout Catholic and Green party leader.) Strauß himself is of course thinking not about this or that upcoming election, but about his own vision, which revolves around conservation of the natural world in the face of uncontrolled exploitation by economic interests, and preservation of the artistic and intellectual achievements of the past, which provide us with the tools for analyzing the foundations and direction of our own society. This is doubtless a minority position in today's Germany; even though environmental consciousness pervades German society, few political figures are willing to criticize the concept of economic growth (and the exports—including armaments—that fuel it). In the cultural sphere, the presence of statues of famous poets and composers in myriad public parks belies the fact that high culture is maintained for tourists but not often patronized by the average German, who has developed an appetite for globalized entertainment purveyed by numerous media outlets. Although many critics have portrayed Botho Strauß as a dangerous figure, he is actually more like the prophetess Cassandra. As an assiduous student of the ancients, Strauß of course knows that Cassandra's warnings were not heeded; this knowledge will probably not stop him from issuing proclamations from his rural refuge.

4

THE VOICE OF THE PEOPLE?
THE ALTERNATIVE FOR GERMANY AND PEGIDA

The controversial and influential Bavarian politician Franz Josef Strauß (1915–1988) often declared that there should never be a political party to the right of his own CSU (Christian Social Union, the sister party of the CDU). There have in fact been such parties in post-1949 West Germany and post-1989 united Germany, but none of them have marshaled enough electoral support to get them the 5 per cent share of the vote they need to gain seats in the *Bundestag*. Writing in 1999, Armin Pfahl-Traughber described three "waves" of right-wing extremism since World War Two.[1] The first involved the *Sozialistische Reichspartei*, a group including many former Nazis that had some success at the regional level in 1951 and was banned in 1952. There followed the founding of the NPD (*Nationaldemokratische Partei Deutschlands*) in 1964; this party entered several regional parliaments in the 1960s, gathered 4.3% of the national vote in 1969, and declined after that; there have been attempts to ban this party as well, but without success: in 2017, the German Constitutional Court decided that, even though the NPD was in fact an enemy of the constitution, racist and anti-Semitic, it was too small and insignificant to be banned.[2] Finally, a third wave brought forth the DVU (*Deutsche Volksunion*), founded by publisher Gerhard Frey in 1971, and the *Republikaner* (known as the REPs), founded in 1983 by, among others, defectors from the abovementioned CSU. The DVU scored the biggest regional electoral victory by a right-wing party to that day (12.9% in Sachsen-Anhalt in 1998), and the REPs reached 7.5% in Berlin in 1989 and 10.9% in Baden-Württemberg in 1992. The DVU ceased to exist after a failed fusion with the NPD in 2011, and the REPs' result in the 2013 federal elections was 0.2%. It could be said that all of these parties represented the 'Old Right,' due in large part to the widespread perception that they were basically closet fascists. As Michael Minkeberg has put it: "the Nazi past puts considerable constraints on openly mobilizing a right-wing electorate."[3] The 'New Right' in Germany appeared in the form of the *Alternative für Deutschland*, usually dubbed the AfD, in 2013; this was quite late, when one considers that similar parties had existed for some time in other European countries, such as Sweden's *Sverigedemokraterna* (1988), Denmark's *Dansk Folkeparti* (founded in 1995 by Pia Kjaersgaard) or Belgium's *Vlaams Belang* (Flemish Interest, reconstituted in 2004 from the earlier *Vlaams Blok*). Marine Le Pen took over and remade her father's *Front National* in France (2011), and Jörg Haider had transformed the Austrian Freedom Party (FPÖ) after taking over as leader in 1986. The appearance of the AfD has been called a "move towards the normal state of affairs in (Western) Europe."[4]

New political parties are often protean, and that has certainly been the case with the young AfD. At the time of its founding, it was widely viewed as a "professors' team"[5] mainly concerned with the Euro and its effects on the German and European economy. One of its founders, who was to become the public face of the party in its early days, was Bernd Lucke (b. 1962), an economist and professor at the University of Hamburg. He appeared on various German talk shows and defended the AfD against the view that it was a right-wing extremist party. A long interview published in the *Frankfurter Allgemeine Zeitung* provides considerable insight into his motivations and values: Lucke and his wife have five children; they are members of the Evangelical-Reformed Church in Hamburg, a congregation that characterizes itself as non-hierarchical, self-administrating, and "grassroots-democratic;"[6] and the family owns neither an automobile nor a television (the quality of the programs is "low," Lucke remarks).[7] At first blush, this appears to be closer to the world of conservative Greens than the extreme right.

Lucke also took time off to help raise his children, not what one would expect from a right-winger; the same can be said of his decision to fulfill his military service obligation as a flautist in a military band. His academic career meant that the family spent a considerable amount of time abroad (in the US, Canada, and France), and his English is quite good; in other words, his is not a background that could be considered provincial. Lucke was a member of the CDU for over three decades, but he became disillusioned with that party's drift toward the political center. This phenomenon highlights the fundamental differences between the situation in Germany and in the US, where the old 'liberal-conservative' wing of the Republican Party has basically disappeared. In the US context, it is unlikely that Lucke would have even considered founding a new conservative party.

Under Lucke's leadership, the AfD managed a surprising 4.7% showing at the 2013 federal election and 7.1% at the 2014 European election; Lucke has been an MEP since then. Despite such success, there was an underground revolt brewing in the party: a so-called "Patriotic Platform" was created in late 2014, and a nationalist faction spearheaded by Björn Höcke and André Poggenburg put forth the "Erfurt Resolution" in March, 2015. The hardliners feared that the AfD was in danger of becoming just another mainstream party instead of a vehicle for radical change.[8] At the Party Congress in 2015, Lucke was deposed as party leader, giving way to Frauke Petry; Lucke subsequently left the AfD and founded a new group initially called *Allianz für Fortschritt und Aufbruch* or ALFA (Alliance for Progress and Awakening), renamed the Liberal-Conservative Reformers (LKR) in November 2016. He was the leading candidate for that party in the run-up to the 2017 German federal elections. In a statement published at the time of Lucke's resignation from the AfD, he explained his decision by pointing to "anti-Islam" and "anti-foreigner" views coming to the fore in the party, as well as irrational criticism of the US and sympathy for Russian political positions; all this he had to reject "out of deep conviction," he emphasized.[9] At the same time, he admitted that he had "recognized too late" to what extent members of the party were attempting to turn the AfD into a "protest and *Wutbürgerpartei*," far from the "objective and constructive" political force that he had envisioned. It was this protest party, however, that enjoyed great success in the 2016 regional elections, winning 15.1% in generally bourgeois-conservative Baden-Württemberg and 12.6% in Rheinland-Pfalz (both in the West), 14.2% in Berlin, 20.8% in Mecklenburg-Vorpommern, and an amazing 24.3% in Sachsen-Anhalt. What were the citizens who chose the newly-radicalized AfD voting for? One way to answer that question is to analyze the party program that was presented in the spring of 2016.[10]

This ninety-six page document touches upon myriad issues in the spheres of culture, politics, and society. (In terms of detail, it is comparable to the 2011 program of the leftist party *Die Linke*, although the latter contains more prose and fewer subsections.) The preamble (p. 6) is preceded by two phrases, namely *"Mut zu Deutschland,"* which can be interpreted as "Have the courage to stand up for your German heritage," and *"Freie Bürger. Keine Untertanen,"* which means that the authors see themselves as "free citizens" who are not "subjects;" this implies that some sort of autocratic system has been set up in Germany since 1949. Many Germans will associate the word *"Untertan"* with the 1918 novel *Der Untertan* by Heinrich Mann (or the 1951 film version directed by Wolfgang Staudte), which provided a satirical portrayal of subservience to the *Kaiser* in pre-1914 Germany. The next three sentences are also telling: "We are liberals and conservatives. We are free citizens of our country. We are democrats out of conviction." This implies that the party still consists of the two factions that existed before the departure of Lucke and his followers. What is meant by the term "democrats out of conviction" is elucidated in the course of the document; in the preamble alone, nevertheless, some basic issues are addressed. The party sees itself as an "alternative" to the mainstream political establishment that claims exclusive representation of the people. For Americans used to a two-party system, one should keep in mind that the German 'mainstream' includes Christian Democrats, Social Democrats, Greens, Leftists, and Free Democrats (Liberals). This coterie is supposedly destroying the rule of law, acting in opposition to "economic rationality," and causing enmity among European nations in the wake of the attempts to save the Euro. There is much boilerplate here that could be found in the program of any democratic party, but there is also an emphasis on German cultural identity; one reads that "democracy and freedom stand on the foundation of shared cultural values and historical memories." That could mean that each country must have a form of democracy appropriate to its individual development, and such a construct would of course no longer be bound by the universal principles of the Enlightenment. Beyond Germany itself, a newly constituted Europe would be a group of "sovereign states" tied to each other in "peace and self-determination as good neighbors." This would be a Europe of independent nation-states, not a European Union; current developments in Hungary and Poland could be viewed as harbingers of such a system. Another paragraph of the preamble provides a vision of the future: "We want to ensure the long-term existence of human dignity, families with children, our occidental and Christian culture, [and] our language and tradition in a peaceful, democratic, sovereign nation-state of the German people." It is clear that the most contentious point here involves the definition of "the German people"—this is no side issue, as illustrated by another statement in the preamble: "We are open to the world, but we want to be and remain Germans." At this juncture, nothing is said about the possibility of "becoming" German.

It is not possible here to discuss every single aspect of the AfD program, so particular attention will be paid to those aspects that reflect a desire to stake out new ground. The first unusual proposal is the introduction of national referendums (*Volksabstimmungen*) patterned after the Swiss model. (Austria also holds referendums, but this is not mentioned, possibly because they have been mainly associated with the right-wing populist FPÖ; indeed, Austria is not touched upon once in the program.) In Germany, this would entail changing the Basic Law, and here the AfD calls for the right of the people themselves to change it, without parliamentary involvement. Given the events of the twentieth century, it is unlikely that such a change could be implemented, since it would raise questions about the stability of postwar German democracy. The AfD would also give the people the right to accept or reject laws passed in parliament, something that would supposedly stop the wave of "nonsensical bills" (p. 9). The reasoning behind this is that the citizens are more concerned with the common good than the "professional politicians," and the overall goal is a "slimmed down state" whose only responsibilities would be "internal and external security, law, foreign relations, and financial administration;" this would entail a return to the nineteenth century. Anthropologically speaking, there seems to be a rather ambivalent view of human nature at work here, perhaps stemming from Martin Luther and Immanuel Kant ("crooked timber"). The word "utopia" only appears once in the document, as a purely negative phenomenon that has brought "great suffering" to human beings (p. 17). It does not occur to the authors that the much-heralded "democracy" of which they speak was once no more than a utopian dream.

The "omnipotence" (*Allmacht*) of the political parties must be broken, it is asserted, because it is connected to "political correctness" and the limited number of viewpoints permitted in "public discourse" (p. 11). In order to facilitate the transformation of politicians into "citizen parliamentarians," terms limits for members of parliament and the Federal Chancellor are to be introduced. The goal is to do away with the "greatest harm" done to democracy, namely that caused by "lobbying and corruption" (p. 13). No one knows, of course, if AfD members who actually enter parliament would be willing to serve there only temporarily, as was once a problem for the Greens. Beyond domestic politics, the AfD opposes the EU in the form of a "centralized federal state" (p. 16). If national sovereignty is regained, European countries will once again become "beacons of freedom and democracy in the world" (p. 17), though it is not stated exactly when these "beacons" existed, and students of colonialism might be somewhat skeptical about the European model. If such beacons have existed, they were first illuminated during the Enlightenment, a period not favored by the AfD. The elephant in the room is globalization, or at least the development of some sort of supranational identity; the AfD makes it perfectly clear that "only national democracies, created by nations through a painful history, are capable of providing their citizens with the necessary and desired spheres of identification and protection" (p. 17). Such pronouncements are part of a widespread reaction against globalization, and they are not limited to those who espouse extreme-right views. The AfD is only willing to accept a European Union that would be a "flexible network" (p. 18) of states without a common currency that would not accept new members from other cultural spheres; thus Turkey would have no place in such a group, but that is a view now shared by many Europeans from all parts of the political spectrum.

On the home front, the AfD wishes to project the image of a strong law-and-order party. The security of individual citizens is supposedly no longer being guaranteed, so certain steps are necessary, including: a larger police force with more modern weapons; trying youth offenders as adults (in light of the "increasing brutality of young criminals"; p. 25); ensuring that judges and prosecutors are free from the influence of political parties; imposing mandatory minimum sentences for attacking a representative of the state; and concentrating on protecting victims rather than perpetrators. The AfD is especially concerned about the involvement of foreigners in "violent and drug-related crime" (p. 26), so strong measures must be taken: it must be easier to deport those involved in crime; to prevent those who have committed crimes from becoming citizens; and to revoke citizenship for certain criminal acts, including membership in groups engaged in organized crime. The society should also be given access to data about the background of perpetrators, something usually proscribed in Germany due to strict privacy rules. Along with such tactics, law-abiding citizens should not have limits put on their ability to obtain weapons; the argument is that criminals will obtain them anyway, so citizens will be more vulnerable. The AfD fears that without weapons, citizens will not be able to resist an "all-encompassing surveillance and nanny state" (p. 26). This is the rhetoric of fear, and it is reminiscent of the world view of the National Rifle Association in the US.

In the area of foreign affairs, the picture is not quite what one would expect. In recognition of Germany as a major economic power, the AfD emphasizes that good relations with "all states" (p. 29) are in the national interest. The United Nations is seen as an "indispensable" institution in which Germany should play an "active and constructive role" (p. 30). Germany should have a permanent seat on the Security Council, and one of the subtexts of such a development would be to acknowledge that the image of the country would no longer be tainted by the events of World War Two; related to this is the AfD's proposal to renegotiate the presence of allied troops in Germany (p. 31). NATO is accepted as a defensive alliance, and the AfD calls for a strengthening of the European contribution to its operations. Germany itself should also rebuild its military capabilities, and this would include an expansion of the domestic armaments industry and a reintroduction of military conscription (neutral Sweden implemented the latter in March 2017); it is worthy of note that the right to conscientious objection would be retained, and women would be allowed to volunteer for service. In a time when Marine Le Pen is a frequent visitor to Moscow, the AfD declares that there can be no real security in Europe without the participation of Russia. This is surely true, but one then reads that conflicts in Europe should be settled "peacefully" (p. 31)—certainly a noble goal, but it can mean that actions like Russia's annexation of the Crimea (and any similar steps in the future) will never be answered with military action.

Since the AfD is dedicated to preserving German cultural identity, it is not surprising that it wishes to encourage Germans to have more children, and views the normative social unit (*Leitbild*; p. 36) as the family. Instead of portraying children as "career hindrances" (p. 37), society must realize that the entire social welfare system will collapse unless the birthrate rises. One proposal is to take childrearing into account when calculating one's (state) pension, and another is to provide extra financial support for large families in order to "encourage [people] to decide to have more children" (p. 37). (Unlike many conservative groups, the AfD also wants to maintain a minimum wage.) In a time when the regard for families is being diminished (from the perspective of the AfD), the forces behind this trend must be countered:

> Gender Mainstreaming and the overall emphasis on individuality are undermining the family as the value-setting basic social unit. The economy wants women as a source of labor. A falsely conceived feminism values working women, but not those who are 'only' mothers and homemakers. The latter are often given less recognition and are disadvantaged financially. (p. 41)

The AfD hopes to promote a "society-wide discussion of values" (p. 41) that would lead to more backing for parents (including single parents, who need "special support"). One could of course argue that immigration could contribute to more favorable demographics, but this is a red flag for the AfD: although a "moderate [amount] of immigration based on qualitative criteria" is deemed acceptable, "mass immigration" is rejected out of hand (p. 62). Given that stance, it is not surprising that the most extensive section of the party program is devoted to "Immigration, Integration, and Asylum."

The authors of the AfD party program realize that they are dealing with a global phenomenon, not a local problem, and are clearly aware of its roots: "population explosion, military and religious conflicts, and climate extremes in many countries, especially on the African continent and in the Near and Middle East" (p. 59). Surprisingly, they even employ the language of the political left when describing these roots in more detail:

> The AfD is committed to avoiding the economic causes of migration, even if this could at first involve disadvantages for Western economies. That entails, for example, stopping the export of highly subsidized agricultural products to Africa, which ruin the local markets and take away the basis of survival for the people there. The same is true for the export of weapons, used clothing, toxic waste, and other Western forms of rubbish as well as for the EU fishing industry active near the African coasts. (p. 61)

They also realize that no one country can come to terms with the current "migration of peoples of historic dimensions." How can Germans and Europeans react to all this? "True refugees" (p. 59)— who are fleeing from political persecution and the horrors of war— must be protected, but not those who abuse the right to asylum in order to take advantage of social welfare. The AfD proposes a two-pronged strategy: on the one hand, the external borders of the EU must be closed to mass migration, and those seeking entry are to be housed in processing centers in "safe states" outside of Europe (p. 59); if international organizations are not able to create such centers, then Germany will do so itself (which would of course entail huge expenditures on the part of the German government). On the other hand, although the AfD recognizes the need for highly-qualified immigrants in small numbers, the emphasis would be on vocational training for native Germans, including the unemployed and those often discriminated against due to their age or their responsibilities as single parents. It is clear that in an ideal world, the AfD would rather not see any immigration to Germany. Beyond a discussion of those who *want* to enter the country, much attention is also paid to those who are already there.

Like many other German and European conservatives, the AfD believes that multiculturalism has failed (even Angela Merkel has said as much); it would ideally like to see the complete assimilation of those who have come to Germany from other countries and cultures, but they realize that this could not be accomplished through coercion (p. 63). To counter the creation of "counter- or parallel societies" (p. 63), all immigrants must recognize that they have the responsibility to pursue integration into Germany society, a process outlined rather succinctly: "[...] learning the German language, respecting our legal and social order, and earning one's own living" (p. 63). Those who refuse to do this could eventually lose their right to remain in Germany. The cultural dimension is not mentioned here, but it is paramount when it comes to deciding whether or not an immigrant may be granted German citizenship, a status that is inseparable from "our culture and language" (p. 65). This is never elucidated, but it is stated that children born in Germany should not be granted citizenship unless one parent is German. But what does it mean to be German? For example, would the AfD consider the children of Polish immigrants (like the renowned soccer player Lukas Podolski) to be German, or is German ethnicity required? (This is perhaps an inappropriate example, since the AfD seems open to qualified immigrants from other EU countries.) Being German does mean to the AfD that one should not (with a few exceptions) have dual citizenship—as many Turkish Germans do.

German identity is the focus in the section entitled 'Culture, Language, and Identity.' The AfD declares that the preservation of the German cultural heritage is one of its "primary political goals" (p. 47); very few mainstream political parties would make such a strong statement, and culture is usually an afterthought in political programs. The CDU did make use of the term "*Leitkultur*" (dominant, leading, or guiding culture) in the 2007 version of its party program, but provided few details. It is significant, however, that the CDU placed this "*Leitkultur*" in the European context:

> These cultural values and historical experiences are the basis for the cohesion of our society, and they shape our *Leitkultur* in Germany. [...] Our culture exhibits, in its history, present, and future, a European character and orientation. This European dimension will, in the course of the ongoing unification of Europe, become more significant.[11]

The AfD also uses the term *"Leitkultur"* (without discussing its origins), but not in exactly the same way. In their version, this culture has three sources, namely "the religious tradition of Christianity, the scientific-humanistic tradition, whose roots were renewed in the Renaissance and the Enlightenment, and [...] Roman law, upon which our legal system is based" (p. 47). This is a remarkable formulation, since the Renaissance and the Enlightenment mark the beginning of modern individualism and secularization, which the AfD rejects. In addition, one does not find the phrase "Judeo-Christian tradition" that is generally used by the contemporary religious and political right; indeed, the Jewish aspect does not appear until later, in the context of a distancing from Islam (p. 48). It is also unclear just what is meant by the "humanistic" tradition, since elsewhere in the document, there is a sharp criticism of "misguided humanitarianism" (p. 59).

If anything is made abundantly clear regarding German culture and identity, it is summed up in one sentence: "Islam is not part of Germany" (*Der Islam gehört nicht zu Deutschland*; p. 49). This is preceded by the declaration that the AfD is committed to religious freedom "without reservation" (p. 48).[12] Most Germans will remember that in 2010 the former federal president Christian Wulff (basically repeating what veteran CDU politician Wolfgang Schäuble had said in 2006) asserted that Islam was in fact part of Germany.[13] From the perspective of the AfD, an "orthodox Islam" that fails to respect or even agitates against "our legal system" and claims to be the one true religion is not "reconcilable" with German law and culture (p. 49). It is conceded that "many Muslims are law-abiding, integrated, and accepted members of our society," but the AfD see the threat of the creation of "parallel societies" with Sharia judges as well as a radicalization process leading to "violent Salafism and terror" (p. 49). It is also emphasized that it must be possible to criticize Islam without being denounced as Islamophobic or racist; since the word "caricatures" is used in this passage, one can assume that the AfD would support the publication of the sort of art that led to waves of protest against the Danish newspaper *Jyllands Posten* in 2005.[14] The original draft of the party program went much further, depicting Islam as a religion in need of a fundamental overhaul: "The AfD supports the efforts of Islam critics to enlighten people about Islam, push for reforms within the Muslim community, and make

Islam conform to the norms and values of enlightened modernity."[15] The final version does include a call to ban minarets, public calls to prayer, full-body covering for women, and the wearing of a head scarf by those in civil service positions (applying the "French model"; p. 50). For the AfD, the wearing of the head scarf is an intolerable symbol of the subordination of women to men. Since these are the final words of the program section revolving around identity questions, it is clear that there is no room for compromise. (This was reflected in the unsuccessful dialog between Frauke Petry and representatives of the Central Council of Muslims in Germany.[16])

In the area of education, one finds a mix of mainstream conservative positions and more radical proposals. The AfD is concerned that the quality of education in Germany is falling, which could eventually lead to an inability to compete on an international scale. It calls both for a further strengthening of the much respected "dual system" of vocational training and a return to the model of elite secondary schools for prospective university students (pp. 53-54); the recently instituted Europe-wide Bachelor's degree would be replaced by the traditional German "*Diplom*" and "*Magister*." Much emphasis is to be placed on the so-called STEM fields (in German: MINT), and there are to be neither quotas for women nor any form of Gender Studies courses. In general, any discussion of gender issues is to be eliminated, because it could "marginalize the natural differences between the sexes and counter traditional value conceptions and sex roles in the family" (p. 55); put another way: "Our schoolchildren should not become objects of the sexual inclinations of a loud minority" (p. 54). Given such language, it is somewhat ironic that the presence of Islam (hardly a faith enamored of Western-style Gender Studies) in the schools is to be severely limited. Koran schools as places of potential anti-democratic radicalization are to be closed "until Islam has gone through a true reformation", and the study of Islam is to be integrated into already existing general courses on ethics. Muslim pupils are to be given no special privileges (such as being excused from swimming classes or class excursions), and female teachers are to be given all due respect by Muslim pupils and their parents (p. 55). (One recalls that there have been cases where the customary handshake between teachers and pupils has been refused by the latter.) It is understandable that the AfD would want to stop the trend toward bullying and violence in the schools, and one can surely agree that the classroom should not be misused for political indoctrination (p. 54), but it is clear that the AfD would prefer that certain topics not be discussed at all, an approach that is not compatible with the—outwardly laudable—goal of ensuring that pupils and students will become "independently thinking citizens" (p. 54).

The AfD's statement supporting the freedom of research and teaching at the universities leads to another conundrum in the party program: "The ethos of science, to which the ability to criticize, impartiality, and respect for other scientists and their achievements belong, must be strengthened" (p. 52). Said conundrum appears in the sections entitled 'Energy Policy' and 'Nature, Environmental Protection, Agriculture, and Forestry.' Here one learns right at the outset that the scientists the AfD respects are the ones who deny that there is such a thing as climate change caused by human activity: this is not characterized as a minority position, but rather as the only scientifically correct position: "The climate has been changing as long as the earth has existed." Therefore:

> We will do away with the view that CO2 is only a harmful substance and put a stop to all national efforts to reduce C02 emissions in Germany. We will not place any financial burden on CO2 emissions. Organizations that work to protect the climate will no longer be supported. (p. 79)

If the AfD had its way, Germany's role as a model for industrialized nations dedicated to stopping global warming and other manifestations of climate change such as extreme weather events would come to an abrupt halt; the Renewable Energy Law (EEG) would be struck from the books; and Germany would return to the halcyon days when electric power production was always "secure, economical, and had a low impact on the environment" (p. 80). Given that many AfD politicians are from Eastern Germany, it is incredible that the memory of the wholesale destruction of entire areas in the wake of strip mining for lignite has somehow been lost. Another 'scientific' argument involves the use of alternative energy sources such as solar and wind: according to the AfD, such sources are only viable if large-scale storage capacity is available. That much is certainly true; we are told, however, that such storage, if it did exist, would be "unaffordable" (p. 80), which ignores the history of technological innovation, in which new methods and products are rather expensive when introduced, but become much less so after widespread adoption. The AfD is also not overly concerned about the negative aspects of nuclear power, calling for an extension of the life cycle of plants that are still running, since the Germans build "the safest [ones] in the world"—a phrase removed from the final version of the program. The AfD clearly believes that such positions are compatible with the statement that, due to our responsibilities to those who come after us, we should preserve an "intact and diverse" natural environment, because "a healthy environment is the basis of life for all human beings and future generations" (p. 85). However, these words are directly followed by something completely different: "Nature protection may not be a burden on human beings" (p. 85). How can these positions be reconciled? Much of the language found in the section on nature and environmental protection could be found in the programs of left-leaning parties: the AfD would preserve intact natural landscapes, reduce toxic substances in the soil and the water, and improve air quality (p. 86); the suffering of animals in industrial-scale agriculture must be ended, and the use of antibiotics must be reduced; genetic engineering research is to be allowed, but tightly controlled until it is clear what the risks would be; GMOs (genetically modified organisms) are to be clearly labeled; the diversity of the seed stock is to be defended against the multinationals' attempts to dominate global agriculture (p. 87); land speculation by international corporations is no longer to be tolerated, and a "sustainable production of healthy, high-quality foodstuffs without toxins at market-based prices" is to be promoted (p. 88); finally, all transport planning should include the needs of pedestrians and bicyclists (p. 92). The Greens could not have said it better.

What is one to make of all this? The one overriding theme is an attempt to reduce the power of the central government, with the pejorative term "planned economy" appearing five times in the party program. The AfD appears to be offering something to everyone, including the elimination of speed limits on the *Autobahn*, fast Internet connections for all citizens, a private-public partnership to fund repairs to the crumbling infrastructure, and the promotion of home ownership as a means to strengthen the citizens' ties to the homeland (*Heimatbindung*). There is even—in contrast to trends in other developed countries—a push to maintain the use of cash for transactions, since this would prevent the government from monitoring all of the economic and financial activities of the populace. (This presumably does not include the drug or fake passport trade.) Even though one finds a commitment to Germany's postwar "social market economy," this is not a plea for its absolute primacy: "The economy is always a means to an end, not an end in itself" (p. 67). What is truly important to the AfD is the project of maintaining a discrete and historically-based German cultural identity (derived from a certain reading of German history); at this point in time, no one can predict to what extent the German people might share this vision. One cannot know if the party's electoral successes in the 2017 regional and national elections will be matched in the future after a period in which the AfD will have to demonstrate what concrete role it wants to play in the German political system.

It might be said that the AfD lives in two worlds. It is one thing to analyze the various points in the party program, and quite another to observe the behavior of party representatives in the public sphere. At least a few of the most notable incidents should be recounted here:

- Probably the most-publicized controversy revolved around Frauke Petry's comments about how to secure the German borders in light of the refugee crisis. On January 30 2016, Petry was interviewed by the newspaper *Mannheimer Morgen*;[17] most observers focused on one section of that interview, in which she was asked how law and order could be restored at the borders. In her response, she said that a border policeman had to prevent illegal border crossings and "if necessary, make use of his weapon. That is the law." When asked if the law ordered officials to shoot at people, she said: "I did not use the word[s] 'order to shoot.' No policeman wants to shoot at a refugee. I don't want that either. But part of the *ultima ratio* [last resort] is the use of firearms. What is key is to not let things get that far [...]." Shortly thereafter, representatives of all the other German parties condemned Petry, using words like "brutalization" and "inhumanity" and drawing parallels to the shooting of East Germans who tried to reach the West. The respected *Süddeutsche Zeitung* began its report about the affair by stating that Petry had "called for the use of weapons against refugees."[18] (Commentator Heribert Prantl spoke of "political obscenity."[19]) Petry disputed this and then issued a different statement declaring that the border officials had a "great responsibility."[20] Unfortunately for her, Beatrix von Storch, a leading figure in the fundamentalist Christian wing of the AfD, came to her defense, saying that to protect the German border from illegal refugees, it would even be justified to shoot at women and children;[21] she later had second thoughts and revised her statement to exclude children.[22] This vignette in all likelihood reflects certain conflicts within the AfD: Petry was at the time the public face of the party, determined to give it legitimacy and a measure of respectability, whereas other more radical members were pushing for an extreme agenda.

- Alexander Gauland, a former long-time CDU member and (at time of writing) the *éminence grise* of the AfD, caused quite a stir when he made a public statement about a player on the German national soccer team not long before the 2016 European Cup. The player in question, Bayern Munich defender Jérôme Boateng, has a German mother and a Ghanaian father, and was born in Berlin. Speaking with two journalists from the *Frankfurter Allgemeine,* Gauland was explaining why the AfD was concerned about the presence of too many foreigners in Germany, especially Muslims: such a presence made AfD supporters feel as if they were gradually losing the identity and everything that they had inherited from their fathers, he said. It was in this context that he added: "People think that he is a good footballer, but they don't want a Boateng as a neighbor."[23] It is difficult to explain why Gauland chose to mention Boateng at all, given that he is native-born, fully assimilated, and a devout Christian (with corresponding tattoos) to boot. Perhaps he thought that he was a Muslim. The two journalists subsequently interviewed Boateng's neighbors in the posh Munich neighborhood Bogenhausen, and no one had anything bad to say about him. After a wave of harsh criticism, Gauland began to retreat; the

Spiegel documented his attempts at damage control.[24] At first, he had no recollection of ever mentioning the name Boateng; then he admitted that his statement might have been made, but it was in the context of a conversation that was not meant to be published; later, he was supposedly only describing common feelings; finally, he claimed that he had known nothing about Boateng's background when he made the initial comment. (In a soccer-crazy society like Germany, even non-fans would surely have come across Boateng's image in some media outlet.) In the end, Frauke Petry had to play mediator, characterizing Boateng as a "top-notch soccer player who is justifiably a member of our national team" and adding that she was looking forward to the European Cup.[25] All of this is reminiscent of the way that the late Austrian populist Jörg Haider used the media: making a controversial statement, reacting to outrage by denying that the statement had been made in the first place, and finally maintaining that he had simply been misunderstood. In the end, the original words are not forgotten.

- It is difficult to misunderstand the AfD member Wolfgang Gedeon (b. 1947), for in his extensive writings, he makes it perfectly clear where he stands. After retiring from medical practice, Gedeon set about to write his magnum opus in three volumes (1,904 pages in all); the part of the title common to all three volumes is *Christlich-europäische Leitkultur. Die Herausforderung Europas durch Säkularismus, Zionismus und Islam* (*Christian-European Leading Culture. Europe Challenged by Secularism, Zionism, and Islam*).[26] He uses the pseudonym "W.G. Meister," somehow implying that he is the master seeking/teaching acolytes. Gedeon's trilogy has been analyzed by the historian Marcus Funck of the Technical University of Berlin's Center for Anti-Semitism Research. Funck's conclusion: "Gedeon's three-volume work is an attempt, in a dialogue between God and world, to reconcile a Christian-volkish world view with right-wing radical positions and to take a stand against modern Western society."[27] According to Funck, Gedeon's most incredible position involves describing the infamous anti-Semitic work *The Protocols of the Elders of Zion* as an authentic program for Jewish world domination.[28] Those who wish to get a taste of Gedeon's *Weltanschauung* can go to his homepage, where one finds the text '*Der Kampf der Kulturen in Europa*' ('The Clash of Cultures in Europe'—a title that demonstrates Gedeon's affinity with Samuel Huntington).[29] Gedeon sees Europe as a battleground, where three models of social organization are attempting to achieve domination: these are a "laicist-American leading civilization," a "Christian-European leading culture," and an "Islamic-Asiatic leading culture." Gedeon wants to free Europe from the "Americanization" that has transformed the continent and at the same time stop the attempts at Islamization via immigration. The only way to do this, in his view, is to restore the central role of Christianity in European society. For him, European culture was formed in a struggle with the "domestic enemy," namely Judaism, and the "external enemy," Islam. Whereas the Jews have had influence in Europe without becoming a major factor, in the United States the Jews have achieved "a dominant position in state and society," especially since 1989. Dismantling the "Americanization" of Europe is thus tantamount to eventually eliminating Jewish influence. When Gedeon's anti-Semitic views became known to a larger public in 2016, there was a discussion in the AfD about what to do about his connection to the party (he joined in 2013); after much back and forth (including a temporary split in the AfD delegation in the state parliament in Baden-Württemberg), Gedeon was removed from his position as speaker of the local party organization in Konstanz. The result of that vote was quite remarkable: even though Gedeon is unrepentantly anti-Semitic, the final tally was sixteen for removal, eleven against, and three abstentions. At time of writing, Gedeon has retained his party membership, even though he has sharply criticized the AfD for refusing to discuss the "taboo" of anti-Semitism and of playing into the hands of the Zionists.[30] How many members of the AfD would agree with this way of thinking?

• Gedeon has also criticized the Holocaust Memorial in Berlin, not because we should forget the victims, but rather because German "memory culture" should foreground "the positive sides" of German history, the "great successes" and "great moments" (*Sternstunden*).[31] Another younger and more prominent AfD member, Björn Höcke (b. 1972) took a similar position in a speech made in Dresden on January 17 2017.[32] Höcke, who is the chair of the AfD faction in the Thuringian regional parliament, is seen as one of the main representatives of the volkish-nationalist wing of the party. At the beginning of his wide-ranging speech before the party youth group (*Junge Alternative*, or JA), he took time to praise the efforts of the PEGIDA movement, describing how he had to make it past "wild hordes" of "so-called anti-fascists" before he could witness one of the early demonstrations of the group. He went on to say that the sort of "fundamental opposition" that he and his comrades envision was actually a positive one ("The AfD is [...] the last peaceful chance for our fatherland"), because it would save the German state from the "worn-out old political elite" supposedly engaged in destroying that very state. These politicians, Höcke asserted, are all "pathetic apparatchiks," meaning that there is no discernible difference between Angela Merkel and (former East German SED leader) Erich Honecker. That assertion itself would have been enough to cause an uproar in Germany, but the real controversy centered around his remarks about the Holocaust Memorial: he asserted that the Germans are unique, but not in a good way:

We Germans [...] are the only people in the world that have placed a monument of shame in the heart of their capital city. And instead of bringing the younger generation into contact with the great philanthropists, the earth-shaking philosophers, the musicians, the ingenious discoverers and inventors—that we have so many of—[...] perhaps more than any other people on earth [...], history, Germany history, is being ridiculed. That cannot and must not continue!

It is hardly inadvertent that Höcke used the words "of shame" rather than "of our shame," since that allows for two completely different interpretations. The one sentence that was cited over and over again in the media was the following: "We need nothing but a 180 degree turn in [our] memory politics!" And what would be the nature of such a turn? Höcke spells it out for his audience: "[W]e need a vibrant culture of memory that brings us above all and first and foremost into contact with the magnificent achievements of our ancestors." As one could well imagine, the Jewish community in Germany reacted without delay: Josef Schuster, the chair of the Central Council of Jews in Germany, declared: "The AfD shows its true face with these anti-Semitic and highly misanthropic words;"[33] Ronald Lauder, the head of the World Jewish Congress, said that the "entire AfD" was a "disgrace," and that he hoped it would disappear from the German political landscape.[34] Once again, it was left to Frauke Petry to find a way to save face, and she did this by going on the offensive: "As a Jewish representative, he [Lauder] should [...] recognize that the AfD is one of the few political guarantors of Jewish life [...] in times of illegal anti-Semitic migration to Germany."[35] Even though Petry intimated in that particular interview that Höcke would be kicked out of the AfD, at time of writing this has not yet happened.

Höcke's Dresden speech provides a useful summary of the positions taken by the radical nationalist wing of the AfD. His praise for PEGIDA brings up an issue that will be crucial in the future, namely the relationship between the party and the grassroots political movement. In the speech, Höcke states very clearly: "In order not to betray its historical mission, the AfD must remain a movement party, that is, it must itself again and again be present on the street and stay in close contact with sympathetic citizens' movements." In postwar West Germany, such movements were generally associated with the political left; these include the so-called Easter Marches opposing war and nuclear armaments (from 1960 to the present, with diminishing participation over time), the student and anti-war/anti-imperialist movement found in many highly-developed countries in the 1960s, feminist protests for equal rights and against abortion restrictions, and the various "citizens' initiatives" (Bürgerinitiativen) of the 1970s that eventually led to the founding of the Green Party. In East Germany, it was impossible for concerned citizens to take to the streets until the years just before the fall of the Berlin Wall. As a movement born in Dresden, PEGIDA is most closely related to the latter, at least in terms of the background of the participants. The push for reunification was of course by no means a purely leftist affair, so it was possible for PEGIDA to copy some of its tactics.

The first protest march organized by PEGIDA[36] took place in Dresden on October 20 2014; this was a complete surprise to most observers, and it was not until the following December that the group articulated its goals in a sort of manifesto called a "Position Paper." This one-page document, consisting of nineteen points, provided more confusion than clarification, as the following analysis will demonstrate. A quick perusal creates the impression that we are dealing with a potpourri encompassing standpoints of the left, the right, and somewhere in between, all arranged in no particular order.[37] A note on the group's acronymic name would be appropriate here: an accurate English translation would be "Patriotic Europeans against the Islamization of the Occident." The German term for "Occident" is *das Abendland*, a rare word in contemporary usage. The authoritative *Duden* dictionary defines the term as "the cultural unity of the European peoples, formed by the ancient world and Christianity."[38] On a scale of one to five, *Abendland* is found in the second-lowest category with regard to usage frequency, and for educated Germans, it conjures up associations with Oswald Spengler's monumental *Der Untergang des Abendlandes* (1918-1922), a work usually translated as *The Decline of the West*. A right-wing twitter feed called "Das Abendland" (@DasAbendland) points us in a more contemporary direction; Hitler used the term, as did conservative anti-communist politicians during the Cold War.[39] Some would trace the term as far back as Charles Martel's defeat of the 'Moors' near Poitiers in 732,[40] which would make PEGIDA a direct descendant of Martel and his grandson Charlemagne.

Charles Martel would have had great difficulty making sense of the PEGIDA "Position Paper," however, since he knew nothing of "sexual self-determination," the right to asylum, "parallel societies," referendums, or "gender mainstreaming." All of this, and more, can be found in the document in question. Even though PEGIDA is routinely characterized as Islamophobic, the word "Islam" does not appear here; the word "Muslim" is used, but only in a positive sense to refer to the Muslims who are "integrating" themselves into German society. Resistance is urged against "a misogynist, violent political ideology" (point 10). Similarly, "Sharia courts" and "Sharia police" are rejected without mentioning Islam (point 16), and the same is true for "preachers of hate, no matter what religion they might belong to" (point 19). The occidental culture found in the group's name is not mentioned until point 13, where its preservation and protection is enjoined. Even though PEGIDA is generally viewed as a radical group, point 18 emphasizes opposition to "radicalism, be it religiously or politically motivated." Should one take such a hastily-constructed hodgepodge seriously? The main theme is the current refugee crisis, and the message is a rather mixed one: most people from all parts of the political spectrum would agree that is our "duty" to take in war refugees and those subject to political or religious persecution (point 1), that it would be logical to provide decent housing for refugees in all parts of the country (point 3), that all EU member states should do their part (point 4), or that more personnel are needed to take care of the asylum seekers (point 5); these are all mainstream proposals. Other aspects are more controversial, such as including the right and duty of refugees to integrate themselves into German society, in other words into the Basic Law (the nature of such integration is not elucidated; point 2), adopting the "Dutch or Swiss model" of dealing with applications for asylum (point 6), or introducing a "zero tolerance policy" toward asylum seekers and migrants who commit crimes (with no mention of what sort of crimes would lead to deportation; point 9). PEGIDA's opposition to "Gender Mainstreaming" and its advocacy for national referendums à la Switzerland, as well as an immigration system patterned on the ones in Australia, Canada, or South Africa can be found in the AfD program. All in all, the "Position Paper" appears to have been written by a committee with no clear political standpoint; it is of course also possible that it was meant to be an exercise in obfuscation designed to conceal a rather sinister agenda. If the founding document is not especially enlightening with regard to the group's aims, the activities of the members in the public sphere certainly are.

Like most protesters worldwide, PEGIDA members carry banners and posters when they take to the streets. The one that initially drew attention to the group featured the phrase *"Wir sind das Volk"* (We are the people); this particular slogan was chanted by East Germans in the period before the fall of the Berlin Wall. At the time, it meant that the functionaries and leaders of the Soviet-style Socialist Unity Party (SED) were a corrupt and authoritarian clique completely isolated from the real concerns of most East Germans. Later on, it was transformed into *"Wir sind ein Volk"* (We are one people), signifying that the ultimate aim of the protests was to overcome the division of Germany; this was of course achieved in 1989/90. What does it mean when protesters use the phrase "We are the people" in united Germany, a Western-style liberal democracy anchored by a so-called "social market economy"? The only possible interpretation is that some citizens of the country feel that their concerns are not being addressed by the 'system.' Such individuals basically have two alternatives: they can organize new movements or political parties with an eye to eventually gaining a majority in parliament, or they can strive to topple the entire system. In postwar (post-Nazi) Germany, this second option is more than a bit dicey. The Basic Law did not contain a right to resist until the 1960s, when various protest movements were seen as a threat to the established order. Article 20 describes the nature of German democracy and concludes (in part 4): "Against anyone who undertakes to do away with this order, all Germans have the right to resist, if no other remedy is possible."[41] In other words, a movement like PEGIDA is entering treasonous territory if it wants to construct a completely new state. It appears that another tactic has been chosen.

The main message is that German leaders, especially the widely admired (if not flawless) Angela Merkel have betrayed the German people and thus must relinquish political power, yielding to the 'true patriots.' PEGIDA posters leave little to the imagination in this regard: Chancellor Merkel is portrayed in nun's garb as "Mother Terrorisia alias Hells Angela," a seemingly benevolent figure who is in fact responsible for importing terrorists to German soil; if this is not clear enough, another version shows her wearing a head scarf. (This is actually quite ironic, given that Merkel refused to wear one during her 2017 state visit to Saudi Arabia.) Such efforts seem tame, however, when German history is brought into play: on one poster, Merkel is shown as a sort of Stasi agent with the words "in IM Erika we trust," implying that she did not resist the East German regime, and moreover supported it as an "informal colleague" of the secret police, and thus could have no democratic legitimacy in united Germany.[42] Even that slander is surpassed by an image of a frowning Merkel in what appears to be a Nazi uniform (where the swastika is replaced by the Euro symbol). This is quite perfidious in light of the presence of neo-Nazis in PEGIDA.[43]

As disgusting as that image was, it was another set of posters that has caused the greatest controversy to date: on Monday, October 12 2015, a protester at the weekly march in Dresden held up a model of a gallows, from which two signs were hanging: "Reserved for Angela "*Mutti*" [mom] Merkel" and "Reserved for Siegmar [sic] "*das Pack*" Gabriel." The latter referred to SPD politician and then economics secretary Sigmar Gabriel, who had referred to xenophobic protesters in the Saxon town of Heidenau as "*Pack*" (rabble or riff-raff).[44] Images of the gallows were widely circulated in the media, and justice minister Heiko Maas declared that people who do such things "don't belong on the street, but in front of a judge."[45] There was an investigation, but in the end no one was prosecuted. The perpetrator claimed that he was simply engaging in "satire," and PEGIDA leader Lutz Bachmann used the occasion to once again castigate the "*Lügenpresse*" (lying press) for an "incredible exaggeration."[46] This is not surprising, since Bachmann's idea of humor includes masquerading as Hitler and posting photos of Klansmen on Facebook.[47]

As is the case regarding the AfD, PEGIDA is an organization in a state of flux. The number of participants in the Monday marches was as high as 18,000 in the early days, but in 2016, only about 2,500 to 3,000 people took part.[48] Dresden remains its center, but attempts have been made to found similar groups in other German cities, both in the new and old federal states; the one in Leipzig, LEGIDA, has gained a reputation for being the most radical, and at times, violent.[49] The question of leadership has also not been resolved: in 2015, Lutz Bachmann stepped down as head of the organization committee, only to return a few weeks later; in 2016, he was sentenced to a fine of 9,600 Euros for having posted xenophobic screeds on his Facebook page (in which he characterized immigrants to Germany as "rabble" [*Gelumpe*] and "bothersome animals" [*Viehzeug*][50]); later in the same year, he moved to the island of Tenerife and was declared *persona non grata* by the regional government there.[51] His background as a former petty criminal and drug dealer[52] does not seem to bother his followers, though, of course, the willingness to separate the message from the behavior of the messenger is hardly a purely German phenomenon. Also in 2016, Bachmann announced the founding of a new political party associated with PEGIDA, the Free Direct-Democratic People's

Party (*Freiheitlich direkt-demokratische Volkspartei*).[53] This happened a year after former PEGIDA spokesperson Kathrin Oertel had decided to leave the group and form a new one called Direct Democracy for Europe (*Direkte Demokratie für Europa*). Given such factional infighting within, it is difficult to imagine that PEGIDA will play a significant role in German politics in the future. However, that does not mean that it is not worth examining. The burning question is: just who are the supporters, and what motivates them to make their views known in public?

At the end of 2014, that is, at the beginning of the movement, the weekly *Der Spiegel* published an unusual editorial. Instead of issuing a blanket condemnation of PEGIDA, the authors tried to come to terms with this new political phenomenon; they asserted that "extreme-right riff-raff" engaged in stirring up resentment against foreigners and asylum seekers were nothing new, as "outrageous" as they might be; what was new was the willingness of "normal" citizens to associate themselves with such figures.[54] The editorialists' prediction: if the mainstream political parties failed to take legitimate concerns of such citizens seriously (such as the failure of the government to deport asylum seekers whose petitions had been rejected), the result would probably be the entry of populist parties like the AfD into parliament and a general shift of the political landscape to the right. Around the same time, Angela Merkel used her annual New Year's speech on German television as a platform against PEGIDA; after mentioning the Monday demonstrations for "democracy and freedom" staged by the East Germans before 1989, she warned:

> Today some are once again proclaiming on Mondays: "We are the people." But actually they mean: You don't belong—because of the color of your skin or your religion. That is why I say to all those who go to such demonstrations: Don't follow those who issue the call! Too often, there is prejudice, coldness, and even hate in their hearts.[55]

This refusal to differentiate doubtless contributed to the success of PEGIDA,[56] but real political analysis followed soon thereafter.

The Dresden political scientist Werner Patzelt published a study entitled *Was und wie denken PEGIDA-Demonstranten?* (What and how do PEGIDA demonstrators think?) in early 2015.[57] On the basis of 242 interviews (roughly the same number of demonstrators refused to answer questions), Patzelt and his students were able to piece together a portrait of the movement: the average age of the interviewees was 46.4 years old, and 72% were men; although many of them could be considered to be members of the working class, quite a few had completed secondary school and even attended the university; most of them had decently-paid jobs; only about 25% had any religious affiliation (not atypical in post-socialist Eastern Germany); 86% were from Dresden or the local area; fully 40% had demonstrated for the reunification of Germany, so the memory of that movement is still present (p. 11). In general, their political views put them somewhere between the center and the right, but some were even left-leaning (p. 7). Only about 46% trusted a political party, and in most cases, that was the AfD (p. 8). Attitudes toward Islam were more mixed than one might expect: when asked if a form of Islam just as peaceful as contemporary Christianity could belong to Germany, 44.6% disagreed absolutely, but 20.9% agreed without reservation. The number of people who felt that there were too many Muslims in Germany, and that they, as Germans, felt like foreigners in their own country, was similar to the attitudes of the populace as a whole (p. 16).

Patzelt came to the conclusion that there were three distinct groups involved in PEGIDA:

> about a third of the PEGIDA demonstrators probably have right-wing nationalist/xenophobic views, somewhat less than two-thirds are "well-meaning, but concerned citizens," and about 10 per cent are "well-meaning citizens" who are driven to solidarity with the PEGIDA demonstrators by considerable anger about distorted media reporting about the movement. (p. 27)

Almost three-quarters of the interviewees felt that media coverage was biased, hence the chanting of the epithet *Lügenpresse* (lying press) at demonstrations. How should civil society react to all this? At the end of his study, Patzelt formulated a strategy that he believed would be more effective than denunciation and marginalization. The major points were: avoid a confrontational mode that only strengthens the movement; encourage PEGIDA to formulate concrete political goals and take responsibility for them; civil society and the political establishment should establish objective and honest communication with the "well-meaning" participants, initiating a society-wide discourse about the problems of integrating new immigrants and avoiding the impression that only political, economic, and cultural elites set the agenda; and finally, demonstrate civil courage in the "struggle against all forms of aggression, intimidation, and marginalization of people of a different sexual orientation, [national] origin, skin color, religion, or political viewpoint." It is important to note that Patzelt did not include "extremists of all types" in his model of societal consensus (pp. 32-33). With regard to PEGIDA, this means that German democracy must make a serious attempt to bring the "well-meaning" members back into the fold, but have no illusions about the destructive potential of the true militants.

CONCLUSIONS AND PROSPECTS

How can one assess the activities and writings of the individuals and groups described above? Firstly, one must decide what to call them, and that entails answering a crucial question: are they populists or not? There is no unequivocal answer, simply because there is no agreement about the nature of populism itself. Two recent publications provide context, but also illustrate the lack of consensus regarding definitions and evaluation; given that populists tend to be skeptical of elites, it is somewhat ironic that both volumes are connected to elite institutions. The first, Jan-Werner Müller's *What is Populism?*,[1] is clearly a partisan exercise.[2] Populism "tends to pose a danger to democracy" (p. 3), it is a "peril" (p. 6), "[I]t is democracy itself that populism damages" (p. 50), it "distorts the democratic process" (p. 57), it is "not a path to more participation in politics" (p. 102), and, once again, it is "a real danger to democracy" (p. 103). On the one hand, Müller summarizes the characteristics of populism accurately for the general reader: it is "antielitist", "antipluralist," "distinctly moral" in tone, and a form of "identity politics" (p. 3). Populism's supporters "are said to be driven by 'fears' (of modernization, globalization, etc.) or feelings of 'anger,' 'frustration,' and 'resentment'" (p. 12). Any claim that populists make is "of a moral and symbolic—not an empirical—nature, it cannot be disproven" (p. 39); populists are "inherently hostile" to "constitutionalism" (p. 60); their "denial of diversity" in the end denies

117

"the status of certain citizens as free and equal" (p. 82). On the other hand, very little is said about the conditions that give rise to populist movements. Müller appears not to believe, for example, that a "silent majority" is being "ignored by elites" (p. 11); this is, of course, a phenomenon that has been endlessly discussed since the election of Donald Trump. Müller does admit, however, that "all is not well with existing democracies in Western Europe and North America" (p. 59), since there exists a "defect": "weaker socioeconomic groups do not participate in the political process and do not have their interests represented effectively" (p. 60). One could add that in an era where 'politics follows money' (especially in the US), these "weaker" groups make up a large segment of the population. Müller outlines the crisis of liberalism, but he does not discuss the concept of economic democracy. Political democracy is praised for incorporating an ongoing process of self-criticism (p. 72), but the distortions caused by increasing income inequality are not addressed; the "broken promises" of democracy are political, not economic. (The latter is at least hinted at in the following statement: "It is necessary [...] to remember one important difference between cultural and economic changes: many of the former do not, in the end, affect many individuals"; p. 92). It is a shame that Müller chose not to grapple with the "deep structural reform" needed in the US (p. 93). His assertion that "populism is not a useful corrective for a democracy that somehow has come to be to 'elite-driven'" (pp. 10-11) makes the reader wish that the developments behind the "somehow" had been examined. Without understanding such developments, one cannot really come to terms with populism.

The second volume in question, *Populism. A Very Short Introduction*, by Cas Mudde and Cristóbal Rovira Kaltwasser,[3] is written from a different perspective. This is illustrated at the beginning of the first chapter, where the authors state: "we neither consider liberal democracy to be flawless, or any alternative democratic system by definition undemocratic, nor apply the approach only within a liberal democratic framework" (p. 2). They refer to their own approach as "ideational," meaning that populism is conceived as "a discourse, an ideology, or a worldview" (p. 5). What is important here is that several other approaches are discussed, and two of them—"popular agency" and "Laclauan"—consider populism to be "essentially a positive force for the mobilization of the (common) people" and "not only the essence of politics, but also [...] an emancipatory force," respectively (p. 3). Neither approach is rejected out of hand: for Mudde and Rovira Kaltwasser, populism is a malleable "thin-centered ideology" that "appears in combination with different, and sometimes contradictory, ideologies" (p. 6); one basis for its appearance is "the gap between governed and governors" (p. 10). Whether it allies itself with "agrarianism," "nationalism," "neoliberalism" or "socialism" p. (19), in its various forms, it does have a "dark side," namely the support of "authoritarian tendencies" (p. 18). Despite this, it is deemed worthwhile to pursue an analysis of "the costs and benefits of democratic responses to populism" (p. 20). This analysis has a global scope (including Latin America), but the section most relevant to the present study concentrates on Western Europe: there, the sort of populism that arose in the 1990s was a "nativist" response to immigration that was based on "an ethnic and chauvinistic definition of the people," thus: "[P]opulism, authoritarianism, and nativism are experiencing a kind of marriage of convenience in Europe nowadays" (p. 34). This is by no means a homogeneous movement, since not all of the parties in question—be it in Austria, Belgium, France, or Italy— share the same characteristics. (One example: the virility cult and vulgar language of a Berlusconi is not typical of the Front National or the AfD.) The "conventional position" (such as that of Müller, who is not mentioned) is that such populism "constitutes an intrinsic danger to democracy" (p. 79); Mudde and Rovira Kaltwasser cite Ernesto Laclau's view that populism "fosters a 'democratization of democracy' by permitting the aggregation of demands of excluded sectors" and state that "Both interpretations are to a certain extent correct" (p. 79). More specifically, they assert that populism is positive in the sense that it promotes "political participation," and negative in that it contributes to "public contestation" (p. 82). The main threat that they see, and rightly so, is the proliferation of attacks on minorities and the erosion of "those institutions that specialize in the protection of fundamental rights" (p. 84). Even though populism may "diminish the quality of liberal democracies," it is unlikely that it could lead to a "breakdown" of a democratic system (p. 96); still, populism is here to stay, so proponents of democracy must attempt to strengthen its "positive effects" and "weaken its negative effects" (p. 98). If populism is in effect "part of democracy"—in that it is "an illiberal democratic response to undemocratic liberalism" (p. 116)—then that degraded liberalism must change. According to the authors, that would involve accepting the fact that "many citizens interpret political reality through the lens of populism" (p. 97), a "lens" that focuses on the perceived dishonesty of the elite political class, its corruption, and its disregard for the "opinions of the majority" (p. 99). Populist-leaning citizens/voters would no longer feel "orphaned" (p. 101) if such phenomena were to disappear from the political landscape or at least be drastically reduced. Put another way, populism "often asks the right questions but provides the wrong answers" (p. 118). Rather than simply attacking populists (the term 'deplorables' comes to mind), true democrats should work to construct democracies (in both the political and economic sense) that are worthy of the name.

How does Thilo Sarrazin fit into all of this? His main aim is to maintain material prosperity in Germany and to preserve the country's cultural heritage as the basis for its national identity. The German economy—especially the export sector—is quite strong at the moment, but the stresses of globalization are impinging upon the quality of life of the 'common people' whom populists usually claim to represent. Sarrazin is more concerned about stopping perceived abuse of the welfare system by immigrants than addressing income inequality. He is aware of environmental issues, but he clearly believes that unlimited economic growth is a sacred cow. Although he laments that the quality of education is not being maintained, he has little to say about the consumer society and the new media that are transforming the cultural landscape across the globe. Despite the strong conviction with which he puts forth his arguments, he is not especially hopeful. His world is gradually fading away, and there is no sign that it might be revitalized in the future; although he is a harsh critic of utopias per se, he lovingly tends his own utopian garden of 'traditional Germany.' The way in which this vision has been ravaged and ridiculed in the German media demonstrates that there is a distortion in the contemporary German public sphere: anyone who dares to wax nostalgic about the German past is immediately under suspicion of fascist tendencies. It is not difficult to imagine, in a not too distant future characterized by the devastating effects of climate change, a scarcity of natural resources caused by mindless waste, and a seemingly endless movement of peoples from one area of the world to another, that many will seek solace in nostalgia, yet it is only in Germany that such an activity will be branded as extremely dangerous. Those who claim that Sarrazin was the "trailblazer of the AfD"[4] simply ignore the fact that he is a man of the past, not the future. He has kept his distance from the AfD (not to mention PEGIDA), and he remains a member of the Social Democratic Party. These are not the credentials of a populist, and even his campaign against political correctness does not suffice to place him in that camp.

Akif Pirinçci, who once aspired to the status of a more radical, more ruthless Sarrazin,[5] has found much resonance in German right-wing circles (despite his disastrous appearance at a PEGIDA rally), but is he a populist? Despite his attempts to present himself as a true German patriot, his absolute detestation of the state and its activities in the spheres of culture, the economy, and politics puts him at odds with the course of German history. There is another aspect of German civilization that he continually disregards, which can be described using the term *dezent*; this word is usually translated as "subdued" or "unostentatious;" it is considered unseemly to stand out too much, to draw too much attention to oneself.[6] (This may well be less desirable among the younger generations, but Pirinçci is nearing the age of sixty.) His vulgarity and use of sexualized language may be tolerated in certain corner pubs, but certainly not in the public sphere; indeed, they are not even really appropriate in right-wing nationalist circles, where people often strive to portray themselves as the 'better,' 'purer' Germans compared to their Americanized compatriots. Pirinçci's idealization of the United States might have seemed strange, even embarrassing, in previous years, but in the Trump era, it actually has an inner logic. Whenever Pirinçci is criticized, he responds with a massive counterattack, often including insults with sexual undertones; he delights in destroying the taboos erected in the name of political correctness; he cultivates an image of male aggressiveness; he is a mortal enemy of the media; and he used Facebook the way Trump uses Twitter. His denigration of women often tests the boundaries of public discourse; he views immigrants—especially those from Muslim-majority countries—as the greatest threat to the prosperity and security of his homeland; he is convinced that he is more knowledgeable than all of the 'experts;' he characterizes environmentalists as dangerous lunatics bent on destroying German society, and dismisses efforts to develop alternative sources of energy as nonsense; if he had a slogan, it would be "Make Germany Great Again."There is an uncanny (fearful?) symmetry at work here; what is absolutely different is, of course, that Pirinçci has no interest in political activity, because his innate fatalism makes that appear meaningless—in other words, he does not really believe that Germany could be made "great" again. His demeanor and temperament are very similar to that of Donald Trump, but his life and career have reached a nadir, and his accumulated outbursts have made him a persona non grata in his own country, because in Germany, there is apparently a line that rabble rousers cannot cross. Trump basically has everything that Pirinçci could ever dream of, and yet his modus operandi[7] has not changed, and it has had only limited effect on his popularity. Perhaps a team of anthropologists, psychologists, and sociologists will choose to study this phenomenon in the future.

Botho Strauß is a unique figure in the contemporary German cultural scene. His veneration of the cultural heritage and distaste for today's consumer society are reminiscent of Éric Zemmour, and both figures would probably feel more comfortable in some past epoch (in the case of Strauß, the Romantic period; in Zemmour's, the Enlightenment). Zemmour is of course a highly public figure, whereas Strauß has chosen to isolate himself intellectually—and physically— from the German public sphere; it is thus puzzling when one reads that representatives of the neonationalist right see him as an inspirational figure. Describing Strauß's essay 'Impending Tragedy' as "even today a kind of credo, a political poetology [for] us," Ellen Kositza calls Strauß "a very prominent prophet (*Vordenker*) of the New Right."[8] Strauß's mode of resistance is, however, not directed towards change, but rather focused on preservation. At some point in the future, Strauß believes, a crisis will bring down the present system, and then the preservers or 'cultural memory keepers' will present a rich legacy to the generation fortunate enough to mount a new beginning. This is all far beyond purely political considerations, and Strauß's concept of culture is also far removed from the thinking of today's German politicians. At the end of April 2017, Interior Minister Thomas de Maizière formulated ten theses on *Leitkultur* (leading culture, as discussed above).[9] He began by describing so-called "constitutional patriotism" (respecting basic rights and the constitution, human dignity, democracy, the rule of law, and speaking German) and then provided the following definition of culture: "unwritten rules of our social existence." What he was really defining here was not culture, but civilization or the everyday way of life. In the fifth thesis, Bach and Goethe are mentioned right after a rather bold assertion: "We are a nation of culture. Hardly any other country is so permeated with culture and philosophy to the extent that Germany is." Such arrogance would not be found in the writings of Strauß, who values his own culture and that of many other lands; de Maizière's muddled thinking is unfortunately evidence of the cultural decline that causes Strauß so much pain. Even though the "Ten Theses" were sharply criticized from practically all quarters (even the AfD's Gauland accused the minister of misusing German culture for election campaign propaganda[10]), little light was shed on the role of culture in contemporary Germany. Ironically, much more attention was paid to a short and rather strange sentence: "*Wir sind nicht Burka*" (We are not [the] Burka). What de Maizière apparently meant to say was that Germans are open with each other in the public sphere and do not hide their identity. It is incomprehensible why he chose to express this in a sort of pidgin German that guest workers were (and sometimes still are) accused of using; Goethe would not have been amused.

The writers discussed above, none of whom can be characterized as true populists (despite assertions to the contrary in the German media), were given attention in the public sphere when they published a book, essay, or even a blog post, although in Germany, books tend to have the greatest impact (and Germans are more reluctant than many others to turn to e-books). It is very different with political parties like the AfD or citizens' movements like PEGIDA. Although the populace is most aware of them during election campaigns, their representatives can gain access to media coverage by making provocative statements or staging what used to be called "happenings" (such as the 'Greenpeace-style' occupation of Berlin's Brandenburg Gate by the relatively new "Identity Movement" [*die Identitären*]).[11] It is difficult to measure how much attention the actions of the populist New Right have gained in the society at large, but there has been intense scrutiny from the ranks of German political commentators and scholars. For the most part, these observers—mainly from the left side of the political spectrum—have made it abundantly clear that the AfD and PEGIDA are first and foremost threats to democracy.

One exception to this is the journalist Melanie Amann, who has written the first book on the AfD aimed at the general reading public. Amann admits that she initially underestimated the AfD, attributing her misjudgment to what she calls "a sort of 'Trump blindness';"[12] she now believes that the party has had both positive and negative effects on German politics. On the plus side: the CDU must now formulate its policies more clearly; more citizens are becoming politically active; more citizens are going to the polls; journalists must do a better job when reporting on politics; exaggerations of "political correctness" have been toned down; and "facts" (such as the necessity to save the Euro) are being questioned. The negatives include a brutalization of political debate, which feeds the fires of citizens' rage; right-wing jargon (such as *Lügenpresse*) becoming part of everyday language; and the fact that ideological excesses such as attacks on scientists who research climate change, or censorship of the arts and the media, might be on the agenda in the future (pp. 306-308). Amann predicts, however, that the "protest voters" who now support the AfD will fade away once the novelty of the party has worn off; once the AfD has found a secure place in the political system, it will be less attractive. The party needs a crisis situation—like the admission of almost a million immigrants and asylum seekers—to survive, and no one can predict what the next crisis might be.

Beyond the reports of journalists and the studies of social scientists, it is significant that politicians from all of the German mainstream parties have contributed to a volume entitled *AfD—Bekämpfen oder ignorieren?* (AfD—fight it or ignore it?).[13] Representatives of the two newest parties in the *Bundestag* (German lower house of Parliament), namely the Greens and the Left, are found right at the beginning of the collection, apparently emphasizing that they are now considered to be just as democratic as anyone else. The Greens make it clear that, for them, the AfD represents "hate, racism, and a societal retreat into pre-modern times,"[14] but they also attribute at least part of the blame for their success to the inability of the opposition parties in parliament to articulate their alternatives to the policies of the reigning grand coalition. For the Left, there would be absolutely no contact with the AfD if it were a "clearly fascist party,"[15] but this is not the case; here, the AfD is characterized as a representative of "a radicalized neo-liberalism, that is, rejection of solidarity" (p. 23). As was true for the Greens, the Left interprets the AfD's ability to attract voters as a failure of "the established [parties]" to perceive the "needs and interests" of certain parts of the populace (p. 25). The AfD is a "symptom of crisis," and the mainstream parties must do a better job of understanding this crisis and coming to terms with it (p. 26).[16]

Given that there is a symbiotic relationship between the AfD and PEGIDA, it is not surprising that the two are analyzed together as part of a "cultural offensive [*Kulturkampf*] from the right."[17] Echoes of the past are unmistakable when it is stated that the AfD must be resisted "before it is too late."[18] Germany is said to be facing "a dangerous development of right-wing populist, right-wing radical and dangerously violent course of events."[19] The electoral success of the AfD is tied to

> the actions of Pegida on the streets [...], the blurring of the boundaries of acceptable speech by persons like Thilo Sarrazin, all the way to Akif Pirinçci [...], the decades-long actions of the New Right in the political and pre-political sphere, and [...] the encouragement from the middle of society.[20]

By far the most accessible contribution to the debate about PEGIDA is a slim volume written by the writer, translator, and Islam specialist Stefan Weidner.[21] In accordance with his background, Weidner chose to focus on the term "Islamization." For him, the critique of Islam is the "think tank for PEGIDA" (p. 40); what distinguishes Weidner from almost all other observers is that he does not include Thilo Sarrazin in this group, remarking correctly that Sarrazin's DSSA is mainly about the threats to the German social welfare system, not Islam (p. 19). Weidner's Islam is in a "wretched state" (p. 73): Muslims are "the losers of history" (p. 49), who, more than others, suffer at the hands of "Islamist terror," and, in countries like Iran and Saudi Arabia, from the abridgement of their "basic rights" (p. 53). Islam's claim to hegemony is "just as justified or outlandish as the Western [one]," but it is "far from any realization" (p. 29). Under such circumstances, one would think that Islam would need some sort of general overhaul, and Weidner agrees with that, but with one proviso: the critique must be "primarily the task of Muslims themselves" (p. 54). In Germany, the 'old' racism (anti-Semitism) has not disappeared, but has undergone a transformation, or "recoding" (p. 35) into something else, namely anti-Islam sentiments. It follows that Germans who criticize Islam have no standing,[22] and the critique of Islam by non-Muslims is the product of a "closed world view" that is immune to facts and arguments (p. 84); thus, those who critique Islam but distance themselves from PEGIDA are in effect deluding themselves. Weidner's anti-racist agenda may be laudable, but he condemns the Germans and other Europeans to absolute passivity. Even though "there is hardly a serious person who denies the dangers of fundamentalist Islam prone to violence" (p. 56), one must simply wait until the Muslims themselves initiate some sort of Enlightenment. Weidner offers little consolation to his readers when he emphasizes that the European version of the Enlightenment is not a completed project, but a "process and method" (p. 80).[23]

———•———

Thilo Sarrazin is an economist and civil servant with a doctorate; Akif Pirinçci is a successful middle-brow author with immigrant parents; Botho Strauß is a celebrated representative of high culture who stems from the educated middle class; Frauke Petry holds a Ph.D. in chemistry; Björn Höcke has taught in a secondary school; Lutz Bachmann comes from the East German working class and was once a petty criminal; Beatrix von Storch is a lawyer and member of the aristocracy: all in all, a rather diverse group. What do they all have in common? Despite differences in temperament and background, they all feel uncomfortable in contemporary Germany, and they have expressed this discomfort in various ways, including the production of fictional and non-fictional works, political organizing, and public demonstrations. The question faced by observers in Germany and abroad is this: to what extent do they represent widespread attitudes in the German populace? There is no simple answer to this question; books by Sarrazin and Pirinçci were certainly bestsellers, but what did the readers do after they had turned the last page (if they in fact reached that point)? Was it simply a matter of letting off steam, of feeling that they were not alone in their negative feelings about current trends in societal development? Were they moved to take some sort of political action? This would be extremely difficult to ascertain. In the case of political parties, things are of course very different, because one can monitor a given party's membership and analyze election results. The AfD has done quite well on the regional level—like other German right-wing parties—but the real watershed was its unexpected success in the 2017 federal elections (see below). Now that the party has entered the *Bundestag*, will it have enough clout to actually influence policymaking, or will it limit itself to disrupting the everyday work of parliament?

What can be stated with some degree of certainty is that none of the figures mentioned above would have come to the attention of the public if the times had been different. To wit: if there had been no 9/11—followed by numerous acts of Islamist terrorism in Europe—and if there had been no mass migration to Germany in the wake of military conflicts in Iraq and Syria, few initiatives conceived as part of the defense of Europe (the *Abendland*, to use the term preferred by PEGIDA) would have seen the light of day. With regard to globalization, the situation is more complicated: Germany is part and parcel of the world economy, but there is a special aspect not found elsewhere in Western Europe, specifically the sudden collapse of the industrial base in former East Germany following the fall of the Berlin Wall. Millions of people who lived in a system that at least appeared to be stable were suddenly faced with the possibility of long-term unemployment. These East Germans also populated the part of the country that had very few residents of foreign origin, which has proved to be a rather toxic combination.

The activities on the far right of the German political spectrum (and in other developed countries, for that matter) will probably never disappear completely, but their significance will be determined by the future political measures taken by the established or mainstream parties like the CDU, the SPD, or the FDP. Will these groups realize that 'business as usual' is not an option in the short or long term? Will they have the farsightedness to attempt a shift away from an economy that depends on the encouragement of ever-expanding consumption and the export of consumer goods (like gas-guzzling cars) and military hardware? The present opposition—the Left and especially the Greens—have proposed alternative models emphasizing social justice and environmental stewardship, but their voices do not carry much weight at the moment. The German parliament has just passed a bill legalizing the long-controversial "marriage for all," but there is no sign of a willingness to address fundamental issues regarding the future of the planet. There was a certain euphoria in Europe following the electoral failures of the far right in the Netherlands and France and the 'Brexit debacle' of the British Tories, but that did not change the overall picture. One often speaks of the 'politics of fear' purveyed by groups like the AfD or PEGIDA, but the irony is that most citizens do not express fear about the real threats confronting all of us, in other words the devastating effects of climate change, the squandering of vital natural resources, and the real danger of overpopulation. A visionary 'politics of fear,' not the one discussed in this study, should be the order of the day. At the same time, it would be naive to believe that a fundamental paradigm shift could take place unless mainstream politicians finally address the anxiety of many citizens about a number of issues, which one observer has summarized in the following manner: "diffuse fears about immigrants, the loss of national identity [...], Euro-skepticism [...], questions of social justice, presumable fear of a loss of social status on the part of the middle class, the regulations governing *Hartz IV*, or the fear of poverty in old age."[24] Such anxiety can only be partially alleviated on a purely national level, so the future role of the extreme right will depend on the extent to which Germany can convince its European partners to make substantial contributions to solving the refugee crisis in a humane manner. Only time will tell if it will be possible to mount a political shift towards "radical reformism" aimed at a society where solidarity is more highly valued.[25]

POSTSCRIPT
THE 2017 NATIONAL ELECTION AND ITS IMPACT

All of the parliamentary elections held in West Germany and subsequently in united Germany after 1989 have certainly been worthy of examination, but not all of them will be remembered as turning points in postwar German history. Only a few resulted in significant political and social change; among these were the success of the Social Democrats in 1969, leading to the reform chancellorship of Willy Brandt, who is now something akin to the patron saint of the SPD; the 1982/83 'surprise' that unseated Helmut Schmidt and paved the way for the long reign of Christian Democrat Helmut Kohl (now viewed as the "chancellor of unification"); the 1998 triumph of the SPD under Gerhard Schröder, leading to government participation by the Greens, a memorable event in national and international terms; and finally the 2017 balloting, which saw the seating of a party to the right of the Christian Democrats, the AfD, for the first time since the founding of the Federal Republic. It is too early to tell whether the presence of the extreme right will have any concrete effects on legislation, but there is no doubt that a long-standing taboo has been pushed aside, a move that is causing concern in many quarters, given the course of twentieth-century Germany history. Is that concern justified?

If one looks at the 2017 voting in all its aspects, it becomes clear that there are trends which may, in the long run, become more significant than the success of the AfD. The most remarkable of these is the decline in popularity of the mainstream parties (*Volksparteien*): for decades, German politics revolved around a struggle for power between the CDU/CSU and the SPD, with minor groupings like the Liberal Democrats (FDP) or the Greens sometimes tipping the balance of power in coalition governments. This time, the CDU/CSU obtained only 32.9% of the vote (compared to 41.5% in 2013), and the SPD fell from 25.7% to 20.5%.[1]

In comparison, the two main blocks garnered 76% in 1998 and still 67.2% in 2013.[2] Some see the shift as a "fatal consequence" of the long years of grand coalitions (CDU/CSU + SPD),[3] whereas others believe that, under Angela Merkel's leadership, the main conservative party has lost much of its conservative identity. Similar developments can of course be found elsewhere, notably in France, where Emmanuel Macron was able to quickly create a 'movement' that simply bypassed traditional party structures. The difference is that, in the case of Germany, when the center no longer holds, others get nervous. (Such unease may have little basis in reality, but old perceptions have a life of their own.)

The smaller parties had mixed results in the 2017 vote. The Left Party (*Die Linke*) received 9.2% (8.6% in 2013), improving slightly, as did the Greens (*Bündnis 90/Die Grünen*), who received 8.9% (8.4% in 2013). Both have become fixtures in German politics, and their success was nothing out of the ordinary. The real story involved two parties that improved their showing drastically: the Liberal Democrats (FDP), who had failed to win parliamentary representation in 2013, made an impressive showing of 10.7% (4.8% in 2013). This has been attributed mainly to the charisma of the young party leader Christian Lindner, who held together a party that propagates both a libertarian-style emphasis on individual rights and lifestyle choices and a strong pro-business stance. If the liberals celebrated their return to the national stage, the AfD managed to enter the *Bundestag* for the first time with 12.6% of the vote (4.7% in 2013). Strangely enough, this was accomplished without a charismatic leader like Lindner, although as a rule, extreme-right parties have such figures at the helm (such as the late Jörg Haider in Austria, Marine Le Pen in France, or Geert Wilders in the Netherlands). The best-known AfD leader of the past few years, Frauke Petry, announced that she was resigning from the party immediately after the 2017 election, with an eye to heading—along with her husband Marcus Pretzell—a new bourgeois-nationalist party dubbed "The Blues" (*Die Blauen*). At time of writing, another newly elected MP has disassociated himself from the AfD, as have numerous officials on the regional level.[4] Petry has stated that the mission of the new party would be to attract "disappointed conservative voters" who see the AfD as being too extremist;[5] the model for the new grouping would be the Bavarian CSU, which does not put forward candidates outside Bavaria. The coming years will show whether or not conservative voters who feel alienated from the increasingly moderate CDU will seek a home in the new party. During the election campaign, the German media routinely portrayed Petry as an extremist pretending to be an establishment conservative, but if her new group were to supplant the 'rump' AfD with its neo-Nazi elements, this would be a positive development. If leading AfD candidate (and disgruntled former CDU member) Alexander Gauland continues to spout venom (see his post-election pledge to "hunt down" Angela Merkel[6]), more AfD members may follow Petry.[7]

The post-balloting decision by the SPD to revitalize itself (à la Labour?) by joining the opposition, rather than participating in a new version of the Grand Coalition with the CDU, meant that the AfD would not be the largest opposition party in the *Bundestag*, a status that carries some political clout, but also that the only viable government not including the AfD would be the so-called "Jamaica Coalition" (named after the colors of that country's flag) consisting of the CDU/CSU, the FDP, and the Greens. If the various negotiators had been able to agree to the terms of such a coalition, the Greens would have been partners in a national government led by the CDU. (A "Jamaica Coalition" has already been tried on the regional level, in the Saarland and in Schleswig-Holstein.) Why would this have been significant? In most countries, conservatives have not supported the environmentalist agenda; the present Trump administration in the US has of course set a new standard, actively pursuing anti-environmentalist policies (such as crippling the EPA and dismissing scientific research about climate change); given this state of affairs, it would have been extremely important for Germany, a leading industrial democracy, to demonstrate that conservatives and environmentalists can work together under the banner of sustainability.[8] It is ironic that the AfD, which has attacked the Greens relentlessly, could actually have made such a project possible; thanks primarily to the recalcitrance of the FDP, however, the "Jamaica" talks broke down, leaving only one alternative: another Grand Coalition or new elections. On March 4 2018, it was announced that the members of the SPD had voted to enter into another version of the previous Grand Coalition with the CDU/CSU, paving the way for Angela Merkel to lead the German government for another four-year term (or rather, almost that long, since it took months of discussion and negotiations after the election to reach that point). As the largest opposition party, the AfD will now have ample opportunity to show its supporters and detractors just how it plans to position itself vis-à-vis German democracy.

What role did the three writers discussed in individual chapters above play in the 2017 election campaign? The short answer is: a very minor one. The most visible was, not surprisingly, Thilo Sarrazin, the one with the largest media presence over time; Sarrazin did not act as an advocate for the AfD (as some commentators had predicted, or in some cases, hoped), but he did make a few public statements. In a TV talk show, he praised Donald Trump's protectionist economic policies and his campaign against illegal immigration, views that were close to those of the AfD (though he did add that he found Trump to be disagreeable, "narcissistic" and "unpredictable");[9] he also gave a talk about his book *Wunschdenken* at the Studienzentrum Weikersheim, a conservative think tank usually associated with the German New Right.[10] When he was criticized for participating in an event where two AfD members (including top co-candidate Alice Weidel) and representatives of the *Republikaner* and the Austrian FPÖ also spoke,[11] Sarrazin stated that although he had no intention of supporting the AfD electoral campaign, he would enter into a dialogue with any "democratic party" and continue to present his ideas "everywhere."[12] In an extensive interview conducted after the election, he provided his own interpretation of the results, especially with respect to the AfD:

> Until now, Germany was the only country in Europe that did not have a national-conservative or right-wing populist party. This special status

is now history. The AfD is everywhere: Even in cities run by the left like Hamburg, Bremen, and Berlin, they got between 8 and 12 percent of the vote. And in Bavaria, especially in the eastern part, they are even stronger. The AfD is here to stay.[13]

He asserted that the success of the AfD would have "long-term effects" on the German political system and added an assessment of Angela Merkel's policies that could have been formulated by the AfD itself: "Merkel is not paying attention to the Germans or the German people. She is pursuing an internationalist and universalist political approach. One can find that good or bad, but many find it bad." This implied critique of the world view of the 'elites' is certainly shared by those who voted for the AfD—or for Donald Trump. With regard to Germany, Sarrazin went on to predict that the AfD could potentially count on about 30 per cent of the vote in the future, as long as it had no "right-wing radical elements" in its ranks. This would of course be tantamount to a dissolution of the AfD that ran in the 2017 election and the ascendancy of the faction supporting Frauke Petry; there is no sign of that at the moment.

Even before the Germans went to the polls, the muckraking SPIEGEL journalist Jakob Augstein characterized Sarrazin as the "godfather of the rightist revolution."[14] No such hyperbole was wasted on Akif Pirinçci, who remained on the sidelines during the run-up to the election. Pirinçci made it clear that he could never join a political party but might entertain the notion of founding a "one-man-party" that would not necessitate any compromises on major issues.[15] This was not meant seriously, but he used the idea as an excuse to once again set out his positions: Germany's exit from the EU and the reintroduction of the D-Mark; radical tax cuts; rather modest pensions to avoid burdening younger Germans; the deportation of about eight million foreigners engaged in criminal behavior or social welfare abuse; the elimination of the right to asylum for the foreseeable future; and the end of abortion (in light of "8 to 10 million murdered children" in Germany). He did not really believe that any of this would become reality, however. In a text published in the summer before the 2017 election (which he called a *Schicksalswahl*, an election that would determine the fate of the nation), he predicted that the Germans would vote "moderately" rather than espousing the radical changes needed to save the country.[16] He attributed this to the fact that most Germans are "*Spießer*," that is to say, petit bourgeois conformists oblivious to the 'big picture' and obsessed with protecting their socioeconomic status at all costs. Such subservient subjects ("*der geborene Untertan*") would vote for their own downfall, ignoring today's supposedly typical German street scene, "a combination of Oriental bazaar and African bush." Aside from writing, Pirinçci himself will not become politically active or join a resistance movement, because he "has already sacrificed enough." He laments that anyone in Germany who declares "Germany first" will be labeled a Nazi.[17]

Botho Strauß also mainly stayed on the sidelines in 2017, but he did publish an essay about the role of intellectuals in contemporary society.[18] Similar to Pirinçci, he used his platform to once again put forth his assessment of conditions in present-day Germany, and his target of choice was anything and everything related to the "social," in other words the entire leftist/humanitarian agenda, which he dubbed "kitschy ideas" (including tolerance, globalism, minority issues, human rights, and quotas). From his perspective, we are living in an age when we are confronted with myriad "irritations," for example: "a world leader who cannot lead," "a referendum (Brexit) against all reason," "a government leader [Angela Merkel] who cannot grasp the implications of her decision [to admit a large number of asylum seekers and refugees]," "a terrorist act [the Christmas market bombing in Berlin?]," and "a New Right." All of this has led to "confusion," but instead of attempting to understand what is behind this confusion, we are reverting to "the old clichés of order;" this includes a sudden skepticism about the role of the common people, transforming a laudable "demos" into a dangerous "populus."[19] The relentless march of technology has deprived us of our instincts, our sensitivity with regard to future developments and threats. According to Strauß, the critical intellectual who appeared in the wake of the French Revolution will soon disappear from history altogether, so one can expect no aid from that quarter; likewise, since no revival of the church, traditional ways of life or authority is on the horizon, there remains only one hope: the "reactionary," the only one left who "cares for our heritage and avoids disposables" (intellectual fads). The "poetic knowledge" of the reactionary will replace the current cult of youth and the new with respect for the past. If this does not occur, Strauß is convinced that the exaggerated self-emancipation of isolated individuals will eventually lead to the rise of "barbarism;" social media have led to a "manic compulsion" to speak, a sort of exhibitionism without content or merit. If the Romantics rebelled against the rise of industrial society, today's "poetic mystics" will turn against the "museless intellectuality of the knowledge society" that is devoid of all "mysteriousness." Surprisingly, Strauß places his hopes for a fundamental transformation of culture and society in the hands of the only group not yet completely co-opted by the system: the cynics.

Much of this can be found in Strauß's other writings, and one would be justified in asking if such musings could possibly have any relevance for German politics in general and the fate of the New Right in particular. But what if Strauß were not actually read, but merely claimed as a kind of countercultural icon? When the Day of German Unity (3 October) was celebrated for the first time after the electoral success of the AfD, party official Beatrix von Storch gave a speech to representatives of the "alternative center," the grouping that supposedly stands for a moderate path in contrast to the nationalist/volkish extremist wing of the party. Von Storch made it perfectly clear that, in her eyes, the policies of the AfD were the "only chance" to put Germany on a path that would ensure national survival, and to add legitimacy to that enterprise, she referred to two Germans with the surname "Strauß." The first was the legendary Bavarian politician Franz Josef Strauß, the former leader of the CSU, who would, she asserted, have founded the AfD himself if he had lived longer. The second was none other than Botho Strauß; von Storch referred to a passage from his 1993 essay 'Impending Tragedy:' just as the "rightist" is no "right-wing extremist," "football fans" are not "hooligans." She then went on to say that "We [the AfD] want the football fans, not the hooligans;"[20] when a journalist asked just who the "hooligans" might be, he was not given a response.[21] Although Strauß has produced many works since 1993—including, as mentioned above, a plea for environmental protection—his most controversial essay (published in *Der Spiegel*, a publication that rejects everything that the AfD stands for) has apparently become a sort of talisman for the New Right. Books have their fates, no matter what their authors might have intended.

One thing that Thilo Sarrazin, Akif Pirinçci, and Botho Strauß have in common is that they were known quantities in German culture and society before they made an unexpected turn toward the right. This is not true of those who aspire to succeed them, as the underground network of the next generation of the New Right is still not widely known in Germany nor abroad. A recent example of investigative journalism might be seen in retrospect as the beginning of a stronger presence in the public sphere: in October 2017, just weeks after the German election, *The New York Times* published a long piece in the magazine section about Götz Kubitschek, the right-wing intellectual and publisher (of Antaios Verlag).[22] (The interviewer, James Angelos, had already discussed the French New Right in the same space earlier that year.[23]) In the print version, the subtitle of his interview reads as follows: 'From a tiny village in Germany's rural east, a leading intellectual of the ascendant far right builds a vision for its future across Europe.' In the online version, the title was changed from 'The Prophet' to 'The Prophet of Germany's New Right,' and the subtitle became 'From a tiny village in the country's rural east, a leading nationalist intellectual builds a vision for the future of his movement across Europe.' Why was the term "ascendant" removed? Perhaps the editors felt that this prospect would be too frightening for their readers; the designation "far right" also was dropped in favor of "nationalist;" at the same time, the possessive "his" that was added in the second version seems to inflate Kubitschek's importance. The two illustrations that accompany the text do not offer much clarification. The first is a full-page image of Kubitschek standing in a grassy field with his goats, wearing a collarless wool cardigan (*Strickjacke*) popular in Southern Germany (and among the followers of the Austrian FPÖ). The second shows a PEGIDA demonstration in Nuremberg, even though that organization is not very present in the western parts of Germany.

Angelos has great difficulty assessing his interviewee, and a reader with little background would probably come away rather confused. It must be said that Kubitschek does not offer many clues to his true political identity; on the one hand, he is concerned about preserving Germany's "ethno-cultural identity," but on the other, he can state:

"The idea that there is such a thing as a pure German is wholly absurd [...], populations migrate and absorb other influences." He also has no trouble envisioning an immigrant becoming a German, if that person "is willing to give everything for this country and is ready to identify with it," a stipulation that does not at all fit in with the concept of "ethno-pluralism" that he espouses. Angelos places Kubitschek in the context of the elitist Conservative Revolution of the 1920s, but Kubitschek believes that elites are destroying Western civilization. He and his wife Ellen Kositza are from the old West Germany, but they choose to live in the east, where "Germany is still Germany." In the traditional Germany of their dreams, however, one would have remained in one's region of origin and cultivated the culture that is rooted there. Kubitschek fears (like Botho Strauß) that the consumer-orientated Germans of today would be incapable of defending themselves, but claims that he is against violence. He leaves the door open for a change of heart, however: "It's not yet a revolutionary situation." All that can be done now is "to prevent the worst." The reader does learn that Kubitschek is active behind the scenes in the AfD (working with his old friend, Björn Höcke, among others), but Angelos's assertion that he "wields considerable influence over far-right thinkers, activists and politicians across Germany," whether it is accurate or not, says little about the scale of the right-wing scene in Germany. The Office for the Protection of the Constitution estimates the number of active rightists to be about 24,000,[24] but that does not include the intellectual New Right and its followers. Still, that number, in a country of 82 million, is relatively insignificant.

A different Götz Kubitschek put in an appearance at the Frankfurt Book Fair in October 2017; as the publisher of Antaios Verlag, he set up a display with new books and arranged for his authors (including Akif Pirinçci) to introduce their work. The night before the event, unknown persons vandalized another right-wing display and stole a large number of books. (Before that, the mayor of Frankfurt had already said that he was against allowing right-wing publishers to take part in the book fair.) Kubitschek went on with the presentation anyway, and disruption began when Björn Höcke spok; a large group of protesters appeared and began yelling "Nazis out of here!" (*Nazis raus!*); Kubitschek's supporters responded with "Everyone hates the

Antifa!" (*Jeder hasst die Antifa!*); the situation escalated, and the police had to separate the antagonists and end the event.[25] Instead of leaving, Kubitschek chose to go ahead with another part of the event, the introduction of two books about the Identitarian movement.[26] Another loud confrontation ensued, and the director of the book fair, Juergen Boos, appeared with a megaphone to call off the presentation; he was stopped by Kubitschek, who at one point grabbed the megaphone. After the fact, Kubitschek gave his version and provided short videos of the incidents, apparently making fun of the 'wimpy' Boos.[27] Any student of German history who has seen these videos will immediately be reminded of the Weimar Republic, when political discussion was gradually replaced with brutal verbal attacks that ended in physical violence. It is difficult to believe that the average German will want to relive that period. Television reports about the recent confrontations in Middlebury, Berkeley, and Charlottesville have given Americans an inkling of what it was like to live during the Weimar years.[28] By the time the next *Bundestag* is elected in 2021, we will know if the deterioration of democracy characteristic of Weimar Germany will have become the preferred mode of operation on a global scale. At time of writing, the Germans are not at the forefront of that movement.[29] That distinction currently applies primarily to Hungary and Poland, with Austria as the only Western European country even remotely comparable,[30] although Italy appears to have aspirations in that direction, given the results of the parliamentary elections on March 4 2018.[31]

A FINAL NOTE

No analysis of contemporary affairs can provide a definitive portrayal of ongoing cultural and political developments, and this is certainly true with regard to the AfD. As this study is being prepared for publication, there is no sign that any sort of normalization is imminent. In January 2019, firebrand André Poggenburg left the party with an eye to founding yet another competing grouping. In February 2019, co-founder Bernd Lucke called upon the moderate members of the party to make a clean break with the extremist right wing. In April 2019, former leader Frauke Petry was convicted of making false statements under oath and was fined 6,000 Euros. In that same month, the AfD was fined over 400,000 Euros for irregularities involving campaign financing. A discussion about some sort of surveillance of the party by the government intelligence services is ongoing. At the 2019 "political Ash Wednesday," newly anointed CSU leader Markus Söder appealed to moderate members of the AfD to come back to the fold, leaving the Nazis in the party behind. (On the same day, AfD leader Jörg Meuthen had nothing but praise for Hungary's Viktor Orbán, leader of the national-conservative, right-wing Fidesz party). It is impossible to predict whether a splintering of the party is on the horizon, but in the fall of 2019, the three regional elections in Eastern Germany will give some sense of future prospects. As for PEGIDA, the demonstrators will have to find new bugaboos now that the old chant "Merkel must go" has lost its impact. It is difficult to imagine a comparable demonization of Merkel's potential successor, Annegret Kramp-Karrenbauer, a more conservative figure, especially since the number of refugees and asylum seekers arriving in Germany has been reduced considerably.

The May 2019 European Parliamentary elections demonstrated very clearly that Europe is deeply divided. The same can be said of Germany. Right-wing populists/nationalists had impressive results in countries like France, Italy, Hungary, Poland, and of course in the Brexit-addled UK, but they were less successful elsewhere (e.g., in Denmark or the Netherlands). The new European parliament will have a stronger oppositional bloc than before, but the pro-European consensus is not (yet) under threat. In Germany, the AfD made modest gains, but these were overshadowed by increased support for the Greens, who surpassed the Social Democrats and finished in second place. However, the division of the country is perhaps more pronounced than ever, since the Greens are popular in the west (especially in metropolitan areas), and the AfD has widespread support in the east. As was discussed above (see the Postscript), the mainstream parties continue to lose support. It is not unimaginable that future German governments will include both the traditionally conservative CDU and the Greens. The AfD may be able to form governments in one or more of the eastern states, but there is presently no indication that this could happen in the west. The recent influence-peddling scandal involving the Austrian FPÖ has dealt a blow to nationalist hopes in the *Alpenrepublik*, and this debacle may influence German voters' view of the AfD.

NOTES

PREFACE

1. Daniel Kehlmann, 'Angela Merkel's Unpopular Goodness', *The New York Times* (1 April 2016). Kehlmann also stated that Merkel's decision "will likely cost her the chancellorship." At time of writing this seems less likely than it did in early 2016. Merkel has, however, decided not to run for reelection in 2021.

2. 'Positive Views of Brazil on the Rise in 2011 BBC Country Rating Poll', BBC World Service (7 March 2011), http://www.bbc.co.uk/pressoffice/pressreleases/stories/2011/03_march/07/poll.pdf, last accessed 21 April 2019.

3. Alison Smale and Steven Erlanger, 'As Obama Exits World Stage, Angela Merkel May Be the Liberal West's Last Defender, *The New York Times* (12 November 2016), http://www.nytimes.com/2016/11/13/world/europe/germany-merkel-trump-election.html?_r=0, last accessed 21 April 2019. In characteristically modest fashion, Merkel immediately dismissed such speculations.

4. The survey results prompted journalistic gadfly Henryk M. Broder to compose an "Obituary for the Ugly German": see H.M. Broder, 'Nachruf auf den hässlichen Deutschen', *Die Welt* (2 May 2011).

5. For an exhaustive depiction of the everyday reality of this *Willkommenskultur* (welcoming culture), see James Angelos, 'Becoming European', *The New York Times Magazine* (10 April 2016), pp. 41-47, 54, 57, 59.

6. See 'Bundespräsident Gauck bei Flüchtlingen: 'Es gibt ein helles Deutschland", *Spiegel Online* (26 August 2015), http://www.spiegel. de/politik/deutschland/joachim-gauck-bei-fluechtlingen-es-gibt-ein-helles-deutschland-a-1049850.html, last accessed 21 April 2019.

7. See James Retallack, *The German Right 1860-1920, Political Limits of the Authoritarian Imagination*, Toronto, Buffalo, London: University of Toronto Press, 2006, p. 16.

8. The latest manifestation of such 'dreaming' is the posthumously published book by the respected historian and sociologist Rolf Peter Sieferle, *Finis Germania*, Schnellroda: Verlag Antaios, 2017. This volume, which has generated much controversy and reached the bestseller lists in Germany, cannot be discussed at length here, but an astute assessment is available in English. See Christopher Caldwell, 'Germany's Newest Intellectual Antihero', *The New York Times* (8 July 2017), https://www.nytimes.com/2017/07/08/opinion/sunday/germanys-newest-intellectual-antihero.html, last accessed 21 April 2019. It is not insignificant that Caldwell's reading is much more objective than that of most German commentators.

Those interested in delving deeper into the issues raised in this study should be aware of two recent publications: In *deutsch, nicht dumpf. Ein Leitfaden für aufgeklärte Patrioten*, München: Albrecht Knaus, 2018, author and critic Thea Dorn (b. 1970) makes the case for enlightened patriotism and the preservation of high culture from a left-liberal perspective. Thilo Sarrazin makes yet another contribution to the 'Islam debate' in his *Feindliche Übernahme: Wie der Islam den Fortschritt behindert und die Gesellschaft bedroht*, München: FinanzBuch Verlag, 2018.

1. THILO SARRAZIN: THE UNLIKELY TRIBUNE

1. 'Sarrazin will Beamtenpensionen abschaffen', *Der Tagesspiegel* (24 February 2004).

2. Gilbert Schomaker, 'Sarrazin entwickelt Hartz-IV-Speiseplan', *Die Welt* (8 February 2008).

3. Thilo Sarrazin, *Deutschland schafft sich ab. Wie wir unser Land aufs Spiel setzen*, München: Deutsche Verlagsanstalt, 2010.

4. The interview appeared in *Lettre international*, vol. 86 (Fall, 2009). The title of this edition was *Berlin auf der Couch. Autoren und Künstler zu 20 Jahren Mauerfall* (Berlin on the Couch: Authors and artists on the 20th anniversary of the fall of the Wall). I am quoting from a reprint in the tabloid *Bildzeitung* (8 October 2009), in which the interview, conducted

by editor-in-chief Frank Berberich, was entitled 'Klasse statt Masse' (in other words, quality, not quantity), https://eppinger.files.wordpress. com/2009/10/klasse-statt-masse.pdf, last accessed 21 April 2019. *Lettre international* demanded damages from *Bild* for reprinting the interview. See 'Sarrazin-Interview. 'Lettre'-Magazin fordert Schadensersatz von "Bild,"' *Spiegel Online* (27 October 2009).

5. In another interview, Sarrazin spoke of a so-called "Jewish gene" (*Juden-Gen*). See Andrea Seibel, 'Mögen Sie keine Türken, Herr Sarrazin?', *Die Welt* (29 August 2010). When asked about the existence of a genetic identity, Sarrazin replied: "All Jews share a certain gene." Although he emphasized in the same interview that he was not a racist, he was accused of this just the same; this led him to publish a clarification. See 'Thilo Sarrazins Erklärung im Wortlaut', *FAZ* (30 August 2010).

He said there that "cultural factors" were important, not genetic identity. One of the studies that provided the supposed basis for his original remark was: Gil Atzmon, et al., 'Abraham's Children in the Genome Era. Major Jewish Diaspora Populations Comprise Distinct Genetic Clusters with Shared Middle Eastern Ancestry', *American Journal of Human Genetics*, vol. 86 no. 6 (2010), pp. 850-859.

Atzmon was also interviewed about the controversy by *Die Welt*. See Hannes Stein, 'Teilen alle Juden wirklich ein bestimmtes Gen?', *Die Welt* (31 August 2010). Atzmon is quoted as saying that the Jews are not a race, but they do "share more genetic material with each other than with their non-Jewish surroundings."

6. Britta Geithe, "'Lettre'-Chef Berberich über das Interview mit Thilo Sarrazin', *tip berlin* (4 October 2009), https://www.tip-berlin.de/lettre-chef-berberich-uber-das-interview-mit-thilo-sarrazin/, last accessed 21 April 2019.

7. 'Umstrittenes Interview. Sarrazin entschuldigt sich', *FAZ* (2 October 2009), http://www.faz.net/aktuell/wirtschaft/wirtschaftspolitik/umstrittenes-interview-sarrazin-entschuldigt-sich-1869514.html, last accessed 21 April 2019.

8. Other sources of inspiration include the Bible, Erasmus, and Shakespeare.

9. See Dieter Groh and Peter Brandt, '*Vaterlandslose Gesellen.' Sozialdemokratie und Nation 1860–1990*, München: C.H. Beck, 1992.

10. This is reminiscent of the lines from Brecht's 1930 play *Die Mutter* (*The Mother*): "*Das Sichere ist nicht sicher / So wie es ist, bleibt es nicht*" (That which is certain is not certain / Things won't stay the way they are). See *Die Gedichte von Bertolt Brecht in einem Band*, Frankfurt am Main: Suhrkamp Verlag, 1981, p. 1160.

11. See Samuel Huntington, *Who Are We? The Challenges to America's National Identity*, New York: Simon & Schuster, 2004.
12. This sounds like a contemporary version of Germany's "militant democracy" (*wehrhafte Demokratie*) from the Cold War era.
13. Gerhard Schröder, 'Das Recht auf Türme', *Die Zeit*, vol. 51 (10 December 2009). Sarrazin discusses this text in *DSSA* (p. 270). At the time, Schröder also wrote about the situation in Turkey, and his words are noteworthy in light of recent political developments there: "And when we focus on Turkey, then we also should see the success of the modernization process. That is attributable almost exclusively to Prime Minister Erdogan and the talks about admitting Turkey to the EU. Under Erdogans' leadership, Turkey has been changed and modernized to an extent that no one could have imagined in his wildest dreams. We see a fundamental democratization of the country."
14. See, for example, Max Horkheimer and Theodor W. Adorno, *Dialectic of Enlightenment*, Stanford UP, 2007. First German edition in 1947.
15. Churchill's defense of democracy comes to mind: "Many forms of Government have been tried, and will be tried in this world of sin and woe. No one pretends that democracy is perfect or all-wise. Indeed, it has been said that democracy is the worst form of Government except all those other forms that have been tried from time to time." Speech in the House of Commons (November 11 1947), from Winston S. Churchill, *His Complete Speeches, 1897–1963*, ed. Robert Rhodes James, Chelsea House Publishers/R.R. Bowker Company, 1974, vol. 7, p. 7566. Analogous to this view, one could say that in the beginning, the Enlightenment was not meant to be valid for all human beings, but it should be expanded and improved, not cast aside.
16. In my view, Sarrazin is justifiably incensed that Kelek and Aayan Hirsi Ali have been characterized as secular fundamentalists (p. 274); he can hardly believe that the two of them have been linked to National Socialism (p. 279). To understand how such an association can be made, see Birgit Rommelspacher, 'Ungebrochene Selbst-idealisierung', *taz* (18 January 2010), http://www.taz.de/!5149236/, last accessed 21 April 2019.
17 Necla Kelek, *Chaos der Kulturen. Die Debatte um Islam und Integration*, Köln: Kiepenheuer & Witsch, 2012, p. 247. In another passage, she writes: "The state's neutrality vis-à-vis religion should not go so far as to limit human rights in the name of religious freedom. If that were to happen, we would renounce the individual freedoms that the Enlightenment has secured in a long historical process. And we would thus be giving up the foundation of our civil society, the rule of law." Necla Kelek, *Die fremde*

Braut. Ein Bericht aus dem Inneren des türkischen Lebens in Deutschland, Köln: Kiepenheuer & Witsch, 2005, pp. 249f.

18. At this juncture, he mentions that the Bill of Rights is the "first political example" of this canon (p. 30).

19. See Ray Furlong, "Honour killing' shocks Germany', *BBC News* (14 March 2005), http://news.bbc.co.uk/2/hi/europe/4345459.stm, last accessed 12 April 2019.

20. In the original, Sarrazin uses the term "*Altbauwohnungen*," which in German cities refers to the roomy old high-ceilinged apartments built in the late-nineteenth and early-twentieth centuries.

21. The old—now tainted—German phrase was "*Am deutschen Wesen soll die Welt genesen.*" A version of this phrase was originally used by the nineteenth-century poet Emanuel Geibel; it later became a rallying cry for German nationalists.

22. Sarrazin is upset that he has fellow citizens who "secretly are in mourning because they were born as Germans" (p. 346). Some observers of the German scene will remember a once-popular sticker found on the back of German cars: "Foreigners! Don't leave us alone with the Germans!"

23. See Richard J. Herrnstein and Charles Murray, *Bell Curve: Intelligence and Class Structure in American Life*, New York: Free Press, 1994. For an overview of the intelligence debate, see David J. Bartholomew, *Measuring Intelligence. Facts and Fallacies*, Cambridge: Cambridge UP, 2004. For an attack on Sarrazin as a misguided eugenicist, see *Der Mythos vom Niedergang der Intelligenz. Von Galton zu Sarrazin. Die Denkmuster und Denkfehler der Eugenik*, ed. Michael Haller and Martin Niggeschmidt, Wiesbaden, Springer VS, 2012.

24. *Sarrazin. Eine deutsche Debatte*, ed. Deutschland Stiftung Integration, München und Zürich: Piper Verlag, 2010.

25. Bubis called Walser a "mental arsonist" because he admitted that he could not stand being constantly confronted with images of the Holocaust. For background on this controversy, see Jay Rosellini, *Literary Skinheads? Writing from the Right in Reunified Germany*, West Lafayette: Purdue University Press, 2000, pp. 179-189.

26. Evelyn Roll demonstrates why this 'invitation' should hardly be taken seriously. See *Sarrazin. Eine deutsche Debatte*, ed. Deutschland Stiftung Integration, p. 47.

27. The association with Hirsi Ali does not necessarily imply a seal of approval. See Patrick Bahners, *Die Panikmacher. Die deutsche Angst vor dem Islam. Eine Streitschrift*, München: C.H. Beck, 2011, pp. 135-137. According to Bahners, Kelek makes "the usual polemics from the rightist fringe against 'Gutmenschentum' [i.e. knee-jerk liberals] palatable to

the very people against whom the polemics were directed" (p. 137). Bahners goes on to say: "She [Kelek] embodies the *telos* of the Islamic Enlightenment that is desired in this country and whose progress is seen by some as the criterion that determines whether or not Islam will continue to be tolerated. Her comrade Ralph Giordano repeats incessantly that Islam is criticized most profoundly by Muslim women like Necla Kelek" (p. 170).

28. Thilo Sarrazin, *Der neue Tugendterror. Über die Grenzen der Meiningsfreiheit in Deutschland*, München: Deutsche Verlags-Anstalt, 2014. Among other things, Sarrazin maintains that the reception "by a certain sector of the media" mainly "did not reach the level of an objective discussion" (p. 56).

29. Klaus J. Bade, *Kritik und Gewalt. Sarrazin-Debatte, 'Islamkritik' und Terror in der Einwanderungsgesellschaft*, Schwalbach: Wochenschau Verlag, 2013.

30. Charlotte Halink, *Kontra Sarrazins Thesen*, Taunusstein: Escritor-Verlag G. Hölling, 2011.

31. Dorothée Lange, *Politisch inkorrekt Oder: Was hat Sarrazin eigentlich mit dem Sturm und Drang zu tun?*, Hannover: Wehrhahn Verlag, 2012.

32. Andreas Kemper, *Sarrazins Correctness. Zur Tradition der Menschen- und Bevölkerungskorrekturen*, Münster: UNRAST Verlag, 2014.

33. Gerd Krell, *Schafft Deutschland sich ab? Ein Essay über Demografie, Intelligenz, Armut und Einwanderung*, Schwalbach: Wochenschau Verlag, 2013.

34. For a detailed discussion of how Germans might criticize Islam, see: *Islamverherrlichung. Wenn die Kritik zum Tabu wird*, ed. Thorsten Gerald Schneiders, Wiesbaden: VS Verlag für Sozialwissenschaften [Springer], 2010, and *Feindbild Islamkritik. Wenn die Grenzen zur Verzerrung und Diffamierung überschritten werden*, ed. Hartmut Krauss, Osnabrück: Hintergrund-Verlag, 2010.

35. Wolfgang Benz, *Die Feinde aus dem Morgenland. Wie die Angst vor Muslimen unsere Demokratie gefährdet*, Munich: C.H. Beck, 2012. The most relevant chapter is entitled 'Die Ideologisierung der Islamfeindschaft' (The ideologization of enmity toward Islam).

For an assessment from the radical right, see: André F. Lichtschlag, *Feindbild Islam. Schauplätze verfehlter Einwanderungs- und Sozialpolitik*, Waltrop und Leipzig: Manuskriptum Buchhandlung, 2010. For Lichtschlag, the 'Muslim question' is no more than a diversion from the fact that the entire system, the social-democratic-Green welfare state, is rotten to the core and on its way out. This is expressed by transforming the entire German (mainstream) political spectrum into one big blob— "CDUCSUSPDFDPGRÜNLINKEN" (p. 51).

36. One example given is the Mohammed caricatures that appeared in the Danish newspaper *Jyllands-Posten* in 2005 (p. 17), an incident which has been hotly debated, to say the least. For an analysis that places the caricatures in the context of restrictive Danish immigration policies, see: Jana Sinram, *Pressefreiheit oder Fremdenfeindlichkeit? Der Streit um die Mohammed-Karikaturen und die dänische Einwanderungspolitik*, Frankfurt/New York: Campus Verlag, 2015.

37. Benz, like Merkel, doubts that one must read *DSSA* in order to evaluate it (p. 94).

38. Thilo Sarrazin, *Wunschdenken*, München: Deutsche Verlagsanstalt, 2016.

39. See his *Guns, Germs, and Steel. The Fates of Human Societies* (New York: W. W. Norton & Company, 1997), and *Collapse: How Societies Choose to Fail or Succeed* (New York: Viking Press, 2005).

40. See his *The Poverty of Historicism* (paper written 1936, book: Abingdon: Routledge, 1957) and *The Open Society and Its Enemies* (Abingdon: Routledge, 1945).

41. In this context Sarrazin mentions Michel Houellebecq's controversial novel *Submission* (in German, *Unterwerfung*), transl. Lorin Stein, New York: Farrar, Straus and Giroux, 2015. The French original, *Soumission*, appeared in January of the same year.

42. In his introduction, Sarrazin had already referred to this decision as "probably the greatest error in postwar German politics" (p. 11).

43. Published in 1944 in both the UK (Abingdon: Rutledge Press) and the US (Chicago: University of Chicago Press).

44. See Francis Fukuyama, *The End of History and the Last Man*, New York: Free Press, 1992. Sarrazin seems unaware that Fukuyama has had a change of heart in the meantime.

45. Sarrazin explains that he is referring to a person in a high-level position that allows for a role in determining governmental policy rather than simply carrying it out (p. 137).

46. Sarrazin confesses that, although he believes that what he is recommending is not tied to any one historical epoch ("überzeitlich"; p. 145), it is clear to him that "a certain developmental stage of society" and "a certain enlightened consciousness" (p. 146) are necessary for its implementation. He is willing to live with this "anachronism" (p. 146), but the reader may not be.

47. At the end of Chapter 3, one finds "maxims" for those who have political responsibility. The very first one ("Watch out whom you let into the country") is very different from the others: "educate well," "act as a servant of your people," or "make sure you have good civil servants" (p. 187).

48. See Immanuel Kant, 'Ideen zu einer allgemeinen Geschichte in weltbürgerlicher Absicht' (Idea for a Universal History with a Cosmopolitan Purpose), 1784, in Was ist Aufklärung? Aufsätze zur Geschichte und Philosophie, ed. Jürgen Zehbe, Göttingen: Vandenhoeck & Ruprecht, 1967, p. 46. In the sixth sentence of Kant's essay, he states:

    "[…] aus so krummem Holze, als woraus der Mensch gemacht ist, kann nichts ganz Gerades gezimmert werden."

    This can be translated as: "Out of the crooked timber of humanity, nothing straight can be made." This phrase was famously used by Isaiah Berlin in his book The Crooked Timber of Humanity: Chapters in the History of Ideas, ed. Henry Hardy, London: John Murray, 1990.

49. For Weber's use of these terms, see his 'Politik als Beruf' (Politics as a vocation) in Geistige Arbeit als Beruf. Vier Vorträge vor dem Freistudentischen Bund, München und Leipzig: Duncker & Humblot, 1919. For an English translation of this text, see 'Politics as a Vocation', polisci2.ucsd.edu/foundation/documents/03Weber1918.pdf, last accessed 21 April 2019.

50. Few right-wing populists can be counted among the number of First Nation proponents.

51. The following passage illustrates Sarrazin's belief that immigrants can be integrated into German society: "The most stable states are those whose inhabitants feel tied to each other by a common national feeling. Linguistic and ethnic homogeneity facilitate the development of a national feeling, but they are not necessary conditions of it" (p. 197).

52. Despite this stance, he admits that globalization and technical progress have exacerbated income and wealth inequality in the developed world (p. 321).

53. He tells us that the "educated American woman apparently finds a life without children incomplete" (p. 389). He can only wonder why this is not the case in Germany.

54. Here is a characteristic assertion: "In the course of history, violence and murder were more the rule than the exception when it came to struggling for power" (p. 458).

55. It is telling that his high praise for democracy is actually a negative one: constitutional democracy "has at least succeeded in placing shackles on politics" (p. 436).

56. See 'Sarrazin rechnet ab!', BILD (19 April 2016), https://www.bild.de/politik/inland/thilo-sarrazin/sarrazi-rechnet-ab-45450514.bild.html, last accessed 24 April 2019.

57. Alexander Kissler, 'Thilo Sarrazins 'Wunschdenken'—Früher war mehr Alarm', Cicero (25 April 2016), https://www.cicero.de/kultur/

thilo-sarrazins-wunschdenken-frueher-war-mehr-alarm/60829, last accessed 21 April 2019.

58. Udo Ulfkotte, "'Wunschdenken:' Der neue Sarrazin als Fundgrube für geistige Schätze', *KOPP Online* (6 June 2016), reposted at http://www.globalecho.org/64402/wunschdenken-der-neue-sarrazin-als-fundgrube-fur-geistige-schatze/, last accessed 21 April 2019.

59. The brief article also noted that the book could be ordered from the "JF Book Service." See "Thilo Sarrazin: 'Wir schaffen das nicht!'", *Junge Freiheit* (20 April 2016), https://jungefreiheit.de/politik/deutschland/2016/thilo-sarrazin-wir-schaffen-das-nicht/, last accessed 21 April 2019.

60. Reposting by Conservo (10 May 2016), https://conservo.wordpress.com/2016/05/10/kositza-ueber-sarrazins-buch-wunschdenken/, last accessed 21 April 2019.

61. 'Thilo Sarrazin's New Book: A Case of Wishful Thinking', Deutsche Welle (28 April 2016), https://www.dw.com/en/thilo-sarrazins-new-book-a-case-of-wishful-thinking/a-19222156, last accessed 21 April 2019.

62. Detlef Esslinger, 'Trotz Unverschämtheiten und Angeberei—Sarrazin hat etwas zu sagen', *Süddeutsche Zeitung* (25 April 2016), http://www.sueddeutsche.de/politik/europa-euro-zuwanderung-alle-krisen-dieser-erde-1.2959991, last accessed 21 April 2019.

63. Arno Widmann, 'Sarrazin und die fehlende Kompetenz', *Frankfurter Rundschau* (25 April 2016), https://www.fr.de/kultur/literatur/sarrazin-fehlende-kompetenz-11132031.html, last accessed 21 April 2019.

64. Nils Minkmar, 'Der Ich-Roman', *Der Spiegel* vol. 17 (23 April 2016), https://magazin.spiegel.de/SP/2016/17/144430255/index.html?utm_source=spon&utm_campaign=centerpage, last accessed 21 April 2019.

65. This sentence does not even work grammatically in German: "Dass diese Flüchtlinge wieder nach Syrien ziehen, wenn in ihrer Heimat Friede herrschen sollte, fließt nicht in die Berechnung ein."

66. Mark Schieritz, "Wunschdenken': An alle: Pullover anziehen!', *Die Zeit* vol. 19 (28 April 2016), http://www.zeit.de/2016/19/thilo-sarrazin-buch-wunschdenken-utopien, last accessed 21 April 2019.

67. Jakob Augstein, 'Gerüchte über Muslime', *Spiegel Online* (9 May 2016), http://www.spiegel.de/politik/ausland/rassismus-in-europa-geruechte-ueber-muslime-kolumne-a-1091398.html, last accessed 21 April 2019.

68. Uwe Schmitt, 'Sarrazins düstere Vision zu den Flüchtlings-"Kohorten"', *Die Welt* (24 April 2016), http://www.welt.de/154704055, last accessed 21 April 2019.

69. Gregor Mayntz, 'Neues Buch 'Wunschdenken:' Thilo Sarrazins Wunsch-Deutschland', *Rheinische Post* (7 May 2016), http://www.rp-online. de/politik/wunschdenken-thilo-sarrazins-wunsch-deutschland-aid-1.5960730, last accessed 21 April 2019.
70. Michael Angele, 'Verkehrtes Wunschdenken', *Freitag* vol. 19 (12 May 2016), https://www.freitag.de/autoren/michael-angele/verkehrtes-wunschdenken, last accessed 21 April 2019.
71. Stefan Wagstyl, 'Homage to Germany before the migrants is an infuriating polemic', *Financial Times* (4 July 2016), https://www. ft.com/content/30e21794-38a3-11e6-9a05-82a9b15a8ee7, last accessed 21 April 2019. The *Financial Times* later added a link to an article about the AfD at the top of the review: "A growing Alternative for Germany attracts some unsavoury members. September 27, 2016."
72. Jürgen Habermas, 'Leadership and Leitkultur', *The New York Times* (28 October 2010), http://www.nytimes.com/2010/10/29/opinion/29Habermas.html, last accessed 21 April 2019.
73. Michael Slackman, 'With Words on Muslims, Opening a Door Long Shut', *The New York Times* (12 November 2010), http://www.nytimes.com/2010/11/13/world/europe/13sarrazin.html?_r=0, last accessed 21 April 2019.
74. One of the manifestations of Sarrazin's ambivalence lies in the fact that even though he wants to maintain Germany as a discrete state and culture, he believes—as an economist—that globalization cannot be reversed.
75. Cited in: Stefan Braun und Evelyn Roll, 'Bundeskanzlerin im SZ-Interview. Merkel: 'Deutschland wird Deutschland bleiben", *Süddeutsche Zeitung* (30 August 2016), http://www.sueddeutsche.de/politik/kanzlerin-merkel-im-sz-interview-deutschland-wird-deutschland-bleiben-1.3141520, last accessed 21 April 2019. Her words in German were: "Deutschland wird Deutschland bleiben, mit allem, was uns lieb und teuer ist."
76. Among these are his critique of the Euro, which is not completely unrelated to the sort of thinking that led to the call for a British exit from the European Union. See: Thilo Sarrazin, *Der Euro: Chance oder Abenteuer?*, Bonn: J.H.W. Dietz, 1997, and *Europa braucht den Euro nicht: wie uns politisches Wunschdenken in die Krise geführt hat*, München: Deutsche Verlags-Anstalt, 2012.

2. AKIF PIRINÇCI: THE MIGRANT PROVOCATEUR

1. 'Multiculturalism Policy of Canada', http://laws-lois.justice.gc.ca/eng/acts/C-18.7/page-1.html#h, last accessed 21 April 2019.

2. Alfred L. Cobb, *Migrants' Literature in Postwar Germany. Striving to Find a Place to Fit In*, Lewiston et al.: Edwin Mellen Press, 2006, p. 81.

3. Miriam Hollstein, 'Katzenkrimi-Autor gibt den neuen Sarrazin', *Die Welt* (4 April 2014), http://www.welt.de/politik/deutschland/article126592871/Katzenkrimi-Autor-gibt-den-neuen-Sarrazin.html, last accessed 21 April 2019.

4. The novel was then printed by Goldmann Verlag in 1981.

5. As one critic noted: "Whoever hopes to find something in his book about the thinking and feeling of the second foreigner generation will be disappointed …" ("Wer hofft, in seinem Buch etwas über das Denken und Fühlen der zweiten Ausländergeneration zu erfahren, wird enttäuscht …"). See Klaus Pokatzky, 'Ich bin ein Pressetürke. Akif Pirinçci und der deutsche Literaturbetrieb', *Transit Deutschland. Debatten zu Nation und Migration*, eds. Deniz Göktürk, David Gramling, Anton Kaes and Andreas Langenohl, München: Wilhelm Fink Verlag / Konstanz University Press, 2011, p. 570. Pokatzky also provides us with a telling statement by Pirinçci himself: "All cultures are similar, culture does not interest me, in the world, everything is a matter of fucking and money and nothing else." ("Alle Kulturen ähneln sich, Kultur interessiert mich nicht, es geht in der Welt nur ums Ficken und ums Geld und um nichts anderes"), p. 570.

   Pirinçci has also been called "the individualistic cosmopolitan of denial." See Tom Cheesman, *Novels of Turkish German Settlement: Cosmopolite Fictions*, Rochester, NY: Camden House, 2007, pp. 58-59.

6. Akif Pirinçci, *Felidae*, München: Goldmann, 1989. I am providing my own translations here, but the book has appeared in English translation (New York: Villard Books, 1993).

7. Religion also plays a role, and at least one passage should be reproduced here (referring to the character Claudandus): "His brain, contaminated by religious mania, strove single-mindedly toward that which constitutes in the end all religious mania, namely bloody orgies" (p. 227).

8. See his *Erbschaft dieser Zeit*, Frankfurt am Main: Suhrkamp, 1962. For an English translation, see *Heritage of our Times*, transl. Neville and Stephen Plaice, Cambridge: Polity Press, 1991. The original edition dates from 1935; at the time, Bloch was discussing how the German Communists utilized 'cold' economic statistics to sway their audiences, whereas the Nazis appealed to rather diffuse emotional needs.

9. Waltrop und Leipzig: Lichtschlag in der Edition Sonderwege, Manuscriptum Verlagsbuchhandlung, 2014, p. 276.

10. The German term *Nazikeule* refers to the practice of smearing opponents by accusing them of being Nazi sympathizers of one degree

or another. It is usually used within the context of a critique of (leftist) political correctness.

11. One journalist has spoken of Pirinçci as "like Sarrazin on speed." See Harald Staun, 'Der Populismus des Akif Pirinçci', *Frankfurter Allgemeine Sonntagszeitung* (5 April 2014), http://www.faz.net/aktuell/feuilleton/der-populismus-des-akif-pirincci-wie-sarrazin-auf-speed-12881608.html, last accessed 21 April 2019.

12. Observers of the 2016 presidential election campaign in the US will recognize a pattern here, namely the practice of making provocative statements and then claiming that they were misinterpreted—or never made in the first place. This is also reminiscent of the rhetorical strategies employed by the late Austrian populist Jörg Haider.

13. Pirinçci's text is archived (25 March 2013) at http://www.achgut.com/artikel/das_schlachten_hat_begonnen\, last accessed 21 April 2019. In the meantime, this site has taken a turn to the right, and one of the original founders, Michael Miersch, has decided to disassociate himself from it. See Christian Bommarius, 'An das deutsch-nationale Pöbel-Pack', *Frankfurter Rundschau* (21 January 2015). For Miersch's own statement, see Michael Miersch, 'Na dann ohne mich' (20 January 2015), archived at http://www.achgut.com/artikel/na_dann_ohne_mich, last accessed 21 April 2019. He states there, among other things: "At the Axis, an atmosphere has taken over that has very little to do with the originally liberal, cosmopolitan, and enlightened stance of this authorial blog." The present driving force behind the site is Henryk M. Broder (see Chapter One).

14. Pirinçci had already placed many other texts online in 2013, the year before the publication of *DvS*. They can be found at http://mohammed.freehostyou.com/akifpirincci/#44, last accessed 21 April 2019. Some of the titles are: 'Fuck you, Facebook!'; 'The Greens—the Party of Liars'; 'Evolution in the Welfare State: Preferential Treatment for the Mediocre'; 'In the end, the Germans will integrate themselves into Islam'; 'From such a book: The mental illness [called] gender mainstream.'

15. The irony here is that Germany's performance in this area has been rather mediocre: according to the European Institute for Gender Equality, Germany's score of 8.5 (on a scale of 0-16) is just above the EU 28 average of 8.4. The leaders are France and Finland (14), Spain and Sweden (13.5), and Austria (13). For the complete results, see: http://eige.europa.eu/gender-mainstreaming/countries, last accessed 21 April 2019.

16. The European Institute for Gender Equality, http://eige.europa.eu/gender-mainstreaming/concepts-and-definitions, last accessed 21 April

2019. What is surprising is that at the same site, "gender" is defined as referring to "the social attributes and opportunities associated with being male and female." There is no mention of gender variance or fluidity, terms that enrage Pirinçci.

17. Pirinçci uses the German word "Geschlecht" here, rather than the current German term "das Gender," which Duden Online defines as "gender identity of a person as a social category (for example, with regard to one's self-perception, one's self-esteem, or one's behavior)" *(Geschlechtsidentität des Menschen als soziale Kategorie (z. B. im Hinblick auf seine Selbstwahrnehmung, sein Selbstwertgefühl oder sein Rollenverhalten.)).* See "Gender" at http://www.duden.de/rechtschreibung/Gender, last accessed 21 April 2019.

18. One sentence in this passage is telling: "I have never seen something that beautiful in my life!" (p. 129). He uses the term "something" *(etwas)* rather than "a woman" or "a person."

19. According to *Der Spiegel,* more and more Germans are opting for the single life. See: Anna Clauß et al., 'Die Sehnsuchenden', *Der Spiegel* vol. 43 (2016), https://magazin.spiegel.de/SP/2016/43/147472091/index.html, last accessed 21 April 2019. Although there are over eighteen million singles in Germany, 72 per cent say that they believe in long-term relationships.

20. Pirinçci does use a phrase from Nietzsche's *Also sprach Zarathustra* as the motto for his afterword: "Somewhere, there are still peoples and herds." *(Irgendwo gibt es noch Völker und Herden …; p. 269.)*

21. The journalist in question is Jochen Grabler, 'Gefährlicher Rassismus', Radio Bremen (6 April 2013), https://web.archive.org/web/20131218094245/http://www.radiobremen.de/politik/themen/pirincci100.html, last accessed 21 April 2019. Grabler pulls no punches: "There is a new hate preacher among the German intellectuals […] inspired by Goebbels's perfidy."

22. There are echoes here of Brecht's 1933 poem 'Deutschland,' which begins with the line "Oh Germany, pale mother" ("*O Deutschland, bleiche Mutter*"). See Bertolt Brecht, 'Deutschland', *Die Gedichte von Bertolt Brecht in einem Band*, Frankfurt am Main: Suhrkamp Verlag, 1981, pp. 487-488. Brecht was of course lamenting the plight of Germany at a time when large families were the rule rather than the exception!

23. We are told in the same chapter that the Greens are "absolutely superfluous" (p. 18).

24. See *Die Grünen und die Pädosexualität: Eine bundesdeutsche Geschichte,* eds. Franz Walter, Stephan Klecha and Alexander Hensel, Göttingen: Vandenhoek & Ruprecht, 2014. A summary of the findings can be

found online at https://www.brd.uy/wp-content/uploads/2016/03/Ergebnisse_Gruenenstudie_2014-2.pdf, last accessed 24 April 2019.

For a helpful review (in German), see Teresa Tammer at http://www.sehepunkte.de/2015/10/26682.html, last accessed 21 April 2019. For assessments in English, see Philip Oltermann, 'German Green party co-leader 'regrets' 1980s paedophilia pamphlet', *The Guardian* (16 September 2013), https://www.theguardian.com/world/german-elections-blog-2013/2013/sep/16/german-green-jurgen-trittin-regret-paedophilia-pamphlet, last accessed 21 April 2019, and Thomas Rogers, 'A Major German Political Party Used to Support Pedophilia — And It's Coming Back to Haunt Them', *The New Republic* (23 November 2014), https://newrepublic.com/article/120379/german-green-party-pedophilia-scandal, last accessed 21 April 2019.

25. To bolster his argument, Pirinçci quotes from a US article: Michael Fumento, 'The Squeaky Wheel Syndrome', *The American Spectator* (December 1998), pp. 24-29. He neglects to mention that Fumento also criticizes breast cancer research. The article is available online in the database Academic Search Complete.

26. In the text, the last word of the previous sentence is "masturbate," which is clearly meant to cause outrage.

27. The author uses a humorous version of an old German saying here. He transforms "Den lieben Gott einen guten Mann sein lassen" into "Allah einen guten Mann sein lassen." The original German saying means to "take things as they come."

28. A different depiction of the same process is found in Michel Houellebecq's novel *Submission*, transl. Lorin Stein, New York: Farrar, Straus and Giroux, 2015. The French original, *Soumission*, appeared in January of the same year.

29. He makes fun of the "German taxpayer" who mistakenly believes that US citizens are subject to "twists of fate [...] or even the economy without protection" (p. 94).

30. He even dreams of abolishing taxes altogether (p. 110).

31. This is more than a bit contradictory, since Pirinçci claims that "no one" in the country feels any such guilt! (pp. 204-205).

32. No such tolerance is granted to Ayatollah Chomeini, who is branded a "bigot" who strove to return his country to the Middle Ages (p. 37). Pirinçci does note that Islamic culture was once more progressive than it is today (p. 43).

33. Eds. Akif Pirinçci and Andreas Lombard, Lichtschlag in der Edition Sonderwege; Waltrop und Leipzig: Manuscriptum Verlagsbuchhandlung, 2014.

34. The German phrase used here is extremely negative: "*Schreiberlinge und Sprecherlinge*." The first word is often used disparagingly, but the second is apparently a neologism of Lombard's own invention. German speakers will inadvertently make the association with the word "*Feigling*" (coward).

35. Like Pirinçci, Lombard immediately adds that such an analogy is "inadmissible" (*unstatthaft*). The strategy is to make outrageous statements and then more or less retract them; the original statement of course is what remains in one's memory.

36. The broadcast is available on YouTube at https://youtu.be/a-f3KDl6QMY, last accessed 2 December 2016.

37. Ijoma Mangold, 'Full Load of Hate', *Die Zeit* no. 13 (4 April 2014). Original title: 'Volle Ladung Hass'.

38. This German site, *Die Freie Welt—Internet- & Blogzeitung für die Freie Welt*, can be found at http://www.freiewelt.net/blog, last accessed 21 April 2019.

39. Akif Pirinçci, *Die große Verschwulung: wenn aus Männern Frauen werden und aus Frauen keine Männer*, Waltrop und Leipzig: Manuscriptum, Edition Lichtschlag, 2015.

40. The entire program presented that evening can be found on YouTube at https://www.youtube.com/watch?v=bAECroAacAU, last accessed 24 April 2019. Pirinçci appears at about the 1'34" mark.

41. See, for example: 'Eklat bei Pegida-Demo', *Spiegel Online* (20 October 2015), http://www.spiegel.de/politik/deutschland/pegida-ermittlungen-wegen-kz-rede-gegen-akif-pirin-ci-a-1058666.html, last accessed 21 April 2019, or 'Pegida: Staatsanwaltschaft ermittelt gegen Akif Pirinçci', *ZEIT ONLINE* (20 October 2015), http://www.zeit.de/politik/deutschland/2015-10/akif-pirincci-pegida-demonstration-fremdenfeindlichkeit-ermittlungen-staatsanwaltschaft-dresden, last accessed 21 April 2019.

42. The media critic Stefan Niggemeier provides a documentation of the way in which the reference to the concentration camps was distorted in various publications, online at http://www.stefan-niggemeier.de/blog/22191/die-unwahrheit-ueber-akif-pirincis-kz-rede/, last accessed 21 April 2019. Niggemeier emphasizes that he has "absolutely no sympathy" with Pirinçci and his hate-filled tirades.

43. See: 'Akif Pirinçci zu hoher Geldstrafe verurteilt', *Sächsische Zeitung* (7 February 2017), http://www.sz-online.de/nachrichten/akif-pirincci-zu-hoher-geldstrafe-verurteilt-3607281.html, last accessed 21 April 2019.

44. Schnellroda: Verlag Antaios, 2016, pp. 160.

45. For an example of how Pirinçci provides a distorted view of events to suit his own purposes, see the following blog post: Frederik Weitz, 'Akif Pirinçci und seine Lügenpresse' (15 November 2015), http://frederikweitz.blogspot.com/2015/11/akif-pirincci-und-seine-lugenpresse.html, last accessed 21 April 2019.

46. See Amy B. Wang, "Post-truth' named 2016 word of the year by Oxford Dictionaries', *The Washington Post* (16 November 2016), https://www.washingtonpost.com/news/the-fix/wp/2016/11/16/post-truth-named-2016-word-of-the-year-by-oxford-dictionaries/?utm_term=.5fffaa9212cf, last accessed 21 April 2019.

47. Jan Fleischhauer, 'Der Aussätzige', *Der Spiegel* vol. 46 (2015), pp. 40-43.

48. He mentioned this in the *Spiegel* interview and also in the magazine *Der Stern*. See: Sophie Albers and Ben Chamo, 'Akif Pirinçci überlegt, das Land zu verlassen', *Der Stern* Online (22 October 2015), http://www.stern.de/panorama/gesellschaft/akif-pirincci-ueber-pegida--sein-titanic-telefonat-und-seine-zukunft---ein-interview-6514746.html, last accessed 21 April 2019.

INTERMEZZO: A FRENCH PIRINÇCI?

1. Éric Zemmour, *Le Suicide français*, Paris: Éditions Albin Michel, 2014.

2. See Laurent Martinet, 'Eric Zemmour: 'Je ne demande pas la francisation des noms'', *L'Express* (11 March 2010), http://www.lexpress.fr/culture/livre/eric-zemmour-je-ne-demande-pas-la-francisation-des-noms_854520.html, last accessed 21 April 2019. The so-called Crémieux decree (1870) granted full French citizenship to Algerian Jews; this was abrogated by the Vichy government in 1940 and reinstated in 1943. See Florence Renucci, 'Le débat sur le statut politique des israélites en Algérie et ses acteurs (1870-1943)', *Contributions du seminaire sur les administrations coloniales* (2009–2010), 2010, France, pp. 31-49, https://halshs.archives-ouvertes.fr/halshs-00599296, last accessed 21 April 2019.

3. Zemmour is course aware that Aznavour was born in France to parents who were Armenian immigrants—another successful example of assimilation! There is no higher praise than when Zemmour lauds the children of immigrants like Yves Montand or Michel Piccoli for showcasing "the language of Racine, the verve of Molière, and the *esprit* of Descartes" (p. 134).

4. This disease has supposedly made France unrecognizable: "French society has swapped heroism for consumerism" (p. 133). Zemmour reports with obvious disdain that the French now consume more

McDonald's hamburgers than any other country outside the US (p. 198). Under American influence, French alimentation has become "a crazy machine for producing maladies (obesity, cholesterol, cancer, diabetes, cardio-vascular illnesses) that the pharmaceutical industry treats with innumerable drugs, providing great profits to its stockholders" (pp. 437-438).

5.   Zemmour prefers the French term *mondialisation*.
6.   Emmanuel Berretta, 'Qui est vraiment Eric Zemmour?', *Le Point* (1 April 2010), https://www.lepoint.fr/societe/qui-est-vraiment-eric-zemmour-01-04-2010-442102_23.php, last accessed 21 April 2019.
7.   At one point, Zemmour uses the term "Lilliputians" to characterize all of these actors, including feminists, gay rights activists, and advocates of decolonization (p. 135).
8.   Like Pirinçci, Zemmour longs for the bygone days when French homosexuals observed "the old manners of discretion" (p. 267).
9.   Zemmour discusses the French soccer team St. Étienne as an embodiment of the 'old France' with its "spirit of abnegation and sacrifice" (p. 154).
10. "Americanization and liberalization are the two teats of the world that is coming. Europe serves as the Trojan Horse" (p. 202).
11. The "destruction" of the "national working class" was caused by the entry of immigrant families into the country (p. 163) and the shift from industrial enterprise to finance (p. 177). Zemmour also laments the decline of small shopkeepers in France (pp. 155, 453).
12. The perpetrators turned out to be skinheads associated with the far-right party PNFE. See Gudrun Lingner, 'Prozeß gegen vier französische Rechtsextreme, die 1990 den jüdischen Friedhof von Carpentras schändeten', *Berliner Zeitung* (19 March 1997), http://www.berliner-zeitung.de/16462898, last accessed 21 April 2019.
13. See Laurent Martinet, 'Eric Zemmour: 'Je ne demande pas la francisation des noms" (endnote 2 above).
14. See, for example, the blog ISLAMNIXGUT, which featured one article about Pirinçci's conviction for disturbing the peace, and another about terrorism in France with a section about Zemmour, https://nixgut.wordpress.com/tag/eric-zemmour/, last accessed 21 April 2019.
15. 'Homophobes de tous les pays', *Le Parisien* (12 May 2015), http://www.leparisien.fr/espace-premium/culture-loisirs/homophobes-de-tous-les-pays-12-05-2015-4764003.php, last accessed 21 April 2019.
16. See Melanie Mendelewitsch, 'Eric Zemmour: The Rush Limbaugh of France', *Observer* (10 February 2015), http://observer.com/2015/02/eric-zemmour-the-rush-limbaugh-of-france/, last accessed 21 April 2019.

17. F. Roger Devlin, 'Forty Years that Unmade France', *American Renaissance* (14 November 2014), https://www.amren.com/features/2014/11/forty-years-that-unmade-france/, last accessed 21 April 2019. The connection is also made by David Pryce-Jones in 'Pangloss's Europe', *The New Criterion* vol. 33 no. 6 (2015), http://www.newcriterion.com/articles.cfm/Pangloss-s-Europe-8091, last accessed 21 April 2019.

18. 'Assaulting Democracy: The Deep Repercussions of the Charlie Hebdo Attack', *Spiegel Online* (9 January 2015), http://www.spiegel.de/international/europe/charlie-hebdo-attack-targets-democracy-and-the-west-a-1012072.html, last accessed 21 April 2019.

19. Robert Zaretsky, 'Do France's Intellectuals have a Muslim Problem?', *Foreign Policy* (8 January 2015), http://foreignpolicy.com/2015/01/08/do-frances-intellectuals-have-a-muslim-problem/, last accessed 21 April 2019. "Zemmourisation" is defined here as a process "that credits racial and ethnic prejudices that, until recently, were limited to the extreme right."

According to Mark Lilla, Zemmour "is less a journalist or thinker than a medium through whom the political passions of the moment pass and take on form." See Mark Lilla, *The Shipwrecked Mind. On Political Reaction*, New York: New York Review Books, 2016, p. 110.

3. BOTHO STRAUß: FROM COSMOPOLITAN FLANEUR TO RURAL PROPHET

1. The only figure who comes to mind is the US poet Robinson Jeffers (1897-1962), for whom Strauß has expressed admiration. Jeffers spent a good part of his adult life in an isolated castle-like house on the California coast. For background on Jeffers, see Charles Simic, 'Divine, Superfluous Beauty', *The New York Review of Books* (11 April 2002), pp. 48-50.

2. For background on this movement, see Roger Woods, *The Conservative Revolution in the Weimar Republic*, New York: St. Martin's Press, 1996, and Jay Rosellini, *Literary Skinheads? Writing from the Right in Reunified Germany*, West Lafayette: Purdue University Press, 2000.

3. Botho Strauß, 'Anschwellender Bocksgesang', *Der Spiegel* vol. 6 (1993), pp. 202-207.

4. *Die selbstbewusste Nation."Anschwellender Bocksgesang" und weitere Beiträge zu einer deutschen Debatte*, eds. Heimo Schwilk and Ulrich Schacht, Frankfurt am Main/Berlin: Ullstein Verlag, 1994. The Strauß essay appears in the title of the volume and is placed directly after the editors'

preface (pp. 19-40). In the following, quoted passages are taken from the *Spiegel* version, the one that was read by a much broader audience.

5. In a later essay, Strauß stated that a young German who is both a Christian believer and someone who values his homeland (*Heimat*) represents only a small minority in Germany. See B.S., 'Der Konflikt', *Der Spiegel* vol. 7 (13 February 2006), http://www.spiegel.de/spiegel/print/d-45889478.html, last accessed 21 April 2019.

6. See, for example, Werner Sombart's volume *Händler und Helden. Patriotische Besinnungen*, München und Leipzig: Duncker & Humblot, 1915.

7. Another statement that would never appear in a text by Pirinçci is the following: "I can see the dignity of the begging gypsy woman at first glance" (p. 203).

8. Peter Glotz, 'Freunde, es wird ernst', *Deutsche Literatur 1993. Jahresrückblick*, Stuttgart: Reclam, 1994, p. 273. Originally published in the *Wochenpost* of 25 February 1993.

9. Klaus Kreimeier, 'Wiedergänger und Nachbereiter', *Deutsche Literatur 1994. Jahresrückblick*, Stuttgart: Reclam, 1995, pp. 266-268. Originally in *Freitag*, 13 May 1994. For a summary of the various reactions to 'Impending Tragedy,' see Jay Rosellini, *Literary Skinheads?*, pp. 105-109.

10. In 1927, the first winner of that prize was poet Stefan George, whose life as an elitist recluse to some extent prefigures that of Strauß. For background on George and his influence, see Robert E. Norton, *Secret Germany. Stefan George and his Circle*, Ithaca and London: Cornell University Press, 2002. One of the terms associated with George is "*geheimes Deutschland*" (secret Germany), and that very term appears at the end of Strauß's 'The Last German' (see note 12 below).

11. Cordt Schnibben, 'Abschwellender Bocksgesang', *Der Spiegel* vol. 39 (2015), pp. 105-108. Schnibben's title changes the one of Strauß's essay from 'Impending Tragedy' to 'Receding Tragedy.'

12. Botho Strauß, 'Der letzte Deutsche. Uns wird die Souveranität geraubt, dagegen zu sein', *Der Spiegel* vol. 41 (2015), pp. 122-124.

13. Botho Strauß, *Die Unbeholfenen. Bewußtseinsnovelle*, Munchen: Hanser, 2007. The subtitle utilizes the older German spelling ("ß" instead of "ss") as an homage to the past. The passage reused in 'The Last German' is found on p. 83. This work portrays the strange interactions of a reclusive group of articulate individualists; the scene is not a "garden" (as in 'Impending Tragedy'), but rather an old-fashioned German house located in a nondescript industrial area. This not-so-subtle scenario is not worthy of the sophisticated Strauß.

14. Botho Strauß, *Der Fortführer*, Reinbek: Rowohlt, 2018.

15. In an earlier essay, Strauß opined that the West's conflict with Islam might put an end to the Western era of "anything goes" (*die herrschende Beliebigkeit*), "syncretism," and "indifference." He characterized that particular era as "a feeble time." See Botho Strauß, 'Der Konflikt', *Der Spiegel* vol. 7 (2006), p. 121.

16. Botho Strauß. *Herkunft*, München: Hanser, 2014, p. 96.

17. Eduard Strauß even petitioned the draft board to exempt his son from military service, citing his own severe war wounds; Botho Strauß was never conscripted into the *Bundeswehr*.

18. German readers will associate this with Nietzsche. The German word used here is *unzeitgemäß*, found in the title of Nietzsche's work *Unzeitgemäße Betrachtungen* (Thoughts out of Season).

19. Hans Hütt, 'Botho Strauß: Die Selbstvernichtung eines Autors', *ZEIT ONLINE* (8 October 2015), http://www.zeit.de/kultur/literatur/2015-10/botho-strauss-glosse-fluechtlingskrise-spiegel/komplettansicht?print=true, last accessed 21 April 2019.

20. Joachim Petrick, 'Botho Strauß: "Hunnengejammer von der Kette"', *der Freitag* (9 October 2015), https://www.freitag.de/autoren/joachim-petrick/botho-strauss-hunnengedanken-von-der-kette, last accessed 21 April 2019. Petrick is a regular contributor to the weekly *der Freitag*.

21. Dietmar Dath, 'Deutschstunde bei Botho Strauß', *FAZ* (7 October 2015), http://www.faz.net/aktuell/feuilleton/debatten/ist-botho-strauss-der-letzte-deutsche-eine-widerrede-13840425-p3.html?printPagedArticle=true#pageIndex_3, last accessed 21 April 2019.

22. Richard Kämmerlings, 'Was ist deutsche Überlieferung?', *Die Welt* (6 October 2015), https://www.welt.de/kultur/literarischewelt/article147264002/Was-ist-deutsche-Ueberlieferung.html, last accessed 21 April 2019.

23. Rüdiger Suchsland, 'Wie rechts ist Deutschland?', *Telepolis* (11 October 2015), http://www.heise.de/tp/artikel/46/46231/, last accessed 21 April 2019.

24. '"Etwas problematisch zu finden, wird als rassistisch gebrandmarkt." Martin Mosebach im Gespräch mit Christopher Heinemann', *Deutschlandfunk*, (28 October 2015), http://www.deutschlandfunk.de/botho-strauss-fluechtlingskulturstreit-etwas-problematisch.694.de.html?dram:article_id=333396, last accessed 21 April 2019.

25. Rolf Schneider, 'Von Kulturbanausen und nationaler deutscher Identität', *Deutschlandfunk* (21 October 2015), http://www.deutschlandradiokultur.de/zum-spiegel-text-von-botho-strauss-von-kulturbanausen-und.1005.de.html?dram:article_id=334533, last accessed 21 April 2019.

26. Botho Strauß, 'Man muß wissen, wie die Sonne funktioniert', *FAZ* (21 October 2005), http://www.faz.net/aktuell/feuilleton/ umweltpolitik-botho-strauss-man-muss-wissen-wie-die-sonne-funktioniert-1280314.html, last accessed 21 April 2019.

4. THE VOICE OF THE PEOPLE? THE ALTERNATIVE FOR GERMANY AND PEGIDA

1. Armin Pfahl-Traughber, *Rechtsextremismus in der Bundesrepublik*, München: C.H. Beck, 1999, pp. 23-39.
2. Wolfgang Janisch, 'NPD—der braune Zwerg darf weiterexistieren', *Süddeutsche Zeitung* (18 January 2017), http://www.sueddeutsche. de/politik/bundesverfassungsgericht-npd-der-braune-zwerg-darf-weiterexistieren-1.3336335, last accessed 21 April 2019. Then Justice Minister (now Foreign Minister) Heiko Maas attempted to revoke state funding for the party. See 'Maas will NPD die Finanzierung entziehen', *Süddeutsche Zeitung* (13 March 2017), http://www.sueddeutsche. de/politik/rechtsextreme-partei-maas-will-npd-den-geldhahn-zudrehen-1.3417031, last accessed 21 April 2019.
3. Michael Minkeberg, 'What's Left of the Right? The New Right and the Superwahljahr 1994 in Perspective', *Germany's New Politics*, eds. David F. Conradt et al., Tempe, AZ: German Studies Review, 1995, p. 223. In contrast to Minkeberg, I refer to the AfD as the "new right," and all post-1945 right-wing parties active before that as the "old right." This is based on the use of modern populist strategies by the AfD and its counterparts in other European countries.
4. Frank Decker, 'Rechts in der Mitte? AfD, Pegida und die Verschiebung der parteipolitischen Mitte', *Aus Politik und Zeitgeschichte* vol. 40, pp. 27-32, http://www.bpb.de/apuz/212360/afd-pegida-und-die-verschiebung-der-parteipolitischen-mitte?p=all, last accessed 21 April 2019.
5. Hajo Funke and Ralph Gabriel, *Von Wutbürgern und Brandstiftern. AfD—Pegida—Gewaltnetze*, Berlin: Verlag für Berlin-Brandenburg [VBB], 2016, p. 73.
6. See the information on the church's website: http://erk-hamburg.de/ verwaltung/, last accessed 21 April 2019.
7. Hendrik Ankenbrand, 'Bernd Lucke: Der Protestant', *Franfurter Allgemeine Sonntagszeitung* (14 December 2013), http://www.faz. net/aktuell/wirtschaft/menschen-wirtschaft/bernd-lucke-der-protestant-12711334.html?printPagedArticle=true#pageIndex_2, last accessed 21 April 2019.
8. See Hajo Funke, *Von Wutbürgern und Brandstiftern*, pp. 74-76.

9. 'Erklärung im Wortlaut. Bernd Lucke zu seinem Austritt aus der AfD', SPIEGEL ONLINE (8 July 2015), http://www.spiegel.de/politik/deutschland/bernd-lucke-erklaerung-zu-austritt-aus-der-afd-a-1042734.html, last accessed 21 April 2019.

10. *Grundsatzprogramm der Alternative für Deutschland*, https://www.afd.de/wp-content/uploads/sites/111/2016/03/Leitantrag-Grundsatzprogramm-AfD.pdf, last accessed 21 April 2019.

11. CDU Party Program, *Freiheit und Sicherheit. Grundsätze für Deutschland*, 2007, p. 16, https://www.cdu.de/system/tdf/media/dokumente/071203-beschluss-grundsatzprogramm-6-navigierbar_1.pdf?file=1&type=field_collection_item&id=1918, last accessed 21 April 2019.

12. Despite this declaration, both the AfD and PEGIDA are secular groups, unlike certain other right-wing populists. See Claus Leggewie, *Anti-Europäer. Breivik, Dugin, al-Suri & Co.*, Frankfurt am Main: Suhrkamp, 2016.

13. See Stephan Detjen, '"Der Islam gehört zu Deutschland." Die Geschichte eines Satzes', *Deutschlandfunk* (13 January 2015), http://www.deutschlandfunk.de/der-islam-gehoert-zu-deutschland-die-geschichte-eines-satzes.1783.de.html?dram:article_id=308619, last accessed 21 April 2019.

14. See Henry Samuel, 'Prophet Mohammed in cartoons: a history', *The Telegraph* (7 January 2015), http://www.telegraph.co.uk/news/worldnews/europe/france/8864935/Prophet-Mohammed-in-cartoons-a-history.html, last accessed 21 April 2019. Jana Sinram (see note 36 to chapter one above) criticizes the "senseless provocations" of the Danish and Western press in the form of such caricatures.

15. *Grundsatzprogramm der Alternative für Deutschland. Leitantrag der Bundesprogrammkommission und des Bundesvorstandes*, p. 34, http://www.welt.de/pdf/1088/Leitantrag-Grundsatzprogramm-AfD.pdf, last accessed 21 April 2019.

16. See Anna Reimann and Fabian Nitschmann, 'Der gewollte Eklat', *Spiegel Online* (23 May 2016), https://www.spiegel.de/politik/deutschland/afd-und-zentralrat-der-muslime-der-inszenierte-eklat-a-1093595.html, last accessed 21 April 2019.

17. Frauke Petry interviewed by Steffen Mack and Walter Serif, 'Sie können es nicht lassen', *Mannheimer Morgen* (30 January 2016), http://www.morgenweb.de/mannheimer-morgen_artikel,-politik-sie-koennen-es-nicht-lassen-_arid,751556.html, last accessed 21 April 2019.

18. Nico Fried, 'CDU/CSU-Fraktionschef Kauder: Äußerungen von Petry "zeigen die wahre Gesinnung der AfD-Führung"', *Süddeutsche Zeitung* (31 January 2016), http://www.sueddeutsche.de/politik/

cducsu-fraktionschef-kauder-aeusserungen-von-petry-zeigen-die-wahre-gesinnung-der-afd-fuehrung-1.2842662, last accessed 21 April 2019.

19. Heribert Prantl, 'AfD-Vorschläge: Auf einmal darf gesagt werden, was unsäglich ist', *Süddeutsche Zeitung* (1 February 2016), http://www.sueddeutsche.de/politik/fluechtlinge-afd-vorschlaege-auf-einmal-darf-gesagt-werden-was-unsaeglich-ist-1.2842762, last accessed 21 April 2019.

20. See Oliver Georgi, 'Petry streicht Aussage zu Waffeneinsatz aus Interview', FAZ (5 February 2016).

21. 'AfD-Vizechefin will Polizei sogar auf Kinder schießen lassen', report from nto/Reuters posted on *FAZ.net* (31 January 2016), www.faz.net/aktuell/politik/fluechtlingskrise/beatrix-von-storch-afd-vizechefin-will-polizei-sogar-auf-kinder-schiessen-lassen-14044186.html, last accessed 21 April 2019.

22. 'AfD: Beatrix von Storch will doch nicht auf Kinder schießen', ZEIT ONLINE/dpa (31 January 2016), http://www.zeit.de/politik/2016-01/alternative-fuer-deutschland-beatrix-von-storch-petry-schusswaffen, last accessed 21 April 2019.

23. See Markus Wehner and Eckart Lohse, 'Gauland beleidigt Boateng', *Frankfurter Allgemeine Sonntagszeitung* (29 May 2016), http://www.faz.net/aktuell/politik/inland/afd-vize-gauland-beleidigt-jerome-boateng-14257743.html, last accessed 21 April 2019.

24. 'Wie sich Gauland zu rechtfertigen versucht', *Spiegel Online* (31 May 2016), http://www.spiegel.de/politik/deutschland/jerome-boateng-wie-sich-alexander-gauland-zu-rechtfertigen-versucht-a-1094988.html, last accessed 21 April 2019.

25. 'Petry entschuldigt sich bei Boateng für Gauland-Beleidigung', *Die Welt* (29 May 2016), https://www.welt.de/politik/deutschland/article155788270/Petry-entschuldigt-sich-bei-Boateng-fuer-Gauland-Beleidigung.html, last accessed 21 April 2019.

26. All three volumes: Frankfurt am Main: R.G. Fischer Verlag, 2009. The full titles are: *Christlich-europäische Leitkultur. Die Herausforderung Europas durch Säkularismus, Zionismus und Islam: Band I: Über Kultur, Geostrategie und Religion*; *Christlich-europäische Leitkultur. Die Herausforderung Europas durch Säkularismus, Zionismus und Islam: Band II: Über Geschichte, Zionismus und Verschwörungspolitik*; *Christlich-europäische Leitkultur. Die Herausforderung Europas durch Säkularismus, Zionismus und Islam: Band III: Über Europa, Globalismus und eine neue Politik der Mitte*.

27. Marcus Funck, 'Wolfgang Gedeon: Wie antisemitisch ist dieser AfD-Politiker?', *Die Zeit* vol. 34 (2016), http://www.zeit.de/2016/34/

wolfgang-gedeon-antisemitismus-afd/komplettansicht, last accessed 21 April 2019.

28. For background, see: Stephen Eric Bronner, *A Rumor about the Jews: Reflections on Antisemitism and the Protocols of the Learned Elders of Zion*, New York: St. Martin's Press, 2000; Hadassa Ben-Itto, *The Lie That Wouldn't Die: The Protocols of the Elders of Zion*, London, Portland OR: Vallentine Mitchell, 2005; and *From the Protocols of the Elders of Zion to Holocaust Denial Trials: Challenging the Media, the Law and the Academy*, eds. Debra Kaufman et al., London and Portland, OR: Vallentine Mitchell, 2007.

29. Wolfgang Gedeon, 'Der Kampf der Kulturen in Europa', http://www.wmg-verlag.de/gedeon-buecher/buchmesse-frankfurt/, last accessed 21 April 2019.

30. Wolfgang Gedeon, 'Das Antisemitismus-Problem nicht unter den Teppich kehren!' (January 2017), http://www.wolfgang-gedeon.de/2017/01/afd-eine-zionistische-partei/, last accessed 21 April 2019.

31. Wolfgang Gedeon, 'Kritik am Holocaust-Mahnmal in Berlin', found on the author's homepage, http://www.wolfgang-gedeon.de/anschuldigungen/mahnmal/, last accessed 21 April 2019.

32. Björn Höcke, 'Gemütszustand eines total besiegten Volkes', transcript initially provided by the journalist Konstantin Nowotny and later reprinted in the Berlin *Tagesspiegel* (19 January 2017), http://www.tagesspiegel.de/politik/hoecke-rede-im-wortlaut-gemuetszustand-eines-total-besiegten-volkes/19273518-all.html, last accessed 21 April 2019.

33. Cited in Matthias Kamann, 'Was Höcke mit der "Denkmal der Schande"-Rede bezweckt', *Die Welt* (18 January 2017), https://www.welt.de/politik/deutschland/article161286915/Was-Hoecke-mit-der-Denkmal-der-Schande-Rede-bezweckt.html, last accessed 21 April 2019.

34. Adrian Arab, Sebastian Gubernator, Tim Osing, 'RONALD LAUDER: "Die AfD ist eine Schande für Deutschland"', *Die Welt* (29 March 2017), https://www.welt.de/politik/ausland/article163246107/Die-AfD-ist-eine-Schande-fuer-Deutschland.html, last accessed 21 April 2019.

35. Matthias Kamann, 'FRAUKE PETRY: "AfD ist einer der wenigen Garanten jüdischen Lebens"', *Die Welt* (6 April 2017), https://www.welt.de/politik/deutschland/article163446354/AfD-ist-einer-der-wenigen-Garanten-juedischen-Lebens.htm, last accessed 21 April 2019.

36. I write the name of the group in capital letters, because that is the format found on the PEGIDA Facebook page, https://de-de.facebook.com/pegidaevofficial/, last accessed 21 April 2019.

37. The document first appeared in the group's Facebook page and was reproduced on many other sites. I am utilizing a copy from i-finger.de/pegida-positionspapier.pdf, last accessed 21 April 2019. In February,

2015, a revised, but quite similar version entitled '*Dresdner Thesen*' appeared, legida.en/images/legida/Dresdner_Thesen_15_02.pdf, last accessed 21 April 2019.

38. The German original is "durch Antike und Christentum geformte kulturelle Einheit der europäischen Völker", http://www.duden.de/rechtschreibung/Abendland, last accessed 21 April 2019.

39. See Rainer Hank, "'Abendland" war stets ein Kampfbegriff', *Frankfurter Allgemeine Sonntagszeitung* (20 December 2014), http://www.faz.net/aktuell/wirtschaft/wirtschaftspolitik/pegida-abendland-war-stets-ein-kampfbegriff-13333220.html?printPagedArticle=true#pageIndex_2, last accessed 21 April 2019. For a discussion of this in English, see Alexander Goerlach, 'Europe, Germany, and "Abendland" Angst. In the Name of Christendom', 10 April 2017, https://en.qantara.de/content/europe-germany-and-abendland-angst-in-the-name-of-christendom, last accessed 21 April 2019.

40. For a recent journalistic account of this event, see Til Biermann, 'Karl 'der Hammer' Martell—Retter des Abendlandes', *Die Welt* (7 March 2013), https://www.welt.de/geschichte/article114207712/Karl-der-Hammer-Martell-Retter-des-Abendlandes.html, last accessed 21 April 2019. Martell's troops are depicted as Christian Spartans.

41. This is my translation from the German original. See *Grundgesetz für die Bundesrepublik Deutschland*, Bonn: Bundeszentrale für politische Bildung, 1994, p. 22.

42. Even the authors of a recent biographical study of Merkel's years in East Germany were not able to find any evidence of her cooperation with the Stasi. See Ralf Georg Reuth and Günther Lachmann, *Das erste Leben der Angela M.*, München: Piper, 2013.

43. Such images have appeared frequently in the Polish media, but that does not make them any less tasteless.

44. See 'Krawalle vor Flüchtlingsheim; "Das ist Pack, das sich hier herumtreibt"', *Frankfurter Allgemeine Zeitung* (24 August 2015), http://www.faz.net/aktuell/politik/inland/merkel-nennt-rechtsextreme-in-heidenau-abstossend-13766082.html, last accessed 21 April 2019.

45. Martin Niewendick et al., 'Pegida-Demo in Dresden: Cem Özdemir: Galgen grenzt an "Aufruf zu Mord"', *Der Tagesspiegel* (14 October 2015), http://www.tagesspiegel.de/politik/pegida-demo-in-dresden-cem-oezdemir-galgen-grenzt-an-aufruf-zu-mord/12441998.html, last accessed 21 April 2019.

46. See 'Galgen auf Pegida-Demo: Staatsanwaltschaft ermittelt wegen Aufrufs zu Straftaten', *Deutschlandfunk* (13 October 2015), http://www.deutschlandfunk.de/galgen-auf-pegida-demo-staatsanwaltschaft-

ermittelt-wegen.2852.de.html?dram:article_id=333790, last accessed 21 April 2019, and 'Keine Strafe für Galgen-Halter', *Bildzeitung* (10 March 2017), http://www.bild.de/regional/dresden/pegida/keine-strafe-fuer-galgenhalter-50791210.bild.html, last accessed 21 April 2019.

47. See 'Das zweite Gesicht des Lutz Bachmann', *Morgenpost Sachsen* (20 January 2015), https://www.tag24.de/nachrichten/bachmann-pegida-dresden-facebook-3958, last accessed 21 April 2019.

48. See 'Statistik zu Pegida in Dresden', *Durchgezählt*, https://durchgezaehlt. org/pegida-dresden-statistik/, last accessed 21 April 2019.

49. See, for example, 'Auflagen für Legida möglich', *Frankfurter Rundschau* (22 January 2015), https://www.fr.de/politik/auflagen-legida-moeglich-11183116.html, last accessed 21 April 2019, and 'Demonstrationsverbot für Legida am Montag in Leipzig', *Frankfurter Rundschau* (7 February 2015), https://www.fr.de/politik/auflagen-legida-moeglich-11183116.html, last accessed 24 April 2019.

50. See 'Lutz Bachmann wegen Volksverhetzung zu Geldstrafe verurteilt', *Spiegel Online* (3 May 2016), http://www.spiegel.de/politik/deutschland/lutz-bachmann-pegida-gruender-wegen-volksverhetzung-verurteilt-a-1090653.html, last accessed 21 April 2019.

51. See '"Pegida"-Mitgründer auf Teneriffa. Bachmann ist eine "unerwünschte Person"', *tagesschau.de* (29 October 2016), https://www.tagesspiegel. de/politik/pegida-mitgruender-teneriffa-erklaert-lutz-bachmann-zur-unerwuenschten-person/14757234.html, last accessed 21 April 2019.

52. One of the placards held up at a PEGIDA march read: 'Ali Baba and the 40 Dealers: Immediate Deportation.' Lutz Bachmann himself was actually deported from South Africa (not for drug dealing, but because of his visa status).

53. For an analysis of the rationale behind the founding of such a party, see 'Lutz Bachmanns "Pegida-Partei"? – Experte: "Eine Totgeburt"', *Sputnik* (20 July 2016), https://de.sputniknews.com/politik/20160720311625196-lutz-bachmann-pegida-partei/, last accessed 21 April 2019.

54. 'Abschreckendes Beispiel', *Der Spiegel* vol. 52 (2014), p. 12.

55. 'Neujahrsansprache von Bundeskanzlerin Angela Merkel zum Jahreswechsel 2014/2015', Berlin: Presse- und Informationsamt der Bundesregierung (30 December 2014), Pressemitteilung vol. 461. Merkel also said that the immigration of people to Germany was a "valuable addition" (*Gewinn*) for all Germans.

56. Alexander Gauland accused Merkel of arrogance: "She condemns people that she does not even know from on high." See 'Neujahrsansprache der Kanzlerin, Selbst Opposition feiert Merkel für Pegida-Kritik', *Spiegel Online* (31 December 2014), http://www.spiegel.de/politik/

deutschland/neujahrsansprache-opposition-feiert-merkel-fuer-pegida-kritik-a-1010882.html, last accessed 21 April 2019.

57. Werner Patzelt, Phillip Buchallik, Stefan Scharf, and Clemens Pleul, *Was und wie denken PEGIDA-Demonstranten? Analyse der PEGIDA-Demonstranten am 25. Januar 2015, Dresden. Ein Forschungsbericht*, Dresden (2 February 2015), https://tu-dresden.de/gsw/phil/powi/polsys/ressourcen/dateien/forschung/pegida/patzelt-analyse-pegida-2015-01.pdf?lang=en, last accessed 21 April 2019.

Patzelt acknowledged the use of earlier research by Hans Vorländer, Dieter Rucht, Franz Walter, and Wolfgang Donsbach; he later published 'Neun unorthodoxe Thesen zu PEGIDA', which he summarized in the following manner: "The key issue is that PEGIDA and AfD are just two distinct appearances of the same phenomenon, that is, the German form of European right-wing populism. Therefore, dealing with PEGIDA as if it was nothing but a local phenomenon, could not avoid failing" (original English). See W. P., 'Neun unorthodoxe Thesen zu PEGIDA', in *Rechtspopulismus zwischen Fremdenangst und 'Wende'-Enttäuschung? Analysen im Überblick*, eds. Karl-Siegbert Rehberg, Franziska Kunz, and Timo Schlinzig, Bielefeld: transcript, 2016, pp. 69-82.

For the reaction of *Der Spiegel* to the position paper, see Christina Hebel, Benjamin Knaack und Christoph Sydow, 'Pegida-Faktencheck. Die Angstbürger', *Spiegel Online* (12 December 2014), http://www.spiegel.de/politik/deutschland/pegida-die-thesen-im-faktencheck-a-1008098.html, last accessed 21 April 2019.

CONCLUSIONS AND PROSPECTS

1. Jan-Werner Müller, *What is Populism?*, Philadelphia: University of Pennsylvania Press, 2016. For an equally partisan interpretation of populism from the opposite perspective, see Adrian Kuzminski, *Fixing the System. A History of Populism, Ancient and Modern*, New York: Continuum, 2008. Kuzminski states therein: "[T]he populist program of decentralizing political and economic power—though marginalized in recent times—continues to hold the greatest promise for ensuring not only political and economic justice, but a sustainable social and natural world" (ix). And further: "In any society, there can and should be richer and poorer, given natural human differences in productive talents, skills, energies, motivations, and knowledge, all of which deserve their suitable rewards. But in a populist democracy there would be neither dramatically rich nor dramatically poor, neither those powerful enough to constitute a coherent and self-perpetuating ruling class nor those

dependent enough to constitute a coherent and self-perpetuating client class" (p. 4).

2. See Müller's various blogs and online essays at Project Syndicate, https://www.project-syndicate.org/columnist/jan-werner-mueller, last accessed 21 April 2019, and *The Guardian*, https://www.theguardian.com/profile/jan-werner-m-ller, last accessed 21 April 2019. At time of writing, one recent piece is 'Fake Volk? Über Wahrheit und Lüge im populistischen Sinne', *Kursbuch* vol. 189 (1 March 2017), https://kursbuch.online/jan-werner-mueller-fake-volk/, last accessed 21 April 2019. His intent there is to show that the populists' 'big lie' about the existence of a homogeneous Volk leads to many other 'little lies.'

3. Cas Mudde and Cristóbal Rovira Kaltwasser, *Populism. A Very Short Introduction*, New York: Oxford University Press, 2017.

4. See, for example, Melanie Amann, *Angst für Deutschland*, München: Droemer, 2017, p. 10. Amann even speaks of AfD activists as "Sarrazin's pupils" (p. 35), just as the Baader-Meinhof terrorists used to be called "Hitler's children."

5. After the appearance of *Deutschland von Sinnen*, Harald Staun wrote in the *Frankfurter Allgemeine Sonntagszeitung* that Pirinçci was "yelling Sarrazin's litany of rage through a megaphone." That is far off the mark, as the reader Andreas Gleim commented: "Der Vergleich mit Sarrazin ist nicht fair, denn S. hat durchaus noch eine wertkonservative Ethik" (The comparison with Sarrazin is not fair, since S. still has ethics based on conservative values).

    See Harald Staun, 'Der Populismus des Akif Pirinçci. Wie Sarrazin auf Speed', *Frankfurter Allgemeine Sonntagszeitung* (5 April 2014), http://www.faz.net/aktuell/feuilleton/der-populismus-des-akif-pirincci-wie-sarrazin-auf-speed-12881608.html?printPagedArticle=true#pageIndex_2, last accessed 21 April 2019.

6. This does not, however, necessarily apply when Germans spend their vacations in other countries.

7. This gruff manner is worlds apart from Éric Zemmour, but that is perhaps not surprising, given that Zemmour is disgusted by the Americanization of France. The only American conservative author and media personality who resembles Zemmour in terms of education and language use is the late William F. Buckley.

8. *Tristesse Droite. Die Abende von Schnellroda*, eds. Ellen Kositza and Götz Kubitschek, Schnellroda: Verlag Antaios, 2015, cited in Andreas Speit, *Bürgerliche Scharfmacher. Deutschlands neue rechte Mitte—von AfD bis Pegida*, Zürich: Orell Füssli Verlag, 2016, p. 144.

9. These theses, 'LEITKULTUR FÜR DEUTSCHLAND, WAS IST DAS EIGENTLICH?', were originally published in *Bild am Sonntag*, a tabloid not known for its promotion of German high culture. I am quoting from a version provided by *Die Zeit*. See 'Thomas de Maizière: "Wir sind nicht Burka"': Innenminister will deutsche Leitkultur', ZEIT ONLINE (30 April 2017), http://www.zeit.de/politik/deutschland/2017-04/thomas-demaiziere-innenminister-leitkultur, last accessed 21 April 2019.

10. See Domenikus Gadermann, 'Leitkultur vor den Wahlen: Gauland wirft de Maizière Missbrauch des Begriffs Leitkultur vor', *Bundesdeutsche Zeitung* (4 May 2017), http://bundesdeutsche-zeitung.de/headlines/national-headlines/leitkultur-vor-den-wahlen-gauland-wirft-de-maiziere-missbrauch-des-begriffs-leitkultur-vor-964119, last accessed 21 April 2019.

11. See Bodo Straub and Ingo Salmen, 'Senat will Brandenburger Tor besser schützen', *Der Tagesspiegel* (28 August 2016), http://www.tagesspiegel.de/berlin/polizei-justiz/nach-aktion-der-identitaeren-bewegung-senat-will-brandenburger-tor-besser-schuetzen/14463426.html, last accessed 21 April 2019. Banners were unfurled with the slogan "Secure borders—secure future."

12. Amann, *Angst für Deutschland*, p. 10.

13. *AfD—Bekämpfen oder ignorieren? Intelligente Argumente von 14 Demokraten*, ed. Christian Nawrocki and Armin Fuhrer, Bremen/Boston: Kellner Verlag, 2016. The editors themselves have a clear position: "AfD is not the same as NSDAP. However, the brown [that is to say, Nazi] ideas that it is bringing to the surface must be withstood by a democracy, but not tolerated or accepted. At the very least, democrats should do everything they can to stop this party from entering the *Bundestag*" (p. 10).

14. Gesine Agena and Anton Hofreiter, 'Ein Weckruf, der gehört werden muss', *AfD—Bekämpfen oder ignorieren?*, p. 18.

15. Dietmar Bartsch, 'Die "Dagegen-Partei"', *AfD—Bekämpfen oder ignorieren?*, p. 24.

16. In another contribution to this volume, Charlotte Knoblauch, a former chair of the Central Council of Jews in Germany, praises the democratic achievements of the postwar *Bundesrepublik* but criticizes the way in which the country deals with the memory of past crimes (*Erinnerungskultur*). Reading her essay, one would think that German democracy is not as stable as it seems to be. See Charlotte Knoblauch, 'Die AfD und wir—die Demokraten dürfen den historischen Moment nicht verpassen', *AfD—Bekämpfen oder ignorieren?*, pp. 67-75.

17. *Kulturkampf von rechts. AfD, Pegida und die Neue Rechte*, eds. Helmut Kellersohn and Wolfgang Kastrup, Münster: UNRAST Verlag, 2016, Edition DISS, vol. 38.

18. Julia Meier, 'Die AfD bekämpfen, bevor es zu spät ist', *Kulturkampf von rechts*, pp. 235-239.
19. Hajo Funke, *Von Wutbürgern und Brandstiftern*, p. 9.
20. Andreas Speit, *Bürgerliche Scharfmacher. Deutschlands neue rechte Mitte— von AfD bis Pegida*, Zürich: Orell Füssli Verlag, 2016, p. 318. Speit's reference to the "middle of society" reflects his skepticism with regard to Germany's relationship to democracy. In this vein, one statement that he makes about the German past is rather provocative, to say the least: "[T]he majority of the 'completely normal people' voted for the NSDAP [...]" (p. 265).
21. Stefan Weidner, *Anti-Pegida. Eine Streitschrift*, Kindle Singles (originally published as an e-Book), 2015. Those who wish to peruse more detailed studies can turn to the following: *Pegida. Die schmutzige Seite der Zivilgesellschaft*, eds. Lars Geiges, Stine Marg, and Franz Walter, Bielefeld: transcript, 2015; *Pegida als Spiegel und Projektionsfläche. Wechselwirkungen und Abgrenzungen zwischen Pegida, Politik, Medien, Zivilgesellschaft und Sozialwissenschaften*, ed. Timo Heim, Wiesbaden: Springer, 2017; Hans Vorländer, Maik Herold, and Steven Schäller, *Pegida. Entwicklung, Zusammensetzung und Deutung einer Empörungsbewegung*, Wiesbaden: Springer, 2016; and *PEGIDA—Rechtspopulismus zwischen Fremdenangst und 'Wende'-Enttäuschung*, eds. Karl-Siegbert Rehberg, Franziska Kunz, and Timo Schlinzig, Bielefeld: transcript, 2016.
22. This also applies to German Muslims like Necla Kelek (pp. 59-62).
23. Another critique of German Islamophobia came from an unexpected quarter: André F. Lichtschlag, who has been associated with the New Right (see his role in the publication of Pirinçci's *DvS*), maintained that the "neo-socialist" welfare state was the problem, not Muslims. See André F. Lichtschlag, *Feindbild Muslim. Schauplätze verfehlter Einwanderungs-und Sozialpolitik*, Waltrop und Leipzig: Manuscriptum Verlagsbuchhaltung, 2010, see note 35 to chapter one.

   The debate about the role of Muslims in German society has brought forth a spate of publications. Among them are: *Feindbild Islamkritik. Wenn die Grenzen zur Verzerrung und Diffamierung überschritten werden*, ed. Hartmut Krauss, Osnabrück: HINTERGRUND-Verlag, 2010; *Islam-Verherrlichung. Wenn die Kritik zum Tabu wird*, ed. Thorsten Gerald Schneider, Wiesbaden: VS Verlag für Sozialwissenschaften, 2010; Wolfgang Frindte, *Der Islam und der Westen. Sozialpsychologische Aspekte einer Inszenierung*, Wiesbaden: Springer VS, 2013; and Hamed Abdel-Samad, *Der islamische Faschismus*, München: Droemer, 2014.
24. Hajo Funke, *Von Wutbürgern und Brandstiftern*, p. 145.

25.   Alexander Häusler, 'Die AfD und der europäische Rechtspopulismus. Krisensymptome politischer Hegemonie', in *Kulturkampf von rechts. AfD, Pegida und die Neue Rechte*, p. 80.

POSTSCRIPT: THE 2017 NATIONAL ELECTION AND ITS IMPACT

1.   These figures are taken from the official site of the *Bundestag*, https://www.bundestag.de/dokumente/textarchiv/2017/kw39-wahlergebnis/527056, last accessed 21 April 2019.

2.   See the statistics provided by the German public broadcaster ARD on the night after the election, http://wahl.tagesschau.de/wahlen/2017-09-24-BT-DE/umfrage-aktuellethemen.shtml, last accessed 21 April 2019.

3.   Sebastian Fischer, 'ZfD—Zäsur für Deutschland', *Spiegel Online* (24 Sept. 2017), http://www.spiegel.de/politik/deutschland/bundestagswahl-2017-analyse-zaesur-fuer-deutschland-a-1169596.html, last accessed 21 April 2019.

   For an in-depth analysis of this phenomenon, see Nicola Abé, Christiane Hoffmann, Veit Medick, Ralf Neukirch, and Christoph Schult, 'Chaostage', Der Spiegel vol. 8 (2018), https://magazin.spiegel.de/SP/2018/8/155846304/index.html, last accessed 21 April 2019. The authors come to the conclusion that the German party system will not return to the "old certainties," even if a new version of the Grand Coalition is installed.

4.   'AfD-Abtrünnige. Petry und Pretzell planen "bundesweite CSU"', *Spiegel Online* (27 September 2017), http://www.spiegel.de/politik/deutschland/afd-abtruennige-frauke-petry-und-marcus-pretzell-planen-bundesweite-csu-a-1170235.html, last accessed 21 April 2019.

   For a list of the 'defectors,' see Maria Fiedler and Matthias Meisner, 'Nach Rückzug von Frauke Petry. "Das Projekt AfD ist beendet"', *Der Tagesspiegel* (12 October 2017), http://www.tagesspiegel.de/politik/ehemalige-afd-vorsitzende-frauke-petry-versucht-es-jetzt-mit-der-blauen-partei/20449136.html, last accessed 21 April 2019.

5.   See Maria Fiedler and Matthias Meisner, 'Nach Rückzug von Frauke Petry' for excerpts from an interview with Petry.

6.   'Reaktionen zur Bundestagswahl: "Wir werden sie jagen"', ZEIT Online (24 September 2017), http://www.zeit.de/politik/deutschland/2017-09/reaktionen-bundestagswahl-cdu-spd-afd, last accessed 21 April 2019.

   Before and after the election, several AfD members joined Gauland in making statements beyond the pale of civilized political discourse: Peter Boehringer, who has been appointed as the chair of the parliamentary budget committee, referred to young Muslim men as a "macho mob of criminal, misogynistic sons of the Suras bound to the Koran" and even called Angela Merkel a whore (*"Merkelnutte"*). See Sebastian Pittelkow, 'Designierter Ausschussvorsitzender der AfD: Islamhetze per E-Mail' (23 January 2018), http://www.tagesschau.de/inland/afd-boehringer-101.html, last accessed 21 April 2019.

Björn Höcke boasted of banning Islam from the Bosporus once the AfD had come to power. See Marc Röhlig, 'Höcke will der Türkei den Islam verbieten, sobald die AfD "an der Macht" ist' (28 January 2018), http://www.bento.de/politik/bjoern-hoecke-will-tuerkei-minarette-verbieten-sobald-afd-an-der-macht-ist-2052499/, last accessed 21 April 2019.

André Poggenburg gave a political speech on Ash Wednesday (14 February 2018) insulting the Turks and demanding that the 'camel drivers get back where they belong.' See 'AfD-Rede von Poggenburg. Steinmeier kritisiert "Hass als Strategie"', (15 February 2018), http://www.tagesschau.de/inland/poggenburg-107.html, last accessed 21 April 2019.

7. One complication lies in the fact that Petry may be convicted of perjury. See 'Staatsanwaltschaft erhebt Anklage gegen Frauke Petry', *Süddeutsche Zeitung* (4 October 2017), http://www.sueddeutsche.de/politik/afd-staatsanwaltschaft-erhebt-anklage-gegen-frauke-petry-1.3693884, last accessed 21 April 2019.

    The AfD has also accused Petry of stealing data from the party's membership list that would facilitate the founding of her new party. See 'Ex-Chefin. AfD wirft Petry Datenklau aus Mitgliederkartei vor', *Spiegel Online* (6 October 2017), http://www.spiegel.de/politik/deutschland/frauke-petry-soll-aus-afd-mitgliederkartei-kopiert-haben-a-1171604.html, last accessed 21 April 2019.

    The *Tagesschau* reported that the Bundestag had lifted Petry's immunity from prosecution. See 'Streit um Markenrechte: AfD verklagt Ex-Parteichefin Petry', *Tagesschau* (24 February 2018), http://www.tagesschau.de/inland/petry-immunitaet-markenrechte-101.html, last accessed 21 April 2019.

8. One figure who might help promote such cooperation is Boris Palmer, the popular Green mayor of the university town Tübingen. He is trying to convince his party that it is necessary to discuss the limits of immigration, something that has been hitherto an absolute taboo in Green circles.

    See Boris Palmer, *Wir können nicht allen helfen. Ein Grüner über Integration und die Grenzen der Belastbarkeit*, München: Siedler Verlag, 2017. It is noteworthy that he—like Sarrazin—uses Max Weber's terminology to describe the Green dilemma 'between conscience and responsibility' (p. 255).

9.   See Sasan Abdi-Herrle, 'Sarrazin gibt bei "Maischberger" den Trump-Versteher', *Westdeutsche Allgemeine Zeitung* (16 February 2017), https://www.waz.de/kultur/fernsehen/sarrazin-gibt-bei-maischberger-den-trump-versteher-id209626831.html, last accessed 21 April 2019.

10. The *Studienzentrum* has provided a video of this talk, https://www.youtube.com/watch?v=Q9f_y4gV7Og, last accessed 21 April 2019.

11. Jürgen Bock, 'Rechtskonservative feiern Thilo Sarrazin', *Stuttgarter Nachrichten* (26 March 2017), http://www.stuttgarter-nachrichten.de/inhalt.kreis-ludwigsburg-rechtskonservative-feiern-thilo-sarrazin.c02945fa-2b22-40c6-8bfd-59af1f0bcd9f.html, last accessed 21 April 2019.

12. See 'Sarrazin verteidigt Auftritt mit AfD-Vorstandsmitglied Weidel', *Journalistenwatch* (30 March 2017), https://www.journalistenwatch.com/2017/03/30/sarrazin-verteidigt-auftritt-mit-afd-vorstandsmitglied-weidel/, last accessed 21 April 2019.

13. Jürg Ackermann (interviewer), 'Autor Thilo Sarrazin zur AfD: "Merkel hat nichts verstanden"', *Luzerner Zeitung* (30 September 2017), http://www.luzernerzeitung.ch/nachrichten/international/merkel-hat-nichts-verstanden;art9640,1111896, last accessed 21 April 2019.

14. Jakob Augstein, 'Angela Merkel: Die Mutter der AfD', SPIEGEL Online (18 September 2017), http://www.spiegel.de/politik/deutschland/bundestagswahl-2017-angela-merkel-die-mutter-der-afd-kolumne-a-1168481.html, last accessed 21 April 2019.

15. Akif Pirincci, 'Die Akif-Partei—Akif for Bundeskanzler', blog post, https://nixgut.wordpress.com/2015/07/15/akif-pirincci-die-akif-partei-akif-for-bundeskanzler, last accessed 21 April 2019.

16. Akif Pirinçci, 'Ein paar Worte zu der "Schicksalswahl"', http://der-kleine-akif.de/2017/07/09/ein-paar-worte-zu-der-schicksalswahl/, last accessed 21 April 2019, and http://www.pi-news.net/akif-pirincci-ein-paar-worte-zu-der-schicksalswahl, last accessed 21 April 2019.

     In a 2011 essay, Botho Strauß portrayed the Germans in a similar manner: "The people (Volk) are spoiled, comfortable, easily irritated, and hypochondriacal." Needless to say, this is not the language of populism. See Botho Strauß, 'Krise des Bürgertums : Klärt uns endlich auf!', *Frankfurter Allgemeine Zeitung* (23 August 2011), http://www.faz.net/aktuell/feuilleton/debatten/krise-des-buergertums-klaert-uns-endlich-auf-11108716.html?printPagedArticle=true#pageIndex_0, last accessed 21 April 2019.

17. See also his latest apocalyptic vision in book form, *Der Übergang: Bericht aus einem verlorenem Land*, Schnellroda, Verlag Antaios, 2017. It does not seem to occur to Pirinçci that if "subservience" is in fact an innate trait of the Germans, then they would have displayed this trait in the phase of the 'old' Federal Republic whose return he yearns for.

18. Botho Strauß, 'Kritisches Denken: Reform der Intelligenz', *Die Zeit* vol. 14 (2017), http://www.zeit.de/2017/14/kritisches-denken-botho-strauss-intelligenz-populismus, last accessed 21 April 2019.

19. This can of course be interpreted as an approval of at least some forms of populism, although Strauß's readers do not as a rule stem from the ranks of the common man (or woman).

20. "Es gibt nur eine AfD!", *Deutschland Kurier* (11 October 2017), http://www.deutschland-kurier.org/es-gibt-nur-eine-afd/, last accessed 21 April 2019.

21. See Marcus Bensmann, 'Gegen die "Hooligans"', Correctiv, (4 October 2017), https://correctiv.org/recherchen/neue-rechte/artikel/2017/10/04/gegen-die-hooligans/, last accessed 21 April 2019.

22. James Angelos, 'The Prophet,' *The New York Times Magazine* (15 October 2017), https://www.nytimes.com/2017/10/10/magazine/the-prophet-of-germanys-new-right.html?emc=edit_mbe_20171013&nl=morning-briefing-europe&nlid=49992931&te=1, last accessed 21 April 2019.

23. James Angelos, 'Will France Sound the Death Knell for Social Democracy?', *The New York Times Magazine* (29 January 2017), https://www.nytimes.com/2017/01/24/magazine/will-france-sound-the-death-knell-for-social-democracy.html, last accessed 21 April 2019.

24. See Bundesamt für Verfassungsschutz, 'Rechtsextremistisches Personenpotenzial [2017]', https://www.verfassungsschutz.de/de/arbeitsfelder/af-rechtsextremismus/zahlen-und-fakten-rechtsextremismus/rechtsextremistisches-personenpotenzial-2017, last accessed 24 April 2019.

25. For accounts of what happened, see the following: 'Lautstarke Tumulte bei Frankfurter Buchmesse', Hessenschau (15 October 2017), http://www.hessenschau.de/kultur/buchmesse/buchmesse-lautstarke-tumulte-bei-antaios-veranstaltung,protest-buchmesse-100.html, last accessed 21 April 2019; 'Tumulte bei Höcke-Auftritt auf der Buchmesse', *Der Tagesspiegel* (15 October 2017), http://www.tagesspiegel.de/kultur/frankfurter-buchmesse-tumulte-bei-hoecke-auftritt-auf-der-buchmesse/20456380.html, last accessed 21 April 2019; 'Eskalation auf der Buchmesse', *Frankfurter Allgemeine Zeitung* (15 October 2017), http://www.faz.net/aktuell/feuilleton/eskalation-auf-der-buchmesse-rechte-verlage-extremer-protest-15247192.html, last

accessed 21 April 2019; Martin Lichtmesz, 'Frankfurter Buchmesse: Opfer- und Tätermythen der Linken' (19 October 2017), https://sezession.de/57451/?komplettansicht=, last accessed 21 April 2019.

26. See Martin Sellner, *Identitär!*, and Mario Müller, *Kontrakultur*, both published by Antaios.

27. The videos are available online at https://www.youtube.com/watch?v=i5y9YVjLDEQ&feature=youtu.be, last accessed 24 April 2019, and https://www.youtube.com/watch?v=d5rJxG5JsPQ&feature=youtu.be, last accessed 24 April 2019. Kubitschek provides the links in his text 'Niederbrüllen—Messetag 4', available online at https://sezession.de/57445/niederbrullen-messetag-4, last accessed 21 April 2019.

28. When Bard College invited the AfD intellectual Marc Jongen to the conference 'Crises of Democracy: Thinking in Dark Times' in October 2017, there was a strong protest against the invitation in the form of an open letter from dozens of academics. The college defended its decision to offer the invitation. For background, see the following: Leon Botstein, 'Bard President Responds to Critics of Far-Right Figure's Talk', The Chronicle of Higher Education (24 October 2017), http://www.chronicle.com/article/Bard-President-Responds-to/241538?cid=pm&utm_source=pm&utm_medium=en&elqTrackId=c7036601c4 14ffbbf7d3c9256bbcd58&elq=8fed52252a654b749aeaa 03ee08bfacc &elqaid=16241&elqat=1&elqCampaignId=7021, last accessed 21 April 2019; 'An Open Letter to the Hannah Arendt Center at Bard College', The Chronicle Review (23 October 2017), http://www.chronicle.com/article/An-Open-Letter-to-the-Hannah/241526?cid=rclink, last accessed 21 April 2019; Roger Berkowitz, 'Against the Tyranny of Intellectual Mobs' (24 October 2017), http://www.chronicle.com/article/Against-the-Tyranny-of/241541?cid=rclink, last accessed 21 April 2019.

29. This should not be taken to mean that 'all is well' in Germany. Most recently, the murder of a German man in Chemnitz (allegedly by two asylum seekers) was followed by a call for vigilante justice supported by the AfD, PEGIDA and others. In light of such provocations, the democratic center must remain alert and counter any attempts to weaken the rule of law or to bypass the state's monopoly of force. For a report on the scene in Chemnitz, see 'Germany migrants: Merkel condemns "vigilantes" after Chemnitz murder', BBC News (27 August 2018), https://www.bbc.co.uk/news/world-europe-45320382, last accessed 21 April 2019. In that article, one finds a statement from AfD politician and MP Markus Frohnmaier, to wit: "If the state is no longer [able] to protect citizens then people take to the streets and protect

themselves. It's as simple as that!" (Other AfD officials later distanced themselves from that statement, but it is unlikely that Frohnmaier's words will be forgotten.)

30. The 2017 Austrian election resulted in a conservative/rightist coalition. The FPÖ's share of the vote (almost 26%, just behind the Social Democrats) is far beyond the AfD's 12.6%, and, unlike the AfD, the FPÖ is too large to be ostracized. The fact that the Greens failed to return to parliament is also not a good sign for the future. One observer's comment on the Austrian election results highlights the difference between the two German-speaking countries: "Voters chose Sebastian Kurz and his People's Party (ÖVP) and the more right-wing Freedom Party (FPÖ) because they are worried about immigration and identity but preferred it with a smiling, unthreatening face." See Stephen Szabo, 'Why Austria Voted the Way It Did', blog post, American Institute for Contemporary German Studies (19 October 2017), http://www.aicgs.org/2017/10/why-austria-voted-the-way-it-did/, last accessed 21 April 2019. So far, the German New Right has preferred the enraged grimace to the trademark engaging smile of young Sebastian Kurz.

31. The electoral success of the populist Five Star movement and the far right (Northern) League led the observers at the newspaper *La Stampa* to proclaim: "Italy is ungovernable." Cited in: 'Italy' election: Populist Five Star and League vie for power', BBC News (5 March 2018), http://www.bbc.com/news/world-europe-43272700, last accessed 21 April 2019.

SOURCES AND FURTHER READING

NB: With some exceptions, articles, essays, interviews, internet resources, etc. are found only in the endnotes.

Abdel-Samad, Hamed, *Der islamische Faschismus*, München: Droemer, 2014.

Amann, Melanie, *Angst für Deutschland. Die Wahrheit über die AfD: wo sie herkommt, wer sie führt, wohin sie steuert*, München: Droemer, 2017.

Ansari, Humayun, and Farid Hafez (eds.), *From the Far Right to the Mainstream. Islamophobia in Party Politics and the Media*, Frankfurt/New York: Campus, 2012.

Bade, Klaus J., *Kritik und Gewalt. Sarrazin-Debatte, 'Islamkritik' und Terror in der Einwanderungsgesellschaft*, Schwalbach: Wochenschau Verlag, 2013.

Bahners, Patrick. *Die Panikmacher. Die deutsche Angst vor dem Islam. Eine Streitschrift*, München: C.H. Beck, 2011.

Bartholomew, David J., *Measuring Intelligence. Facts and Fallacies*, Cambridge: Cambridge UP, 2004.

Ben-Itto, Hadassa, *The Lie That Wouldn't Die: The Protocols of the Elders of Zion*, London, Portland OR: Vallentine Mitchell, 2005.

Benz, Wolfgang, *Die Feinde aus dem Morgenland. Wie die Angst vor Muslimen unsere Demokratie gefährdet*, München: C.H. Beck, 2012.

Berlin, Isaiah, *The Crooked Timber of Humanity: Chapters in the History of Ideas*, ed. Henry Hardy, London: John Murray, 1990.

Bloch, Ernst, *Erbschaft dieser Zeit*, Frankfurt am Main: Suhrkamp, 1962.

Böckelmann, Frank, *Jargon der Weltoffenheit. Was sind unsere Werte noch wert?*, Waltrop und Leipzig: Edition Sonderwege bei Manuscriptum, 2014.

Brecht, Bertolt, *Die Gedichte von Bertolt Brecht in einem Band,* Frankfurt am Main: Suhrkamp, 1981.

Bronner, Stephen Eric, *A Rumor about the Jews: Reflections on Antisemitism and the Protocols of the Learned Elders of Zion,* New York: St. Martin's Press, 2000.

Cheesman, Tom, *Novels of Turkish German Settlement: Cosmopolite Fictions,* Rochester, NY: Camden House, 2007.

Cobb, Alfred L., *Migrants' Literature in Postwar Germany. Striving to Find a Place to Fit In,* Lewiston et al.: Edwin Mellen Press, 2006.

Conradt, David F., et al. (eds.), *Germany's New Politics,* Tempe, AZ: German Studies Review, 1995.

Der Fall Sarrazin. Eine Analyse (4th Revised Edition), Albersroda: Institut für Staatspolitik, Arbeitsgruppe 3, Zuwanderung und Integration, 2010.

Diamond, Jared, *Guns, Germs, and Steel. The Fates of Human Societies,* New York: W.W. Norton, 1997.

Diamond, Jared, *Collapse: How Societies Choose to Fail or Succeed,* New York: Viking, 2005.

Dorn, Thea, *deutsch, nicht dumpf. Ein Leitfaden für aufgeklärte Patrioten,* München: Albrecht Knaus, 2018

Frindte, Wolfgang, *Der Islam und der Westen. Sozialpsychologische Aspekte einer Inszenierung,* Wiesbaden: Springer VS, 2013.

Funke, Hajo, with Ralph Gabriel, *Von Wutbürgern und Brandstiftern. AfD— Pegida—Gewaltnetze,* Berlin: Verlag für Berlin-Brandenburg, 2016.

Fukuyama, Francis, *The End of History and the Last Man,* New York: Free Press, 1992.

Gedeon, Wolfgang. *Christlich-europäische Leitkultur. Die Herausforderung Europas durch Säkularismus, Zionismus und Islam: Band I: Über Kultur, Geostrategie und Religion; Christlich-europäische Leitkultur. Die Herausforderung Europas durch Säkularismus, Zionismus und Islam: Band II: Über Geschichte, Zionismus und Verschwörungspolitik; Christlich-europäische Leitkultur. Die Herausforderung Europas durch Säkularismus, Zionismus und Islam: Band III: Über Europa, Globalismus und eine neue Politik der Mitte,* Frankfurt am Main: R.G. Fischer Verlag, 2009.

Geiges, Lars, Stine Marg, and Franz Walter (eds.), *Pegida. Die schmutzige Seite der Zivilgesellschaft,* Bielefeld: transcript, 2015.

Göktürk, Deniz, David Gramling, Anton Kaes, and Andreas Langnohl (eds.), *Transit Deutschland. Debatten zu Nation und Migration.* München: Wilhelm Fink Verlag / Konstanz University Press, 2011.

Groh, Dieter, and Peter Brandt, *'Vaterlandslose Gesellen.' Sozialdemokratie und Nation 1860-1990,* München: C.H.Beck, 1992.

Grundgesetz für die Bundesrepublik Deutschland, Bonn: Bundeszentrale für politische Bildung, 1994.

Grundsatzprogramm der Alternative für Deutschland, https://www.alternativefuer. de/wp-content/uploads/sites/111/2017/01/2016-06-27_afd-grundsatzprogram, last accessed 24 April 2019.

Grundsatzprogramm der Alternative für Deutschland. Leitantrag der Bundesprogrammkommission und des Bundesvorstandes, http://www.welt. de/pdf/1088/Leitantrag-Grundsatzprogramm-AfD.pdf, last accessed 24 April 2019.

Halink, Charlotte, *Kontra Sarrazins Thesen,* Taunusstein: Escritor-Verlag G. Hölling, 2011.

Haller, Michael and Martin Niggeschmidt (eds.), *Der Mythos vom Niedergang der Intelligenz. Von Galton zu Sarrazin. Die Denkmuster und Denkfehler der Eugenik,* Wiesbaden, Springer VS, 2012.

Hayek, Friedrich von. *The Road to Serfdom,* Chicago: U. of Chicago Press, 1944.

Heim, Timo (ed.). *Pegida als Spiegel und Projektionsfläche. Wechselwirkungen und Abgrenzungen zwischen Pegida, Politik, Medien, Zivilgesellschaft und Sozialwissenschaften,* Wiesbaden: Springer, 2017.

Heisig, Kirsten, *Das Ende der Geduld. Konsequent gegen jugendliche Gewalttäter,* Freiburg, Basel, Wien: Verlag Herder, 2010.

Herrnstein, Richard J. and Charles Murray, *Bell Curve: Intelligence and Class Structure in American Life,* New York: Free Press, 1994.

Horkheimer, Max and Theodor W. Adorno, *Dialectic of Enlightenment,* Stanford: Stanford UP, 2007. (First German edition in 1947).

Houellebecq, Michel, *Submission,* transl. Lorin Stein, New York: Farrar, Straus and Giroux, 2015.

Huntington, Samuel P., *The Clash of Civilizations and the Remaking of World Order,* New York: Simon & Schuster, 1996.

Huntington, Samuel P., *Who Are We? The Challenges to America's National Identity,* New York: Simon & Schuster, 2004.

Kant, Immanuel, '*Ideen zu einer allgemeinen Geschichte in weltbürgerlicher Absicht*' (Idea for a Universal History with a Cosmopolitan Purpose), 1784, in *Was ist Aufklärung? Aufsätze zur Geschichte und Philosophie,* ed. Jürgen Zehbe, Göttingen: Vandenhoeck & Ruprecht, 1967, pp. 40-54.

Kaufman, Debra et al. (eds.), *From the Protocols of the Elders of Zion to Holocaust Denial Trials: Challenging the Media, the Law and the Academy,* London and Portland, OR: Vallentine Mitchell, 2007.

Kelek, Necla, *Die fremde Braut. Ein Bericht aus dem Inneren des türkischen Lebens in Deutschland,* Köln: Kiepenheuer & Witsch, 2005.

Kelek, Necla, *Chaos der Kulturen. Die Debatte um Islam und Integration,* Köln: Kiepenheuer & Witsch, 2012.

Kellersohn, Helmut and Wolfgang Kastrup (eds.), *Kulturkampf von rechts. AfD, Pegida und die Neue Rechte*, Münster: UNRAST Verlag, Edition DISS, vol. 38, 2016.

Kemper, Andreas, *Sarrazins Correctness. Zur Tradition der Menschen- und Bevölkerungskorrekturen*, Münster: UNRAST Verlag, 2014.

Kießling, Friedrich, *Die undeutschen Deutschen. Eine ideengeschichtliche Archäologie der alten Bundesrepublik 1945–1972*, Paderborn, München, Wien, Zürich: Ferdinand Schöningh, 2012.

Kositza, Ellen and Götz Kubitschek (eds.), *Tristesse Droite. Die Abende von Schnellroda*, Schnellroda: Verlag Antaios, 2015.

Krauss, Hartmut (ed.), *Feindbild Islamkritik. Wenn die Grenzen zur Verzerrung und Diffamierung überschritten warden*, Osnabrück: Hintergrund-Verlag, 2010.

Krell, Gerd, *Schafft Deutschland sich ab? Ein Essay über Demografie, Intelligenz, Armut und Einwanderung*, Schwalbach: Wochenschau Verlag, 2013.

Kuzminski, Adrian, *Fixing the System. A History of Populism, Ancient and Modern*, New York: Continuum, 2008.

Lange, Dorothée, *Politisch inkorrekt Oder: Was hat Sarrazin eigentlich mit dem Sturm und Drang zu tun?*, Hannover: Wehrhahn Verlag, 2012.

Leggewie, Claus, *Anti-Europäer. Breivik, Dugin, al-Suri & Co*, Frankfurt am Main: Suhrkamp, 2016.

Lichtschlag, André F., *Feindbild Islam. Schauplätze verfehlter Einwanderungs- und Sozialpolitik*, Waltrop und Leipzig: Manuskriptum Buchhandlung, 2010.

Lilla, Mark, *The Shipwrecked Mind. On Political Reaction*, New York: New York Review Books, 2016.

Meyer, Frank, *Der lange Abschied vom Bürgertum. Joachim Fest und Wolf Jobst Siedler im Gespräch*, Berlin: wjs verlag, 2005.

Mudde, Cas and Cristóbal Rovira Kaltwasser, *Populism. A Very Short Introduction*, New York: Oxford University Press, 2017.

Müller, Jan-Werner, *What is Populism?*, Philadelphia: University of Pennsylvania Press, 2016.

Nawrocki, Christian and Armin Fuhrer (eds.), *AfD—Bekämpfen oder ignorieren? Intelligente Argumente von 14 Demokraten*, Bremen/Boston: Kellner Verlag, 2016.

Nietzsche, Friedrich, *Also sprach Zarathustra. Ein Buch für alle und keinen*, Leipzig: Alfred Kröner Verlag, 1930.

Nietzsche, Friedrich, *Unzeitgemäße Betrachtungen* [*Thoughts out of Season*], München: Goldmann, Gesammelte Werke 2, 1964.

Norton, Robert E, *Secret Germany. Stefan George and his Circle*, Ithaca and London: Cornell University Press, 2002.

Palmer, Boris, *Wir können nicht allen helfen. Ein Grüner über Integration und die Grenzen der Belastbarkeit*, München: Siedler Verlag, 2017.

Pfahl-Traughber, Armin, *Rechtsextremismus in der Bundesrepublik*, München: C.H. Beck, 1999.

Pokatzky, Klaus, "'Ich bin ein Pressetürke.'" Akif Pirinçci und der deutsche Literaturbetrieb', in *Transit Deutschland. Debatten zu Nation und Migration*, eds. Deniz Göktürk, David Gramling, Anton Kaes and Andreas Langenohl, München: Wilhelm Fink Verlag / Konstanz University Press, 2011.

Popper, Karl, *The Open Society and Its Enemies*, London, G. Routledge & Sons, Ltd., 1945.

Popper, Karl, *The Poverty of Historicism*, Boston: Beacon Press, 1957.

Pirinçci, Akif, *Felidae*, München: Goldmann, 1989.

Pirinçci, Akif, *Deutschland von Sinnen. Der irre Kult um Frauen, Homosexuelle und Zuwanderer*, Waltrop und Leipzig: Lichtschlag in der Edition Sonderwege, Manuscriptum Verlagsbuchhandlung, 2014.

Pirinçci, Akif and Andreas Lombard (eds.), *Attacke auf den Main-Stream. "Deutschland von Sinnen" und die Medien*, Waltrop und Leipzig: Manuscriptum Verlagsbuchhandlung, Lichtschlag in der Edition Sonderwege, 2014.

Pirinçci, Akif, *Die große Verschwulung: wenn aus Männern Frauen werden und aus Frauen keine Männer*, Waltrop und Leipzig: Manuscriptum (Edition Lichtschlag), 2015.

Pirinçci, Akif, *Umvolkung. Wie die Deutschen still und leise ausgetauscht warden*, Schnellroda: Verlag Antaios, 2016.

Pirinçci, Akif, *Der Übergang: Bericht aus einem verlorenem Land*, Schnellroda: Verlag Antaios, 2017.

Rehberg, Karl-Siegbert, Franziska Kunz, and Timo Schlinzig (eds.), *PEGIDA. Rechtspopulismus zwischen Fremdenangst und 'Wende'-Enttäuschung? Analysen im Überblick*, Bielefeld: transcript, 2016.

Retallack, James, *The German Right 1860-1920, Political Limits of the Authoritarian Imagination*, Toronto, Buffalo, London: U. of Toronto Press, 2006.

Reuth, Ralf Georg and Günther Lachmann, *Das erste Leben der Angela M.*, München: Piper, 2013.

Rosellini, Jay Julian, *Literary Skinheads? Writing from the Right in Reunified Germany*, West Lafayette: Purdue University Press, 2000.

Sarrazin, Thilo, *Der Euro: Chance oder Abenteuer?*, Bonn: J.H.W. Dietz, 1997.

Sarrazin, Thilo, *Deutschland schafft sich ab. Wie wir unser Land aufs Spiel setzen*, München: Deutsche Verlagsanstalt, 2010.

Sarrazin, Thilo, *Europa braucht den Euro nicht: wie uns politisches Wunschdenken in die Krise geführt hat*, München: Deutsche Verlags-Anstalt, 2012.

Sarrazin, Thilo, *Der neue Tugendterror. Über die Grenzen der Meinungsfreiheit in Deutschland*, München: Deutsche Verlags-Anstalt, 2014.

Sarrazin, Thilo, *Wunschdenken*, München: Deutsche Verlagsanstalt, 2016.

Sarrazin, Thilo, *Feindliche Übernahme: Wie der Islam den Fortschritt behindert und die Gesellschaft bedroht*, München: FinanzBuch Verlag, 2018.

Sarrazin. Eine deutsche Debatte, ed. Deutschland Stiftung Integration, München und Zürich: Piper Verlag, 2010.

Schneiders, Thorsten Gerald (ed.), *Islamverherrlichung. Wenn die Kritik zum Tabu wird*, Wiesbaden: VS Verlag für Sozialwissenschaften [Springer], 2010.

Schwilk, Heimo and Ulrich Schacht (eds.), *Die selbstbewusste Nation. "Anschwellender Bocksgesang" und weitere Beiträge zu einer deutschen Debatte*, Frankfurt am Main/Berlin: Ullstein Verlag, 1994.

Sieferle, Rolf Peter, *Die konservative Revolution. Fünf biographische Skizzen*, Frankfurt am Main: Fischer, 1995.

Sieferle, Rolf Peter, *Das Migrationsproblem: Über die Unvereinbarkeit von Sozialstaat und Masseneinwanderung*, Erste Ausgabe der Werkreihe TUMULT, Waltrop/ Berlin: Manuscriptum, 2017.

Sieferle, Rolf Peter. *Finis Germania*. Schnellroda: Verlag Antaios, 2017.

Sinram, Jana, *Pressefreiheit oder Fremdenfeindlichkeit? Der Streit um die Mohammed-Karikaturen und die dänische Einwanderungspolitik*, Frankfurt/New York: Campus Verlag, 2015.

Sombart, Werner, *Händler und Helden. Patriotische Besinnungen,* München und Leipzig: Duncker & Humblot, 1915.

Speit, Andreas, *Bürgerliche Scharfmacher. Deutschlands neue rechte Mitte—von AfD bis Pegida*, Zürich: Orell Füssli Verlag, 2016.

Strauß, Botho, '*Anschwellender Bocksgesang*', *Der Spiegel* vol. 6 (1993), pp. 202-207.

Strauß, Botho, 'Man muß wissen, wie die Sonne funktioniert', *Frankfurter Allgemeine Zeitung* (21 October 2005).

Strauß, Botho, 'Der Konflikt', *Der Spiegel* vol. 7 (2006), pp. 120-121.

Strauß, Botho, *Die Unbeholfenen. Bewußtseinsnovelle*, Munchen: Hanser, 2007.

Strauß, Botho, 'Krise des Bürgertums : Klärt uns endlich auf!', *Frankfurter Allgemeine Zeitung* (23 August 2011), http://www.faz.net/aktuell/ feuilleton/debatten/krise-des-buergertums-klaert-uns-endlich-auf-11108716.html?printPagedArticle=true#pageIndex_0, last accessed 24 April 2019.

Strauß, Botho, *Herkunft*, München: Hanser, 2014.

Strauß, Botho, 'Der letzte Deutsche. Uns wird die Souveränität geraubt, dagegen zu sein', *Der Spiegel* vol. 41 (2015), pp. 122-124.

Strauß, Botho, *Oniritti Höhlenbilder*, München: Hanser, 2016.

Strauß, Botho, 'Kritisches Denken: Reform der Intelligenz', *Die Zeit* vol. 14 (2017), http://www.zeit.de/2017/14/kritisches-denken-botho-strauss-intelligenz-populismus, last accessed 24 April 2019.

Strauß, Botho, *Der Fortführer*, Reinbek: Rowohlt, 2018.

Ulfkotte, Udo, *Vorsicht Bürgerkrieg! Was lange gärt, wird endlich Wut*, Rottenburg: Kopp Verlag, revised edition 2014. (First printing in 2009.)

Vorländer, Hans, Maik Herold, and Steven Schäller, *Pegida. Entwicklung, Zusammensetzung und Deutung einer Empörungsbewegung*, Wiesbaden: Springer, 2016.

Walter, Franz, Stephan Klecha and Alexander Hensel (eds.), *Die Grünen und die Pädosexualität: Eine bundesdeutsche Geschichte*, Göttingen: Vandenhoek & Ruprecht, 2014.

Weber, Max, 'Politik als Beruf', *Geistige Arbeit als Beruf. Vier Vorträge vor dem Freistudentischen Bund*, München und Leipzig: Duncker & Humblot, 1919. For an English translation of this text, see 'Politics as a Vocation', polisci2.ucsd.edu/foundation/documents/03Weber1918.pdf, last accessed 21 April 2019.

Weidner, Stefan, *Anti-Pegida. Eine Streitschrift*, Kindle Singles (originally published as an e-Book), 2015.

Weiß, Volker, *Deutschlands Neue Rechte. Angriff der Eliten—Von Spengler bis Sarrazin*, Paderborn, München, Wien, Zürich: Ferdinand Schöningh, 2011.

Woods, Roger, *The Conservative Revolution in the Weimar Republic*, New York: St. Martin's Press, 1996.

Zemmour, Èric, *Le Suicide français*, Paris: Èditions Albin Michel, 2014.

INDEX

185